P9-CKH-474

MANAGEMENT LAUREATES:

A Collection of Autobiographical Essays

VOLUME 5

Editor: ARTHUR G. BEDEIAN, *Boyd Professor*
Ourso College of Business Administration,
Louisiana State University

MANAGEMENT LAUREATES:

A Collection of Autobiographical Essays

by

ARTHUR G. BEDEIAN   THOMAS A. MAHONEY

C. WEST CHURCHMAN   ANDREW M. PETTIGREW

DAVID J. HICKSON   KARLENE H. ROBERTS

WICKHAM SKINNER

 JAI PRESS INC.

Stamford, Connecticut   *London, England*

Copyright © 1998 JAI PRESS INC.
100 Prospect Street
Stamford, Connecticut 06901-1640

JAI PRESS LTD.
38 Tavistock Street
Covent Garden
London WC2E 7PB
England

ISBN: 0-7623-0178-3

Manufactured in the United States of America

CONTENTS

PREFACE

Management Laureates: A Collection of Autobiographical Essays
(Bedeian, 1992-1996) is now in its fifth volume. As with its predecessors, the current volume continues in the belief that it is difficult to fully
understand the work of the management discipline's leading thinkers
without knowing more about them as individuals. Hence, like its predecessors, the goal of this volume is to present autobiographies of the discipline's most distinguished laureates.

Contributing laureates were selected not only because of their promi-
nence, but also for their behind-the-scenes insights into the management
discipline's historical development. As such, the essays that follow do
not mirror the typical academic career, but rather reflect a collage of
extraordinary and exemplary achievements. At the same time, each
essay highlights the ways in which all persons, individually and collec-
tively, share imperatives that shape their common being.

By definition, autobiographies (as life histories) require the recollection, reconstruction, and interpretation of past experiences. In this
regard, laureates were encouraged to introspectively consider connec-
tions between their life experiences and the development of their
careers. It is this probing of one's own past, as a way of identifying and

analyzing determinants of one's present, that mark autobiographical narratives as the most individualistic of all undertakings.

The difficulty and trepidations of preparing a history of oneself have been noted in prior Prefaces. Likewise, the risk in conducting a review of one's life has been also acknowledged. An immersion in the self, in order to prepare a candid account of one's life for public disclosure, demands both confronting the meaning of one's existence and openly acknowledging one's own imperfections—no mean task.

With this said, the inherent limitations in retrospective recollections cannot be denied. Simply put, memory can be inaccurate. Details of personal experiences may be forgotten or become distorted, their source and sequence may be misremembered, and completely new details may enter into one's memory (cf. Conway, Collins, Gathercole, & Anderson, 1996). At the same time, as with other self-narrative methods, the "slippage and slipperiness" inherent in autobiographical portrayals are themselves revealing (Batteson & Ball, 1995, p. 204).

Indeed, it has been argued that as self-profiles, "perhaps the most important information people convey when they write life history...is their life theme" (Howard, Maerlender, Myers, & Curtin, 1992, p. 404). That is, by weaving the "matter" of their experience into a life story, autobiographers depict their lives' core issues and values and, in so doing, engage in the ongoing and irremeable "discovery" of their personal history and experience (cf. Batteson & Ball, 1995). It is perhaps for this very reason that autobiography has been regarded as "the highest and most instructive form in which the understanding of life confronts us" (Dilthey 1926/1961, p. 85).

As in preceding volumes, editorial intervention has been kept at a minimum. Once again, all essays open with a photograph and conclude with a complete bibliography of the author's published works. Laureates remained free to choose their manner of presentation and the aspects of their lives they wished to emphasize. Although it has been suggested that autobiographies generally portray their subjects as "highly efficacious, rather than benefiting from luck" (Baumeister & Newman, 1994, p. 685), the present essays (as do those in previous volumes) defy this contention. Most describe uncanonic careers largely shaped by chance encounters and consequential choices, and not by anything resembling a carefully designed cursus.

Special thanks goes to the contributing laureates. It is hoped that they will find satisfaction in the immortality that their essays provide. All have hereby gained a medium of access that will allow them, decades from now, to speak to those management scholars who will be heirs to their intellectual legacy.

Arthur G. Bedeian
November 1997

REFERENCES

Batteson, C., & Ball, S.J. (1995). Autobiographies and interviews as means of 'access' to elite policy making in education. *British Journal of Educational Studies, 43*, 201-216.

Baumeister, R.F., & Newman, L.S. (1994). How stories make sense of personal experiences: Motives that shape autobiographical narratives. *Personality and Social Psychology Bulletin, 20,* 676-690.

Bedeian, A.G. (Ed.). (1992-1996). *Management laureates: A collection of autobiographical essays (*Vols. 1-4). Greenwich, CT: JAI Press.

Conway, M.A., Collins, A.F., Gathercole, S.E., & Anderson, S.J. (1996). Recollections of true and false autobiographical memories. *Journal of Experimental Psychology: General, 125,* 69-95.

Dilthey, W. (1961). Extracts from Dilthey's works. In H.P. Rickman (Ed. and Trans.) *Meaning in history: W. Dilthey's thoughts on history and society* (pp. 66-168). London: George Allen & Unwin. (Original work published 1926)

Howard, G.S., Maerlender, A.C., Myers, P.R., & Curtin, T.D. (1992). In stories we trust: Studies of the validity of autobiographies. *Journal of Counseling Psychology, 39,* 398-405.

And Fate Walked In

ARTHUR G. BEDEIAN

One might suppose that when the writer is not only a historian, but someone who has edited the autobiographies of a majority of his generation's leading scholars, the task of recounting his own life would be comparatively easy. At the moment, as I sit alone in my study with pen in hand, this supposition seems doubtful for several reasons. Chief among these is that to include one's own intellectual history in a volume of one's own editing may seem not only egotistical, but even of dubious propriety. The danger in this being the case is enhanced by the fact that as I view my life in retrospect, I find myself once again experiencing emotions and strivings that remain very intimate. This intimacy deepens as I contemplate ideals that have yet to be fulfilled and reactions to past encounters that still stir deep feelings.

The preparation of a self-portrait invites one to pause, to look before and after. To the extent that the contemporary self recollects a plausible past, intellectual journeys of the present kind are invariably composed of denied truths and illusory fancies. As inevitable as this may be, the realization that neither the events nor the people will be in the following representation what they were when experienced prompts a measure of

Management Laureates, Volume 5, pages 1-40.
Copyright © 1998 by JAI Press Inc.
ISBN: 0-7623-0178-3

discomfort. In this respect, the past is invariably interpreted in terms of the present.

CHILDHOOD AND YOUTH

I was born on December 22, 1946, in Davenport, Iowa, to Arthur Bedeian and Varsenick Bedeian, née Donjoian. As the names suggest, the Bedeians and Donjoians are of Armenian origin, my father's and mother's parents having immigrated to the United States to escape Turkish persecution.[1] My father (the third youngest of fourteen brothers and sisters and the first born in America) retired in 1979 from the International Harvester Company, after 42 years as a tool-and-die department supervisor. He continues as an avid near-scratch golfer. My mother (one of six brothers and sisters) remains a warm and caring individual devoted to her family's well-being. I find it very easy to see in myself a mosaic of both complementary and contradictory parental influences, especially my mother's industriousness and my father's temper.

My memories of childhood and youth remain warm after 50 years. I have delightful recollections of my maternal grandparents and numerous aunts, uncles, and cousins. Dominant among my recollections are the many summers spent directly across the Mississippi River from St. Louis, Missouri, in Granite City, Illinois, with my maternal grandparents. Their home, a block from the American Steel Foundries, where my grandfather worked for 35 years as a core maker, was situated in a section of town populated by other immigrant Armenians, as well as by foreign-born Hungarians, Bulgarians, Mexicans, and others, all drawn to the nearby steel plants, rolling mills, and foundries looking for work. This admixture of nationalities made for a rich milieu of grocery stores, taverns, barber shops, and other small businesses frequented by a steady stream of family members and friends. If it were possible to return to one's youth, it is to the summers spent long ago with my grandparents, parents, and other family and childhood friends that I would gladly retreat. Even now, these many years later, I can recall the sounds and smells, the voices and faces, the food and frolic of those halcyon times.

In 1947 my family moved from Bettendorf, Iowa, to Memphis, Tennessee, where my father participated in the opening of a new International Harvester plant for the manufacturing of cotton pickers, hay balers, and cultivators. It was in Memphis that I attended school as a child and young adult and where my parents and younger sister still live.

There being a nine-year gap between my sister and me, for all practical purposes, I grew up as an only child.

I entered first grade when I was five, attending the Memphis City Schools until my freshman year, at which time I enrolled in the all-boys Catholic-sponsored Christian Brothers High School. I attribute much of the success that I may enjoy today to the education I received at Christian Brothers. Discipline was strict and expectations high. Whereas I was not the finest student, my name did regularly appear on the B-honor roll. More importantly, the preparation I received, especially in learning to write, made my transition to college quite easy.

My memories of growing up in Memphis in the 1950s and early 1960s also remain warm. I played sports, especially baseball, in both intramural and church leagues. As a Boy Scout, I was active in camping and other outdoor pursuits. For a time, I delivered the now defunct afternoon city newspaper, the *Memphis Press-Scimitar*, to some 75 neighborhood homes. At the time, one of my regular customers was only distinguished by the fact that he took two copies of each day's paper. It wasn't long thereafter, however, that this customer and his wife sprang to fame as country-music stars Johnny Cash and June Carter Cash. The second paper I delivered each day went to Mother Maybelle Carter, then living with her daughter and son-in-law. After all these years, I can still remember that on the third Thursday of each month when I collected payments, the Cashs and Mrs. Carter wrote separate checks and always paid on time. Bill collection was an important lesson in commerce learned early by a young newsboy who would someday seek a doctorate in business administration.

Socially, I was a member of a high-school fraternity and dated like most other teenagers. Fraternity dances and high-school football games were the order of the day. It was, however, while attending a Saturday sorority car wash that I was introduced to a shy beauty by the name of Lynda Kennon. Little did I then realize that some six-years later, after dating through high school and college, she would become my matchless wife of now almost 30 years.

UNDERGRADUATE YEARS (1964-67)

Although neither of my parents had attended college, it was taken for granted that I would do so, as both stressed the importance of "getting an education." Thus, during my senior year in high school, I applied to both the University of Illinois and the University of Iowa, and was accepted by both. Without much information other than Illinois seemed such a large school and my father had once been considered for a baseball scholarship at Iowa, without even having visited either campus, I chose to attend the latter. So, in September, 1964, at the age of 17, I drove with my father to Iowa City, in our family's new Volkswagen bug. All my belongings were packed in my father's World War II navy sea chest. I still remember the bright sunny Iowa Sunday afternoon and our poignant good-byes.

I earned my undergraduate degree in management and industrial relations, completing the graduating requirements in three years by attending classes each summer at what was then known as Memphis State University. What prompted me to select my major remains unclear. I wanted to major in business administration, and management and industrial relations seemingly held the greatest interest. During my freshman year, I joined Sigma Chi Fraternity and have fond memories of friends and good times. I cannot say that the substance of my College of Business Administration school courses was memorable. The Management Theory and Practice textbook was Henry H. Alber's *Principles of Management*. This was the first management book I ever read. Albers taught the course to a class of several hundred students. He lectured twice weekly, and one hour a week was devoted to attending a discussion group under the direction of a Ph.D. student. James W. Walker, who went on to Towers Perrin (management consultants), was my discussion group leader. A continuing friendship that has its roots in my undergraduate days at Iowa involves Max S. Wortman. As a young faculty member, Max taught the required course in Personnel and Industrial Relations and served as Chapter Advisor for the Alpha Kappa Psi business fraternity of which I was a member. As I write these words, I am reminded that 30 years ago (1966) this very semester, every Monday, Wednesday, and Friday, at 8:30 a.m., I would sit in Max's class in Phillips Hall wading through Wendell L. French's *The Personnel Management Process*.

Even before beginning my freshman year at Iowa, I knew that I wished to obtain a master's degree. In this respect, I was greatly influenced by my mother's brother who lived with our family while he attend Memphis State. He went on to obtain a master's degree at George Peabody College. Needing letters of recommendation to accompany my application to the MBA program at Memphis State, I approached Chester A. Morgan and Max Wortman. Professor Morgan taught the required Labor Economics course, using his textbook by the same title. To my good fortune, he had been an Iowa Ph.D. classmate of Herbert J. Markle, then dean of the Memphis State College of Business Administration. Max's advice was to stay at Iowa and he kindly offered to arrange for me to obtain an assistantship in the College of Business Administration's Bureau of Labor and Management. Love and a desire to escape the Iowa winters, however, prevailed. Lynda and I had corresponded during my three years at Iowa and dated during my visits home. It was thus through Max's and Professor Morgan's letters of recommendation, and a fairly respectable grade-point average, that I received a graduate assistantship at Memphis State.

MEMPHIS STATE UNIVERSITY (1967-1968)

During my graduate days at Memphis State, fate seemingly again intervened. By chance, I was assigned to serve as graduate assistant to Ralph W. Williams. A newly hired assistant professor, Ralph had recently completed his Ph.D. at the University of Oregon. Ralph's interests reflected his solid training, as well as prior experience as a system engineer with the Boeing Company in Seattle. Both as Ralph's graduate assistant and as a student in his Seminar in Management (in which we used Paul R. Lawrence et al.'s *Organizational Behavior and Administration*), I was exposed to a part of the academic world that I had no idea existed. Grading exams, conducting library research, and having the opportunity to prepare a case study for Ralph to use in a management development program were all activities that I greatly enjoyed. Moreover, Ralph by his professional demeanor and enthusiasm for teaching was an exemplary role model. Unknowingly, my initial interest in a possible academic career was beginning to take shape.

My year at Memphis State was also exciting for other reasons. First, I found myself in able company. Of my MBA cohort, no fewer than seven others went on to obtain terminal degrees, including Dub Ashton, Carmen Coleman Reagan, Bob Colvard, Jim Hadaway, Tony Koonce, and Hillman Willis. An eighth, Bob Clement (D-Tenn.), is currently a U.S. Congressman. From this group of students I received much. We all shared a large office and an *esprit de corps* quickly developed. Our classes were both challenging and enjoyable.

One memory that particularly stands out as reflecting the times involves the early evening of April 4, 1968, the date on which Martin Luther King was assassinated in downtown Memphis. As one of the few graduate assistants still in my office after 6:00 p.m., I was directed by campus security to go from classroom to classroom throughout the business building with the news that classes were to be dismissed and the campus was to close immediately.

The 1967-68 school year was also exciting for a second reason. On October 19, 1967, Lynda and I became engaged. We were married in Memphis at St. Mary's Episcopal Cathedral on the evening of June 29, 1968. It is an understatement of the highest order to say that over the years she has put up with my idiosyncracies as few in her place would have done.

SELF-APPRAISAL

This leads me quite naturally to say a few words in self-appraisal. Fully recognizing that self-appraisal can more often than not delude the self, I readily recognize a number of limitations in myself which I would prefer to overcome, but also—after some debate with my alter ego—admittedly take satisfaction. Whereas the interconnections that structure my personality are beyond my ability to unravel, as a person I see myself as capable of a steadfast determination in achieving goals and, thus, unafraid of hard work and long hours. Whereas I am somewhat reclusive by nature and, at times, even insular, I enjoy close relationships. This may, in part, be explained by the fact that I am at first uneasy with people on a purely social basis, being more comfortable initially interacting on a task-oriented basis. I have definite opinions and am far from accomplished at disguising my beliefs with empty words. My emotions generally ride close to the surface and spike—both up and down—easily. My tendency to "shoot from the hip" has, however, lessened with the years. Nevertheless, I continue to require the approval of my own judgment over that of others.

Others, I am sure, often see me quite differently and may see such self-appraisal as egotistical. Long ago I acquired the habit of second guessing my thoughts, feelings, and attitudes. At the same time, I have come to accept the inevitability of my own personality and, in truth, I have become rather fond of certain attendant characteristics that seem to guide my life and, I believe, are a principal reason for whatever career success I may have enjoyed.

MLG&W (1967)

During my final summer of study at Memphis State, I accepted a position as a job analyst in the Wage and Salary Department at the City of Memphis Light, Gas & Water Division (MLG&W). As such, my duties involved researching and preparing job descriptions for the company's some 600 job titles, participating in wage and salary determination hearings, and collecting data for the company's annual wage and salary survey. Lynda and I were beginning our life together as an up-and-coming couple. Each morning I commuted to my office in downtown Memphis and each evening I returned home. Surveying the scene, I soon began to realize how I missed the excitement of learning and the immediate feedback received from exams and papers. Moreover, as I judged my prospects for advancement and monetary gain, I also soon realized that, as I then jested, someone above me was going to have to die before I was ever going to be promoted. My boss was perhaps 15 years older than me, his boss about the same, and the vice president one level up wasn't that much older. And, not one of the three were about to go anywhere. All the while, however, I was gaining valuable experience, and I was also able to take advantage of the company's tuition reimbursement program by enrolling in a computer programming course offered locally by the University of Tennessee. Simultaneously, I had enlisted in the U.S. Army Reserves. Whereas I had yet to be called for a draft physical, the Vietnam War and draft made young people my age restless. Facing the uncertain prospect of the military draft, I enlisted and began six years of military service as a Special Agent in U.S. Army Counterintelligence.

In general, life was good. Lynda was working as a billing agent at Humko Products (a division of Kraftco) and, beyond our jobs, other demands on our time were limited. As fate would have it, however, one Wednesday afternoon, in November, 1968, I stopped by Memphis State to visit Sid Johnson, an MBA classmate. I just wanted to catch-up on the latest news. There wasn't much news to speak of—Sid was teaching accounting and thinking about pursuing a doctorate. In fact, he was going down to Mississippi State University on Friday. Why didn't I go along and keep him company? Sure, why not, I thought. I'd never been to Starkville and Friday was always a slow day at the office.

To make a long story short, we did visit State. While Sid was meeting with Loomis Toler, chairman of the Accounting Department, I wandered in and spoke with Graduate Program Coordinator Don Doty. After general pleasantries, Don sent me on to see Dennis Ray in the Management Department to discuss course work.

As with "all things great and wonderful," two months later, a week past my 22nd birthday, I became a student majoring in Management at Mississippi State. At times, it would seem that much of what happens in life results through chance encounters. As seems to be true of many contributors to the *Management Laureates* volumes, I did not deliberately choose management education as a career path. I literally stumbled into it. In case the reader is wondering, Sid Johnson—the cause of it all—did finally enter State, but some two years later. He correctly reasoned that if I could do the work, he certainly could as well.

MISSISSIPPI STATE UNIVERSITY (1969-1971)

My choice of Mississippi State for graduate study in Management was obviously very much a happenstance. Knowing very little about the journey on which I was embarking, I blithely resigned my position at MLG&W and headed for Starkville. Whereas Lynda and I had hoped to move to Starkville and live on the income from an assistantship I had accepted in the College of Business and Industry's Bureau of Business and Economic Research, we were unable to find an apartment within our limited means. Consequently, she remained in Memphis and each weekend I made the 185 mile drive home from Starkville, living on campus during the week. Although my memory is fuzzy about how it happened, I was soon appointed a Resident Assistant for the graduate floor in Dorman Hall. The additional income this generated easily covered my weekly expenses.

As we were soon to learn, fate had intervened by keeping Lynda in Memphis. By this time, I had been in the Reserves for over a year with no word on when I might be called to basic training. The odds suggested that this might occur during the coming summer and, thus, would not disturb my studies. To my dismay, however, some two months into my DBA career, I was ordered to report on April 3, 1969, to Fort Leonard Wood, Missouri, for the beginning of four months' active duty. At the time, this seemed to be a disaster, but again fate intervened on our behalf. Before leaving Starkville, Dean of Men Harold D. Hall asked if

I would like to return in the fall and continue working in an on-campus residence hall. He, however, allowed that what he had in mind was Lynda and I serving as Head Residents for Evans Hall, a men's athletic dorm that housed the basketball, baseball, golf, tennis, and track teams. The position included a rent-free apartment and $200 a month in salary. With this offer, Lynda would now be able to move to Starkville and we could both enroll in school. Moreover, the two months during which I attended classes had been an excellent realistic preview of what was needed to succeed in graduate school. I now had a much clearer idea of the trek on which I was about to embark.

My nine weeks at Fort Leonard Wood passed and were followed by a nine-week session at the Camp McCoy (Wisconsin) Intelligence School, where I completed the Intelligence Research course. Good to his word, Dean Hall held the Head Resident position for my return and September found Lynda and me living together and both enrolled in classes. Just as I had first encountered at Memphis State, I again experienced an intellectual excitement that soon became addictive. Because of the small enrollment in the State DBA program, an intimate association existed among the students, giving rise to many lifetime friendships. Contemporaries such as Achilles Armenakis, Roy Carpenter, Bill Roe, Jerry Kinard, Bill Richmond, Pete Mears, Jim Corprew, Ernest Jobe, Ronnie Weir, and Allen Bizzell kept the atmosphere charged. Achilles was later to become a faculty colleague, and our friendship remains especially close. (Some years back, I introduced Achilles to golf. Whereas neither of us is favored to win this year's PGA Championship, I suspect we both envision heaven as one endless fairway.)

Instead of cutthroat competition, there was always helpful cooperation among our "merry band" of graduate students. It has been observed that as a rule graduate students educate one another. True to form, our group was at times an even more potent source of influence than our classes. Indeed, the stimulation we received from one another moved us to ever greater efforts as we absorbed more and more from our madhouse exchanges.

When State students of my generation get together, their conversation invariably turns to Joyce Bateman Giglioni's Seminar in Personnel Administration. It was a unique experience and the most influential course in my plan of study. Joyce's seminar boiled over with provocative ideas, with its participants arguing vehemently and, often, simultaneously. I readily recall, after receiving back my first seminar paper,

Joyce asking if she might arrange to have it published in the *Mississippi Business Review.* This was my first publication and I was, indeed, proud.

A second fruit of my graduate work was a paper written for Guy Peden's Seminar in Price Policies. I still chuckle thinking about how naive I was at the time, not even knowing how to submit a manuscript for publication. It so happens, however, that one day I noticed the Management Department secretary typing a manuscript submission letter. This was the first such letter I had ever seen, but by week's end I had composed a similar letter and, for the price of postage, was on the way to my second publication. Although the manuscript was rejected from the first journal to which it was submitted, it was promptly accepted by *MSU Business Topics* at Michigan State University. Fate again seems to have intervened. I've since wondered if the manuscript would have ever seen the light of day if the Management Department secretary had just been typing class notes.

With this initial success, 2 for 2, I was on my way. Who said this publishing stuff was difficult, anyway? In fact, I was soon to go 3 for 3, as a paper I had prepared for Paul Pietri's Seminar in Communications was shortly thereafter accepted for publication in *Personnel Administration-Public Personnel Review.*

Following two years of coursework, I sat for my comprehensive exams. Given the nature of a DBA program, I was examined not only in my major, Management, but in three minors: Economics, Marketing, and Business Statistics and Data Processing. As was customary at the time, my thoughts not only turned to a dissertation topic, but to finding a job. Lynda was completing her undergraduate degree in Education, with an emphasis in Library Science. I had interviewed at the 1970 Southern Management Association meeting for various positions, but my "big" break came when Gene Trotter, the current Graduate Program Coordinator, received a call from the dean of the School of Business Administration at Georgia Southern College in Statesboro. He was attempting to fill two positions and Gene had given him my and Bob Bretz's names. Bob and I visited Georgia Southern together and, given the poor job market, we both gladly accepted assistant professorships.

Before proceeding to my years at Georgia Southern, however, something should be said about my dissertation. I spent two years on its completion while teaching full-time at Georgia Southern. Titled *The Standardization of Managements Concepts,* it was supervised by Giovianni B. Giglioni and selected by Garland Publishing for the series

Outstanding Dissertations in American Business History. Although a history dissertation did little to enhance my research skills for competing in an empirically driven profession, I can nevertheless readily appreciate the advantages that resulted. Beyond an understanding of our profession's etiology, my dissertation was an incredibly productive publishing platform, giving initial conception to no fewer than seven publications, including four articles in the *Academy of Management Journal* (AMJ) and two in the *Academy of Management Review* (AMR) within four years of receiving my degree. Of particular pride is an acceptance letter from *AMJ* editor John B. Miner, dated less than a month after my May 13, 1973, graduation from State. In commenting on the reviews for my dissertation-based manuscript, "A Historical Review of Efforts in the Area of Management Semantics," he wrote: "Both reviewers were extremely impressed, and voted for publication without qualification. I can assure you that this happens only very rarely." No written reviewer comments accompanied Jack's letter and not a single revision was required. The manuscript was published as submitted.

As I look back on my graduate days at State, it is clear how my training gave me both various points of view and values that have been influential in all my later work. It is also clear for all but the influence of my assistantship experience at Memphis State under Ralph Williams and a Wednesday afternoon chance encounter with Sid Johnson, I might still be commuting each day to an office at the MLG&W, with a sheaf of incomplete job descriptions in hand. Oh, but for the hand of fate!

GEORGIA SOUTHERN COLLEGE (1971-73)

Lynda and I arrived in Statesboro in August, 1971. Our two-year stay in Statesboro had both its ups and downs. Lynda obtained a position as librarian at Southeast Bullock County High School in nearby Brooklet and enjoyed her work very much. Virtually all of my time was devoted to completing my dissertation. My class schedule was relatively heavy, including an off-campus course to be taught two nights a week at Brunswick Naval Air Station, some 115 miles away, or 54 miles away in Savannah at Armstrong State College. My daily on-campus courses allowed me to finish teaching by noon, at which time I would hurry home and begin writing as late as the evening allowed. Aesthetically, living in Statesboro, with coastal destinations such as Savannah, Hilton

Head, Jekyll Island, and Sea Island only hours away, was a delight. We enjoyed the mild climate and beautiful surroundings.

Academically, however, GSC was a nightmare. The culture within the School of Business Administration was rife with backbiting and politics, every bit the stereotype at that time of a small regional school where the infighting is made worse because there is so little to fight over. Much of this emanated from the management style of the School's dean, who seemed to dole out the available limited resources based on whim. Upon arriving, I learned that the text I had selected for my course had not been to a colleague's liking and another had been selected in its place. My cry that if I was competent enough to teach the course, I was competent enough to select a text, fell on deaf ears. It also quickly became evident that the dean's antics had resulted in the formation of two principal coalitions whose members literally would not speak to one another. As a new faculty member, any attempt on my part to communicate with either group was seen as siding with the "enemy." It was a lose-lose situation.

To make matters worse, my success in publishing was a threat to all sides. By "speeding up the race," I had inadvertently discredited the self-serving belief that by being at a small school with limited resources and a heavy teaching load, one couldn't be expected to do much more than meet classes. As a "rate-buster," I had become a threat to the status quo and was subject to the very shunning discussed in our own textbooks. It was obvious that the future career I had envisioned wasn't going to become a reality in such a setting. This realization was cemented when Bob Trent (University of Virginia) called me aside at an Academy of Management meeting and bluntly told me that if I was going to have a future, I needed to relocate at a "name-brand" school. Thanks to Bob's interest, I was quickly learning the ins and outs of the academic pecking order. Soon, however, I would also learn that it is much more difficult to "trade up" than "trade down" in moving to a new position.

One very important event that occurred while we were in Statesboro was the birth of our first child. Katherine Nicole was born on December 4, 1972. Together, Lynda and I experienced all the excitement, apprehension, and satisfaction of caring for our first born. Today, Katherine, a graduate of Rhodes College, is active in her own career in the field of public relations and is a lovely young lady of whom her mother and I are most proud. In the way of all things, she and her husband, George

Kingsmill, are now expecting their first daughter. (*N.B.*: Anna Kennon Kingsmill made her world debut on April 2, 1997.)

Going back a step to Bob Trent's advice, during my second year at GSC, I began to apply for positions at various other schools. At the time, former Academy of Management President Ron Shuman was retiring from the University of Oklahoma and his position as Curator of the Harry W. Bass Business History Collection was thus open. Lynda (now seven months pregnant with Katherine) and I were invited to Norman for a campus interview. We were, of course, excited. Oklahoma meant the "big time." During one of my last interviews, Dean Horace B. Brown offered me the position from which Ron was stepping down. For some reason, for which we've never received an explanation, the offer did not materialize. We simply did not hear another word about the position. Hence, another lesson learned—an offer is not an offer until it is in writing. As a result of this experience, in all my interviewing as a department chairman, I have always tried to avoid misleading job candidates. Fate, however, again seems to have played a hand. I've often wondered how different my career would have been had I become curator of the Bass Collection and had focused my interests solely in the area of management history. In any event, Oklahoma went on to hire Dan Wren, then at Florida State University, for the position. It definitely got the best person for the job. Since our paths first crossed at the 1974 Southern Management Association meeting in Atlanta, Dan and I have remained close, as he has been both a friend and mentor. Without question, he is our generation's foremost management historian.

Beyond applying for the Oklahoma position, I had also inquired about a position with the Boston University Overseas Program and, much to my surprise, one afternoon I received a call from Yu Sang (Charlie) Chang inquiring about my interest. He had noted my experience teaching at Brunswick Naval Air Station and, given that most of BU's overseas programs were military affiliated, thought I might have the experience necessary to work in such a setting. A campus interview in Boston was scheduled, a position was offered, and soon Lynda, Katherine, and I were on our way to Frankfurt am Main, West Germany.

In retrospect, I marvel at our courage. With Bob Trent's admonishment ringing in my ears, I resigned my position at GSC with no future beyond a one-year contract with BU. I, however, was again fortunate because before leaving for West Germany on September 2, 1973, Lynda and I stopped in Auburn, Alabama, to visit Achilles and Wilma

Armenakis. Achilles had accepted a position at Auburn University for the fall term. John Henry and Bill Holley had recruited Achilles from East Carolina University, based on a recommendation from Don Mosley at Mississippi State. Don had been Achilles's major professor and also had been influential in Bill finishing his undergraduate and master's degrees at State and going on to complete a Ph.D. at Alabama (as had Don). In addition, Junior Feild had just joined the Auburn faculty, having been recruited as a new Ph.D. in Industrial/Organizational Psychology from the University of Georgia. Junior had received both his undergraduate and master's degrees from State and had worked with Achilles and me in the Bureau of Business and Economic Research. At the prompting of Achilles, Bill, and Junior, an informal round of interviews was scheduled for me to meet various faculty members. Little did I then realize how significant their actions on my behalf would soon prove.

BOSTON UNIVERSITY OVERSEAS PROGRAM (1973-74)

Looking back, our young family tremendously enjoyed our year together in Europe. It was a chance for our young family to strike out on its own. We spent Thanksgiving and Christmas in Frankfurt, the location of my first teaching assignment. Easter found us in the snowy mountains of Baumholder, my second assignment. Finally, we spent the summer in Wildflecken, among the Bavarian Alps.

My schedule required that I teach a graduate course three evenings a week. The students were primarily U.S. airmen and soldiers of all ranks, with an occasional spouse and German national. This schedule not only meant our days were open for local exploring, but normally left four uninterrupted days (Thursday through Sunday or Friday through Monday) for side trips. We traveled all over Europe, including England, Holland, Luxembourg, Belgium, France, Austria, Switzerland, and Italy. We missed very few sights and delighted in the pastry shops and local restaurants. The freedom and novelty were a wonderful experience for a young couple beginning to make their own way in the world.

Being in Europe also allowed me to pursue several research interests. Working at the Goethe University library in Frankfurt, I was able to begin a bibliography of the complete writings of Henri Fayol, to inspect much of Kurt Lewin's work in its original German, and to complete a paper comparing the attitudes of German and U.S. managers toward the legitimacy of various organizational influences. This paper was my first empirical analysis and became my fifth *AMJ* article in four years.

During this entire time, the question of where the coming fall would find our family loomed unanswered. Arranging for job interviews in the States was, understandably, quite difficult and costly. To my thrill, however, whereas other BU faculty were facing the prospects of a second year in Europe, a letter arrived from John Henry at Auburn offering me an assistant professorship. He requested that I call him collect to discuss the offer. I can remember trekking through the snow to use a phone at the local post office. Ours was a short conversation—I'd be thrilled to accept the offer and join what would soon become known as the "Auburn Mafia," our own early version of what more recently have been tagged "hot groups."[2]

AUBURN UNIVERSITY (1974-1985)

On August 8, 1974, the Bedeians moved to Auburn and bought their first home. Though Auburn was our home for only eleven years, it seems longer because it was a period of intense personal and professional growth. Auburn remains a college town of unique charm. Of all the places we've lived, I think of Auburn with the greatest nostalgia and affection. It represents much of my professional youth and some of the most pleasant and productive years of my life. It was also in Auburn in 1979 that our son Thomas Arthur (known by his initials as Tab) was born. Currently a senior in high school, Tab is an outstanding young man with a special interest in music. As with Katherine, we take enormous satisfaction in his integrity and accomplishments.

I gave my best to Auburn University and received incomparably more from the rich friendships and intellectual stimulation than I could give in return. As I have noted before, there is no doubt that whatever career success that I may have enjoyed was largely determined by being able to spend the first years of my career in such fine company. The environment within the Management Department was one of nourishment, excitement, and collegiality. Above all, no one was afraid of excellence and achievement in others. My debt, both academic and personal, to my original academic family—Achilles Armenakis, Junior Feild, Bill Holley, Bill Giles, and later on, Kevin Mossholder, may be acknowledged, but can never be repaid. My development as a scholar was immeasurably enhanced by the learning opportunities afforded me while working alongside these men of such personal quality and creativeness as are seldom found in an academic group. Recalling our daily lunches and our monthly dinner meetings, it would be difficult to adequately express what our friendship (which has included our wives and children) has meant to me. There has not been a year, since 1985, when we have not visited Auburn or had Auburn guests. We all remain close friends and colleagues.

LOUISIANA STATE UNIVERSITY (1985-PRESENT)

I hated to leave Auburn University. At the same time, however, the University as a whole seemed without leadership. A vote of confidence in the University's president had resulted in his resignation and his successor seemed unable to articulate a clear vision for the University's future. Likewise, I was developing a mild case of claustrophobia. In a small university town, one's academic affiliation often becomes a defining feature of social and community interactions. Thus, in 1984, I began to selectively seek out other career opportunities. This led, in the spring of 1985, to an invitation to become the first Ralph and Kacoo Olinde Distinguished Professor of Management at Louisiana State University.

With my move to the LSU College of Business Administration in the fall of 1985, at age 39, my professional life was changed significantly. Heretofore, most of my energy had gone to my own professional activities and research. At LSU, I was expected to help revive a department that seemed to have been in a 15-year time warp. Jim Henry had arrived, as new dean, 18-months prior with a similar charge for the entire College. These were stirring times, as Jim's efforts to transform the College prompted strong resistance and resentment. Despite prior assurances that my joining the Management Department faculty was welcomed by my new colleagues, much of the prevailing resentment associated with Jim's efforts to rebuild the College spilled over to other newcomers—including me.

Also joining the Management Department my first fall was a new chairman. It may be impossible to write of these events with objectivity. Within the first year, signs of a serious crisis within the Department began to surface, ultimately ending in an open revolt among the Department's members and a faculty vote demanding that the chair resign. In his place, an associate professor who had been in the Department for several years was appointed chairman. With the deposed chairman still in residence and an inexperienced hand at the helm, circumstances continued to deteriorate. The atmosphere in the Department was unlike any other place I had worked. In some ways it resembled Georgia Southern, but the open skepticism, criticism and antagonism were much more damaging. As the senior (in position) member of the Department, much of the blame for its inability to right itself fell at my feet. The situation was beyond my ken and totally alien to anything I had experienced at Auburn. Events reached a head when the replacement chairman accepted a position elsewhere and Dean Henry immediately removed him from the chairmanship. With no one else to turn to, I was drafted as the Department's fourth chairman in three years. The Department was an interpersonal mess. I had not come to LSU to be an administrator and had no desire to become one. As I write this, however, I am within a month of completing my third (and final!) three-year (elected) term as the Department's chairman.

DEPARTMENT CHAIRMAN (1988-1997)

Although I admittedly dislike doing work of an administrative nature, I have nevertheless derived a great measure of pride in helping to build an outstanding department at LSU. For my own part, from the beginning of my chairmanship, I had determined that the Department would have high standards and have them on honest terms. The only thing that matters is excellence. Excellence in teaching, research, and service. This requires an insistence on the public getting what it pays for, and more if possible.

In my own mind, my chief accomplishments as chairman lie in working to surround myself with talented colleagues and staff, setting them free to excel, and making us all jointly responsible for the Department's welfare. In this respect, I've attempted to build upon the heritage of my Auburn years to create an environment where we all take pride in the accomplishments of one another and our focus is on "why" (rather than "why not") we can achieve excellence in all that we do.

My department colleagues have contributed greatly to my personal growth. We have become a close and nourishing group. Perhaps nothing has given me deeper satisfaction than watching young colleagues begin their careers and families as they embark upon their personal odysseys. The successes of my current colleagues, Cheryl Adkins, Nate Bennett, Tim Chandler, Courtland Chaney, David Deephouse, Paul Jarley, Dave

Ketchen, Dan Marin, Kevin Mossholder, Tim Palmer, and Kerry Sauley, have given me a great deal of pride. Kevin, of course, a colleague from my Auburn days, is someone whom I've had the good fortune of successfully recruiting on two occasions. His many accomplishments speak for themselves.

For those contemplating an administrative career, I offer a bit of counsel. Based on my experience, I firmly believe that those who do seek administrative venues should bring with them a measure of "academic credibility." For me, this is especially important for it avoids situations where administrators demand that faculty colleagues do things, such as conduct research, publish, and secure grants that they haven't and, perhaps, couldn't do themselves. Moreover, having one's performance judged by a chairman who has never sat pen in hand in front of a blank page, collected data, negotiated a book contract, or responded to reviewer comments on a pet manuscript is much different than being judged by a chairman who has successfully done these things and appreciates the sacrifices involved.

It may seem strange at first, but let me also note that whereas I believe being a scholar makes one a better administrator, being an administrator can also make one a better scholar. I'll forever be a better faculty member, classroom instructor, and management researcher by virtue of my experiences as a department chairman. The reader has no doubt heard it said that its much easier to run for president than be president. Well, based on my experience, it's a whole lot easier to "bitch" about what one's department chairman should have done than to be charged with actually doing it oneself. If management professors simply practiced what they taught, being a department chair would be a *much more* desirable position. But, then again, I have long believed that, for some people, bitching is a form of job enrichment.

TEACHING

It would seem appropriate to also mention my classroom experiences. Throughout my career, I have maintained a special interest in teaching, having lectured to thousands of students in both traditional and executive education programs. As an educator, I have attempted to be keenly aware of the impact I might have on my students' lives, realizing as historian Henry B. Adams once observed, "A teacher affects eternity; he can never tell where his influence stops."[3]

This thought reminds me of a story told by columnist Sydney Harris in which he recounts the recent obituary of a deceased University of Chicago professor.[4] The obituary concluded with the bleak sentence: "He left no survivors." Such a statement is, of course, ridiculous for, as Harris went on to observe, "A great teacher, even if he writes not a word, may be survived by generations, even centuries." My survivors will be those students whose thoughts, feelings, and, sometimes, character I have helped shape, for better or worse. This is a teacher's ultimate reward and glory.

In retrospect, relationships with students have been a major source of professional satisfaction for me. I have watched their careers with anticipation. Indeed, I count the life-long friendships that I have established with many as among the most precious of my satisfactions. The pleasure of observing their career progress and knowing that so many have turned out so well has given me immeasurable fulfillment. I am proud of all, in one way or another. Among those for whose dissertations I have been responsible are (in approximate order of date): Allayne B. Pizzolatto, Kerry D. Carson, Antoinette S. Phillips, Rebecca G. Long, and Franz T. Lohrke. To be able to work with such brilliant and interesting students has been an extremely rewarding experience.

PUBLICATIONS

A consideration of my classroom experiences leads me to say a few words concerning my publications. Rather than make an effort to review my publications, I will simply note that the focus of my work has been determined not only by my innate personality, but also by a multitude of stimuli from all directions. My much-ramified writings reflect whatever has caught my fancy. Whereas some academics have spent years carving out a single scholarly niche for themselves, my inclination has been to follow my interests and, above all, work with good people.

Over the years, fate has been quite generous in providing me with talented partners. I have collaborated with more than 65 colleagues—several of whom I've never met face-to-face. Playing to each other's strengths, we've complemented one another quite nicely. I can only hope that my co-authors have shared my satisfaction in our joint labors.

Turning for a moment to my various textbooks, as is often the case, each grew out of courses I have taught over the years. All have been used widely around the world, both in English- and foreign-language editions. One gratification of being a textbook author is realizing that thousands of readers one will never know have been influenced by one's written words. This said, however, the labor of love that I have found most gratifying is the *Management Laureates* series of which this volume is a part. The opportunity the series has provided to work closely with so many of the management discipline's leading contributors has been a unique privilege.

PROFESSIONAL SERVICE

This would be an incomplete story if I did not at least comment on my involvement in academic organizations. During much of my professional life, I have been active in management and other kinds of organizations. This experience has been invaluable in widening my circle of acquaintances and providing exposure to new ideas and developments within the academic world, as well as also calibrating my standards of academic excellence.

Throughout the years, I have had the honor of serving as President of the Southeastern Institute for Decision Science (1979), the Southern Management Association (1983), the Allied Southern Business Association (1983), the Foundation for Administrative Research (1990), and the Academy of Management (1989). In addition, I have had the privilege of serving as editor of the *Journal of Management* (1978-79), as well as serving in numerous other editorial roles.

Of all the organized groups to which I have belonged, none has been more important to me than the Academy of Management. If I were listing the kudos that have fallen to me, I should place first that of being elected the Academy's youngest-ever President. I remain similarly proud of being the youngest person ever elected an Academy of Management Fellow, generally regarded as the highest distinction a member of the discipline can receive. At the time (1979), I was 32-years old. My DBA had been awarded only six-years prior. I am particularly gratified to be presently serving as the Fellowship's tenth Dean. The formal recognition of my professional colleagues has been a signal honor that I continue to deeply appreciate.

Finally, closer to home, being named a Boyd Professor this past spring by the LSU Board of Supervisors provides an additional measure of gratification. A lifetime appointment, in recognition of national and international contributions to one's discipline, this is the University's highest professorial rank, now held by only 12 active members of its over 1300 faculty members. Being recognized by one's own carries special significance.

CONCLUSION

The preceding pages tell more than enough about my life, my interests, and my beliefs. On most of my accomplishments, I place a modest estimate. It is no doubt evident to any reader that has persevered thus far, I have been extremely fortunate—fortunate in my nativity, in my marriage and family, in my education, in my colleagues, in my opportunities, and in achieving success beyond any justifiable expectation. As I look back over these pages and contemplate my past life, I marvel at what I didn't know that I didn't know and can only wonder what someday I will know that *now* I don't know that I don't know. The future, therefore, promises to be equally exciting, with hard work, fate, and fortune continuing to play a hand.

December 1996
Baton Rouge, Louisiana

PUBLICATIONS

1970

Cultural influences on minority group self-concept. *Mississippi Business Review, 32*(2), 9-11, 14.

1971

Consumer perception of price as an indicator of product quality. *MSU Business Topics, 19*(3), 59-65.

1972

Relationship in organization: A clarification. *Academy of Management Journal, 15,* 238-239.

Superior-subordinate role perception. *Personnel Administration-Public Personnel Review, l*(3), 4-11.

1973

Management theory: A pediatric note. *Business Perspectives, 10*(4), 2-5.

Red Dot Drug Stores, ICH 9-473-736. Intercollegiate Case Clearing House, Harvard University, Cambridge, MA. February, 2 pages. [Revised and reprinted as: "Red Dot Drug Stores: The polygraph test" in R.L. Hilgert, S.H. Schoen, & J.W. Towle (Eds.), *Cases and policies in human resources management,* 3rd ed., 1978, pp. 197-199; *idem.,* 4th ed., 1982, pp. 170-171; 5th ed., 1986, pp. 177-178, Boston: Houghton-Mifflin; W.H. Holley & K.M. Jennings (Eds.), *Personnel management: Functions and issues.* Hinsdale, IL: Dryden Press, 1983, pp. 556-557; *idem.,* 2nd ed., 1987, pp. 584-585.]

1974

A historical review of efforts in the area of management semantics. *Academy of Management Journal, 17,* 101-114.

With G.B. Giglioni. A conspectus of management control theory: 1900-1972. *Academy of Management Journal, 17,* 292-305.

Vytautas Andrius Graicunas: A biographical sketch. *Academy of Management Journal, 17,* 347-349.

With R.D. Coston. Managerial perspectives of the shorter workweek in Georgia manufacturing firms. *Atlantic Economic Journal, 2*(1), 62-69.

A bibliographic investigation of the writings of Henri Fayol. *The N-File,* (2), (Suppl., Research Note #1), pp. 1-6.

1975

A comparison and analysis of German and United States managerial attitudes toward the legitimacy of organizational influence. *Academy of Management Journal, 18,* 887-904.

With A.A. Armenakis. Male-female differences in perceived organizational legitimacy. *Human Resource Management, 14*(4), 5-9.

With A.A. Armenakis, H.S. Feild, & W.H. Holley. The effects of anonymity versus identified but confidential response conditions in
organizational research. *Management, l*(l), 45-49.

A selected bibliography of theses and dissertations in the area of management history. *The N-File,* (4), 14-17.

With D.T. Grider. Personnel practices in Georgia manufacturing companies: I. Hiring. *Atlanta Economic Review, 25*(2), 36-39.

With D.T. Grider. Personnel practices in Georgia manufacturing companies: II. Development. *Atlanta Economic Review, 25*(3), 36-39.

With D.T. Grider. Personnel practices in Georgia manufacturing companies: III. Employee relations. *Atlanta Economic Review, 25*(4), 52-
54.

With D.T. Grider. Personnel practices in Georgia manufacturing companies: IV. The personnel manager. *Atlanta (Economic Review, 25*),
44-45.

With A.A. Armenakis, W.H. Holley, Jr., & H.S. Feild, Jr., (Eds.), *Proceedings of the annual meeting of the Academy of Management* (p.
494). Auburn, AL.

1976

Management history thought. *Academy of Management Review, 1*(1),
96-97.

Organizational socialization: A cross-cultural comparison. *Management International Review, 16*(2), 73-80.

Finding 'the one best way'—An appreciation of Frank B. Gilbreth, the
father of motion study. *Conference Board Record, 16*(6), 37-39.

Relationship of need achievement to self-esteem: Evidence for validity
of form B of Coopersmith's self-esteem inventory. *Perceptual and
Motor Skills, 43*, 1219-1220.

Rater characteristics affecting the validity of performance appraisal.
Journal of Management, 2(l), 37-45.

With A.A. Armenakis, & B.W. Kemp. Relation of sex to perceived legitimacy of organizational influence. *Journal of Psychology, 94*, 93-
99.

With H.S. Feild. Institutional participation in the Academy of Management: A 40-year perspective. *Academy of Management Newsletter,
6* (May) 5.

With J.R. Harris, R.E. Anderson, & H.C. Schneider (Eds.), *Proceedings of the Southeastern American Institute for Decision Sciences* (p. 278), Auburn, AL.

1977

The roles of self-esteem and N achievement in aspiring to prestigious vocations. *Journal of Vocational Behavior, 11*, 109-119.

With A.A. Armenakis, H.S. Feild, W.H. Holley, & B. Ledbetter. Human resource considerations in textile work redesign. *Human Relations, 30,* 1147-1156.

With A.A. Armenakis. A program for computing Fisher's exact probability test and the coefficient of association M for n X M contingency tables. *Educational and Psychological Measurement, 37,* 253-256.

With R.W. Zmud. Some evidence relating to convergent validity of form B of Coopersmith's self-esteem inventory. *Psychological Reports, 40,* 725-726.

With M.J. Zarra. Sex-role orientation: Effect on self-esteem, need achievement and internality in college females. *Perceptual and Motor Skills, 45,* 712-714.

With J.L. Hyder. Sex-role attitude as a moderator in the relationship between locus of control and N achievement. *Psychological Reports, 41,* 1172-1174.

With R.J. Teague, Jr., & R.W. Zmud. Test-retest reliability and internal consistency of short-from of Coopersmith's self-esteem inventory. *Psychological Reports, 41,* 1041-1042.

With K.R. Davis. Southeast AIDS udate. *Decision Line, 8*(2), 2.

With R.J. Teague, Jr. Internal consistency of the Coopersmith self-esteem inventory (form B). JSAS *Catalog of Selected Documents in Psychology, 7,* 41. (Ms. No. 1471)

With S.W. Harden. An investigation of leadership attitudes, political orientation and need for achievement (n Ach). JSAS *Catalog of Selected Documents in Psychology, 7,* 108-109. (Ms. No. 1592)

With J.R. Harris (Eds.), *Proceedings of the annual meeting of the Southeastern American Institute for Decision Sciences* (p. 260), Auburn, AL.

1978

Historical development of management. In L. R. Bittel (Ed.), *Encyclopedia of professional management* (pp. 645-650). New York: McGraw-Hill.

With A.A. Armenakis. Relationships between age and adjective check list scale scores. *Psychological Reports, 43,* 821-822.

With J. Touliatos. Work-related motives and self-esteem in American women. *Journal of Psychology, 99,* 63-70.

With D.D. Van Fleet. Span of management: Its current status and future. *Akron Business and Economics Review, 9*(1), 25-30.

The management crossword puzzle. In R.M. Fulmer & T.T. Herbert (Eds.), *Exploring the new management* (2nd ed., pp. 318-320; 3rd ed., 1983, pp. 344-346). New York: Macmillan. [Reprinted from the *Academy of Management Newsletter, 7* (March), 4; *Solution, 7* (May), 7.]

1979

With A.A. Armenakis, & R.E. Niebuhr. Planning for organizational intervention: The importance of existing socio-psychological situations in organizational diagnosis. *Group & Organization Studies, 4,* 59-70.

With S.G. Green, A.A. Armenakis, & L.D. Marbert. An evaluation of the response format and scale structure of the job diagnostic survey. *Human Relations, 32,* 181-188.

With L.D. Marbert. Individual differences in self-perception and the job-life satisfaction relationship. *Journal of Social Psychology, 109,* 111-118.

1980

With A.A. Armenakis & R.W. Gibson. The measurement and control of beta change. *Academy of Management Review, 5,* 561-566.

With H.S. Feild. Academic stratification in graduate management programs: Departmental prestige and faculty hiring pattern. *Journal of Management, 6,* 99-115.

With R.E. Niebuhr, & A.A. Armenakis. Individual need states and their influence on perceptions of leader behavior. *Social Behavior and Personality, 8*, 17-25.

With A.A. Armenakis, & S.M. Curran. Personality correlates of role stress. *Psychological Reports, 46*, 627-632.

Organizations: Theory and analysis (339 pp.); *Instructor's manual* (88 pp.). Hinsdale, IL: Dryden Press.

1981

With A.A. Armenakis. A path-analytic study of the consequences of role conflict and ambiguity. *Academy of Management Journal, 24*, 417-424.

With K.W. Mossholder, & A.A. Armenakis. Role perceptions, satisfaction, and performance: Moderating effects of self-esteem and organizational level. *Organizational Behavior and Human Performance, 28*, 224-234.

With A.A. Armenakis, & S.M. Curran. The relationship between role stress and job-related, interpersonal and organizational climate factors. *Journal of Social Psychology, 113*, 247-260.

Foreword. In D.F. Ray (Ed.), *The relationship between theory, research, and practice: An assessment of fundamental problems and their possible resolution* (p. ii). Mississippi State, MS: Southern Management Association.

1982

With K.W. Mossholder, & A.A. Armenakis. Group process-work outcome relationships: A note on the moderating impact of self-esteem. *Academy of Management Journal, 25*, 575-585.

Suicide and occupation: A review. *Journal of Vocational Behavior, 21*, 206-223.

With N. Schmitt. A comparison of LISREL and two stage least squares analysis of an hypothesized life-job satisfaction reciprocal relationship. *Journal of Applied Psychology, 67*, 806-817.

With A.A. Armenakis. On the measurement and control of beta change: Reply to Terborg, Maxwell, and Howard. *Academy of Management Review, 7*, 296-299.

With J. Touliatos. Material achievement expectancies, IQ, and autonomous achievement motivation in kindergarten children. *Psychological Reports, 50*, 51-54.

Counterpoint (A rejoiner). *Personnel Psychology, 35*, 247-249.

On "Karayan's histories of Armenian communities in Turkey." *Armenian Review, 35*, 100-101.

1983

With A.A. Armenakis, & S.B. Pond, III. Research issues in OD evaluation: Past, present, and future. *Academy of Management Review, 8*, 320-328.

With K.W. Mossholder, & A.A. Armenakis. Role perception-outcome relationships: Moderating effects of situational variables. *Human Relations, 36*, 167-184.

With K.W. Mossholder. Cross-level inference and organizational research: Perspectives on interpretation and application. *Academy of Management Review, 8*, 547-558.

With K.W. Mossholder. Group interactional processes: Individual and group-level effects. *Group & Organization Studies, 8*, 187-202.

Communication. *Armenian Review, 36*(3), 102.

With W.F. Glueck. *Management* (3rd ed., 672 pp.). Hinsdale, IL: Dryden Press. *Instructor's manual* (255 pp.); Transparency masters (104 pp.); *Test bank* (235 pp.); *Computerized test bank*; all with D.R. Norris.

With L.R. Jauch, S.A. Coltrin, & W.F. Glueck. *The managerial experience: Cases, exercises, and readings,* (3rd ed., 469 pp.); *Instructor's manual* (195 pp.). Hinsdale, IL: Dryden Press.

With S.A. Coltrin, L.R. Jauch, & W.F. Glueck. *Study guide to accompany management* (3rd ed., 253 pp.) Hinsdale, IL: Dryden Press.

With W.F. Glueck. *Management* (3rd ed., 672 pp.). Tokyo: Holt-Saunders. [International edition]

1984

Henry Plimpton Kendall. In L.F. Urwick & W.B. Wolf (Eds.), *The golden book of management* (rev. ed., pp. 337-340). New York: AMACOM.

Ordway Tead. In L.F. Urwick & W.B. Wolf (Eds.), *The golden book of management* (rev. ed., pp. 389-392). New York: AMACOM.

With J. Touliatos, K.W. Mossholder, & A.I. Barkman. Job-related perceptions of male and female government, industrial, and public accountants. *Social Behavior and Personality, 12*, 61-68.

In Memoriam: Lyndall F. Urwick (1891-1983). *Academy of Management Newsletter, 14* (October), 10.

Organizations: Theory and analysis (2nd ed., 513 pp.). Hinsdale, IL: Dryden Press.

With W.R. Langford. *Instructor's manual* (117 pp.). Hinsdale, IL: Dryden Press.

Organizations: Theory and analysis (2nd ed., 513 pp.). Tokyo: Holt-Saunders. [International edition]

1985

With E.R. Kemery, K.W. Mossholder, & J. Touliatos. Outcomes of role stress: A multisample constructive replication. *Academy of Management Journal, 28*, 363-375.

With K.W. Mossholder, & J. Touliatos. An examination of intra-occupational differences: Personality, perceived work climate, and outcome preferences. *Journal of Vocational Behavior, 26*, 164-175.

Historical development of management. In L.R. Bittel & J.E. Ramsey (Eds.), *Handbook for professional managers* (2nd ed., pp. 491-496). New York: McGraw-Hill.

1986

The serial transmission effect: Implications for academe. *The Bulletin of the Association of Business Communication, 49*(1), 34-36.

With A.A. Armenakis & M.R. Buckley. Survey research measurement issues in evaluating change: A laboratory investigation. *Applied Psychological Measurement, 10*, 147-157.

In Memoriam: Richard J. Whiting. *Academy of Management Newsletter, 16* (May), 9.

With A.I. Barkman, J. Touliatos, & K.W. Mossholder. Females and males in accounting: A profile. *Government Accountants Journal, 35*, 24-32.

Contemporary challenges in the study of organizations. In J.G. Hunt &
J.D. Blair (Eds.), *1986 Yearly Review of Management, Journal of
Management, 12,* 185-201.
With K.W. Mossholder, J. Touliatos, & I.G. Barkman. The accountant's
stereotype: An update for vocational counselors. *Career Develop-
ment Quarterly, 35,* 113-122.
A standardization of selected management concepts. Garland Series of
Outstanding Dissertations in American Business History. New
York: Garland Publishing.
Management (666 pp.). Hinsdale, IL: Dryden Press. *Instructor's man-
ual* (397 pp.) with L. A. Zienert; *Transparency acetates* (50 pp.)
with P. L. Wright; *Test bank* (pp. 150) and *Computerized test bank*
both with J. C. McElroy.
With L.R. Jauch, & S.A. Coltrin. *The managerial experience: Cases,
exercises, and readings* (4th ed., 276 pp.). Hinsdale, IL: Dryden
Press. *Instructor's manual* (162 pp.).
With J.A. Coltrin, & L.R. Jauch. *Study guide to accompany management* (361 pp.). Hinsdale, IL: Dryden Press.

1987

With E.R. Kemery, & K.W. Mossholder. Role stress, physical symptom-
atology, and turnover intentions: A causal analysis of three alternative specifications. *Journal of Occupational Behaviour, 8,* 11-
23.
Organization theory: A review of the field. In C.L. Cooper & I.T. Rob-
ertson (Eds.), *International annual review of industrial and organizational psychology—1987* (pp. 1-33). Chichester: Wiley.
With H.S. Feild, & R.D. Gatewood. Inferring employee specifications
from job analysis data: Some example applications. In R.S.
Schuler & S. Youngblood (Eds.), *Readings in personnel and
human resource management* (3rd ed., pp. 121-137). St. Paul, MN:
West Publishing.
With K.W. Mossholder, & J. Touliatos. Individual propensities for emotional supportiveness within a dual career context: Work and non-
work reactions. *International Journal of Manpower, 7*(4), 7-12.
Knowing oneself: An exercise in perceptual accuracy. *Organizational
Behavior Teaching Review, 11*(4), 137-139.

With R. Kalwa. Parental leave: New challenge in the U.S. workplace. *Equal Opportunities International*, *6*(3), 1-3.

With J.H. Greenhaus, & K.W. Mossholder. Work experiences, job performance, and feelings of personal and family well-being. *Journal of Vocational Behavior*, *31*, 200-215.

An interactionist perspective on organisational adaptation. *Leadership & Organization Development Journal*, *8*(3), 31-32.

With A.S. Phillips (Eds.), *Proceedings of the annual meeting of the Southwest division of the Academy of Management* (236 pp.). Baton Rouge, LA.

1988

With J. Farh & J.D. Werbel. An empirical investigation of self-appraisal-based performance evaluation. *Personnel Psychology*, *41*, 141-156.

With C.C. Wilhelm. In Memoriam: Jane S. Mouton. *Academy of Management Newsletter*, *18*(March), 3.

With J. Farh. Understanding goal setting: An in-class experiment. *Organizational Behavior Teaching Review*, *12*(3), 75-79.

With K.W. Mossholder, D.R. Norris, & W.F. Giles. Job performance and turnover decisions: Two field studies. *Journal of Management*, *14*, 403-404.

With B.F. Burke, & R.G. Moffett, III. Outcomes of work-family conflict among married male and female professionals. *Journal of Management*, *14*, 475-491.

With C.P. Neck. Maunsell White III: Louisiana inventor and victim of the Matthew effect. *New Orleans Genesis*, *27*, 399-404.

With A.A. Armenakis & W.A. Randolph. The significance of congruence coefficients: A comment and statistical test. *Journal of Management*, *14*, 559-566.

With H.S. Feild. Relationships between age and California Psychological Inventory Scale scores. *Psychological Reports*, *63*, 696-698.

With A.S. Phillips, K.W. Mossholder, & J. Touliatos. Birth order and selected work-related personality variables. *Individual Psychology*, *44*, 492-499.

With J.A. Buford, Jr. *Management in extension* (2nd ed., 264 pp.). Auburn: Alabama Cooperative Extension Service, Auburn University.

1989

With E.R. Kemery, & K.W. Mossholder. Testing for cross-level interactions: An empirical demonstration. *Behavioral Science, 34,* 70-78.

With R.W. Griffeth. Employee performance evaluations: Effects of ratee age, rater age, and rater gender. *Journal of Organizational Behavior, 10,* 83-90.

With S. Parasuraman, J.H. Greenhaus, S. Rabinowitz, & K.W. Mossholder. Work and family variables as mediators of the relationship between wives' employment and husbands' well being. *Academy of Management Journal, 32,* 185-201.

With J.D. Werbel. Intended turnover as a function of age and job performance. *Journal of Organizational Behavior, 10,* 275-281.

With A.A. Armenakis. Progress and promise: The case of the alpha, beta, gamma change typology. *Group & Organization Studies, 14,* 155-160.

With K.S. Sauley. .05: A case of the tail wagging the distribution. In R. Griffin & D.D. Van Fleet (Eds.), *1989 Yearly Review of Management, Journal of Management, 15,* 335-344.

With T.M. Dockery. Attitudes versus actions: LaPiere's (1934) classic study revisited. *Social Behavior and Personality, 17,* 9-16.

With E.R. Kemery & W.P. Dunlap. The employee separation process: Criterion-related issues associated with tenure and turnover. *Journal of Management, 15,* 417-424.

Totems and taboos: Undercurrents in the management discipline. (Presidential Address.) *Academy of Management Newsletter, 19* (October), 1-6.

With A.S. Phillips. PMS and the workplace. *Social Behavior and Personality, 17,* 165-174.

Management, 2nd ed. Hinsdale, IL: Dryden Press. *Instructor's manual and transparency masters* with A. S. Phillips and R. G. Long (368 pp.); *Transparency acetates*; *Test bank* and *Computerized test bank* both with R. Lester.

With L.R. Jauch, & S.A. Coltrin. *The managerial experience: Cases, exercises, and readings* (5th ed., 331 pp.). Hinsdale, IL: Dryden Press. *Instructor's manual* (188 pp.).

With J.A. Coltrin, & L.R. Jauch. *Study guide to accompany management* (327 pp.). Hinsdale, IL: Dryden Press.

Management (2nd ed., 671 pp.). Tokyo: Holt-Saunders. [International edition]

1990

With K.W. Mossholder, & J. Touliatos. Type a status and selected work experiences among male and female accountants. In M.J. Strube (Ed.), Special Issue, *Journal of Social Behavior and Personality, 5,* 291-305.

With K.W. Mossholder, & E.R. Kemery. On using regression coefficients to interpret moderator effects. *Educational and Psychological Measurement, 50,* 225-263.

With K.H. Roberts, P. Weissenberg, D. Whetten, J. Pearce, W. Glick, H. Miller, & R. Klimoski. A history of organizational behavior (invited paper). *Journal of Management Systems, 2,* 25-38.

With C.R. Phillips. Scientific management and stakhanovism in the Soviet Union: A historical perspective. *International Journal of Social Economics, 17,* 28-35.

With A.S. Phillips. Understanding Antonio Gramsci's ambiguous legacy. *International Journal of Social Economics, 17,* 36-41.

With J.L. Colbert, & K.W. Mossholder. Characteristics of professionals in public accounting firms. *Managerial Auditing Journal, 5,* 22-24.

With A.S. Phillips, & R.G. Long. Type A status: Birth order and gender effects. *Individual Psychology, 46,* 365-373.

Choice and determinism: A comment. *Strategic Management Journal, 11,* 571-573.

With J.A. Buford, Jr. *Management in extension* (2nd ed.). Bangkok, Thailand: Ministry of Agriculture and Cooperatives, Department of Agricultural Extension. [Thai translation]

1991

Behavioral foundations of human resource management. In J.A. Buford, Jr., *Personnel and human resources in local government: Concepts and techniques for local governments* (pp. 52-75). Auburn: Center for Governmental Services, Auburn University.

With C.R. Phillips, & C. Molstad. Repetitive work: Contrast and conflict. *Journal of Socio-Economics, 20,* 73-82.

With A.B. Pizzolatto, R.G. Long, & R.W. Griffeth. The measurement and conceptualization of career stages. *Journal of Career Development*, 7, 153-166.

With W.J. Duncan, & K.M. Bartol. In memoriam: Dalton Edward McFarland, 1919-1991. *Academy of Management Newsletter*, 21, (May), 20.

With D.V. Day. Work climate and Type A status as predictors of job satisfaction: A test of the interactional perspective. *Journal of Vocational Behavior*, 38, 39-52.

With D.V. Day. Predicting job performance across organizations: The interaction of work orientation and psychological climate. *Journal of Management*, 17, 589-600.

With J.L. Far, & A.A. Canaille, Jr. Peer ratings: Impact of purpose on rating quality and user acceptance. *Group & Organization Studies*, 16, 367-386.

In memoriam: Edmund P. Learned. *Academy of Management Newsletter,* 21(October), 29.

With E.R. Kemery, & A.B. Pizzolatto. Career commitment and expected utility of present job as predictors of turnover intentions and turnover behavior, *Journal of Vocational Behavior*, 39, 331-334.

With R.F. Zoomed. *Organizations: Theory and design* (654 pp.). Hinsdale, IL: Dryden Press. *Instructor's manual, Test bank,* and *Transparency masters* (402 pp.), with R.F. Zoomed, J.E. Gold, & S.C. Whittington.

With J.A. Buford, Jr. *Management in extension* (2nd ed.). Riyadh, Saudi Arabia: Extension and Agricultural Services Department, Ministry of Agriculture and Water. [Arabic translation]

1992

With G.R. Ferris, & K.M. Kacmar. Age, Tenure, and job satisfaction: A tale of two perspectives. *Journal of Vocational Behavior*, 40, 33-48.

With K.W. Mossholder, E.R. Kemery, & A.A. Armenakis. Replication requisites: A second look at Klenke-Hamel and Mathieu (1990). *Human Relations*, 45, 1093-1105.

With A.A. Armenakis. The role of metaphors in organizational change: Change agent and change target perspectives. *Group & Organization Management, 17,* 242-248.

In memoriam: Franklin G. Moore. *Academy of Management Newsletter, 22*(October), 39.

With R.F. Zoomed. *Organizations: Theory and design* (654 pp.). Tokyo: Holt-Saunders. [International Edition]

[Editor]. *Management laureates: A collection of autobiographical essays* (Vol. 1, 420 pp.). Greenwich, CT: JAI Press.

[Editor]. *Management laureates: A collection of autobiographical essays* (Vol. 2, 438 pp.). Greenwich, CT: JAI Press.

[Editor]. *Management laureates: A collection of autobiographical essays* (Vol. 3, 414 pp.). Greenwich, CT: JAI Press.

1993

With L.L. Cummings. Meet the fellows of the Academy of Management. *Academy of Management Newsletter, 23*(March), 1-3.

In memoriam: Luther H. Gulick, Jr. *Academy of Management Newsletter, 23*(June), 22.

In memoriam: Eric L. Trist. *Academy of Management Newsletter, 23*(October), 44.

Management (3rd ed., 745 pp.) Fort Worth, TX: Dryden Press. *Instructor's manual* and *Transparency masters* with F. D. Alexander; *Transparency acetates* (519 pp.); *Test bank* (391 pp.), and *Computerized test bank* both with G. Foegen (319 pp.); *Video instructor's manual* with W. D. Schulte, Jr. & L. A. Woehrle (377 pp.).

With L.R. Jauch, & S.A. Coltrin. *The managerial experience: Cases, and exercises* (5th ed., 203 pp.). Fort Worth, TX: Dryden Press.

With S.A. Coltrin, & L.R. Jauch. *Study guide to accompany management* (3rd ed., 360). Fort Worth, TX: Dryden Press.

With L.R. Jauch, & S.A. Coltrin. *Management: An experiential approach* (98 pp.). Fort Worth, TX: Dryden Press. *Instructor's manual* (67 pp.)..

With L.R. Jauch, & S.A. Coltrin. *Management: A case approach* (69 pp.). Fort Worth, TX: Dryden Press. *Instructor's manual* (48 pp.).

Management (3rd ed., 745 pp.). Tokyo: Holt-Saunders. [International Edition]

1994

With K.W. Mossholder. Simple question, not so simple answer: Interpreting interaction terms in moderated multiple regression. *Journal of Management, 20,* 159-165.

With K.D. Carson. Career commitment: Construction of a measure and examination of its psychometric properties. *Journal of Vocational Behavior, 44,* 237-262.

With A.S. Phillips. Leader-follower exchange quality: The role of personal and interpersonal attributes. *Academy of Management Journal, 37,* 990-1001.

With D.V. Day, J.R. Edwards, C.S. Smith, & J. Tisak. Difference scores: Rationale, formulation, and interpretation. *Journal of Management, 20,* 673-698.

Foreword. In M. J. Alexander, *A general theory of corporate strategy and business policy* (pp. x-xi). Auburn, AL: University Publications.

With K.W. Mossholder, R.E. Niebuhr, & M.A. Wesolowski. Dyadic duration and the performance-satisfaction relationship: A contextual perspective. *Journal of Applied Social Psychology, 24,* 1251-1269.

In memoriam: Karl D. Reyer. *Academy of Management Newsletter, 24*(December), 23.

1995

With D.J. Woehr, D.V. Day, & W. Arthur, Jr. The systematic distortion hypothesis: A confirmatory test of the implicit covariance and general impression models. *Basic and Applied Social Psychology, 16,* 417-434.

With D.V. Day. Personality similarity and work-related outcomes: A test of the supplementary model of person-environment congruence among African-American nursing personnel. *Journal of Vocational Behavior, 46,* 55-70.

Workplace envy. *Organizational Dynamics, 23*(4), 49-56.

With D.A. Wren, & A.A. Bolton. In memoriam: Ronald Guy Greenwood (1941-1995). *The Chronicles* [Academy of Management History Division Newsletter], (Autumn), 3-4.

With D.A. Wren, & A.A. Bolton. In memoriam: Ronald Guy Greenwood. *Academy of Management Newsletter, 25*(December), 23.

With K.D. Carson, & P.P. Carson. Development and construct validation
of a career entrenchment measure. *Journal of Occupational and
Organizational Psychology, 68,* 301-320.

With J.A. Buford, Jr. *Management in extension* (2nd ed., 492 pp.) M.
Chizari, Trans. Tehran, Iran: Iranian Ministry of Jahad Sazandegie. [Persian translation]

With J.A. Buford, Jr., & J.R. Lindner. *Management in extension* (3rd
ed., 357 pp.). Columbus, OH: Extension Service, Ohio State University.

1996

With E.R. Kemery & S.R. Zacur. Expectancy-based job cognitions and
job affect as predictors of organizational citizenship behaviors.
Journal of Applied Social Psychology, 26, 635-651.

With C.P. Neck. Frederick W. Taylor, J. Maunsell White III, and the
Matthew effect: The rest of the story. *Journal of Management History, 2,* 20-25.

With H.S. Feild, & G.B. Childress. Locating measures used in I/O psychology: A resource guide. *The Industrial-Organizational Psychologist, 34,* 103-107.

Lessons learned along the way: Twelve suggestions for optimizing
career success. In P.J. Frost & M.S. Taylor (Eds.), *Rhythms of academic life: Personal accounts of careers in academia* (pp. 3-9).
Thousand Oaks, CA.

Improving the journal review process: The question of ghostwriting.
American Psychologist, 51, 1189.

[Editor]. *Management laureates: A collection of autobiographical
essays* (Vol. 4, 322 pp.). Greenwich, CT: JAI Press.

With W.M. Fox, & R.H. Trent. In memoriam: Claude Swanson George,
Jr. (1920-1995). *Academy of Management Newsletter, 26*(December), 22.

In memoriam: Ernest Dale (1917-1996). *Academy of Management
Newsletter, 26*(December), 23.

Thoughts on the making and remaking of the management discipline.
Journal of Management Inquiry, 5, 311-318.

1997

With D.V. Day, & E.K. Kelloway. Correcting for measurement error attenuation in structural equation models: Some important reminders. *Educational and Psychological Measurement, 57,* 785-799.

With K.W. Mossholder, J. Touliatos, & A.I. Barkman. The accountant's stereotype: A look back at Granleese and Barrett (1990). *Personality and Individual Differences, 23,* 897-898.

Of fiction and fraud. *Academy of Management Review, 22,* 840-842.

In memoriam: Burnard H. Sord (1915-1997). *Academy of Management Newsletter, 27*(December), 31.

1998

Exploring the past. *Journal of Management History, 4,* 4-15.

With A.A. Armenakis. The cesspool syndrome: How dreck floats to the top of declining organizations. *Academy of Management Executive, 12*(1), 58-63.

With F.T. Lohrke. Managerial responses to declining performance: Turnaround investment strategies and critical contingencies. In D. Ketchen (Ed.), *Advances in applied business strategy* (Vol. 5, pp. 3-20). Stamford, CT: JAI Press.

In Press

With R.G. Long. Internal labor markets: Labor-process and market-power effects. *Advances in Industrial and Labor Relations.*

Management (2nd ed.). Djakarta, Indonesia: Binarupa Aksara. [Indonesian translation]

With J.A. Buford, Jr., & J.R. Linder. *Management in extension* (3rd ed.). M. Chizari, Trans. Tehran: Iranian Ministry of Jahad Sazandegie. [Persian translation]

With J.A. Buford, Jr., & J.R. Linder. *Management in extension* (3rd. ed.). M. Drygas, Trans. Warsaw: Foundation of Assistance Programs for Agriculture. [Polish translation]

With D.V. Day, & J.M. Conte. Personality as predictor of work-related outcomes: Test of a mediated latent structural model. *Journal of Applied Social Psychology.*

With A.S. Phillips. PMS in the workplace: Myth or method? *Social and Personality.*

ACKNOWLEDGMENTS

I thank Achilles A. Armenakis, Lynda Kennon Bedeian, Hubert S. Feild, Jr., William H. Holley, Jr., and Kevin W. Mossholder for checking a draft manuscript against their recollections. The editorial assistance of Katherine Bedeian Kingsmill is likewise gratefully acknowledged. Correspondence concerning this manuscript should be addressed to the author at the Department of Management, Louisiana State University, Baton Rouge, LA 70804-6312 or via Internet to ABEDE@LSU.EDU.

NOTES

1.   The Bedeian genealogy, from 1650, has been compiled by my cousin Torcom Bedayan and me and was deposited in certain historical societies and the Library of Congress in 1981.

2.   See, H. J. Leavitt & J. Lipman-Blumen (1995), Hot groups. *Harvard Business Review, 73*(4), 109-116; H.J. Leavitt (1996), The old days, hot groups, and managers' lib. *Administrative Science Quarterly, 41*, 288-300.

3.   H.B. Adams (1918), *The education of Henry Adams: An autobiography* (p. 300). Boston: Houghton Mifflin.

4.   S.J. Harris (1982). *Pieces of eight* (pp. 174-175). Boston: Houghton Mifflin.

MANAGERIALISM:
THE MANAGEMENT
OF HUMAN KNOWLEDGE

C. WEST CHURCHMAN

My story of my life with management should begin with one of my earliest beliefs about reality: When I came to believe that there is a God and God is the manager of humanity. That belief was a gift—a magnificent gift. I'm in my mid-eighties and soon going to leave, and my farewell is a hope mixed with a faith. Both packages, hope and faith, can now be opened, having been partially tied up by the strings of academic caution and skepticism. There is a God. A wonderfully, kind God. I no longer have any obligation to define God. My God tells me that my God is not he, she, it, but infinite kindness. And finally, always, with a magnificent sense of humor and seriousness melded perfectly.

> To begin with, God manages with infinite kindness.
> But not all powerful, the way we humans who live now, mean "power."
> Nor is God the creator, the way we mean creator.
> Because these two descriptions are not kind, the way we mean them.

But the God of Infinite Kindness is not the creator of what we humans call reality. Reality may be spiritual, but that doesn't solve the problem

Management Laureates, Volume 5, pages 41-92.
Copyright © 1998 by JAI Press Inc.
All rights of reproduction in any form reserved.
ISBN: 0-7623-0178-3

of my inquiring mind. I've read the literature of past and present spiritualism, and keep asking how the poems help starving babies. But can a kindness that is able to move without boundaries help?

I don't know. Yet or ever. To be able to manage, not with power that dominates (pushes, squashes, increases), but transforms to higher, more aesthetic, exciting, loving works, constitutes not a mathematical but a spiritual infinity, for example, a living ideal.

That's the statement of an ignorant academic. I've probably sounded superior or even supreme at times and I'm sorry. I'd rather sound joyous, as a deaf Beethoven suggests in the Ninth Symphony and the last piano concerto. I don't agree with Tchaikovsky that I have to end it like the last movement of his Sixth Symphony.

I also became familiar with the "proofs" of the existence of God that occupied the minds of philosophers and scientists in the sixteenth to the nineteenth centuries (e.g., Descartes, Leibniz, etc.). I studied the proof from causality, which at best establishes a first cause, but not a first good cause, or the "ontological" proof, which defines God as perfect, but assumes that supreme perfection implies existence. I agreed with Kant that no existing proof succeeds, because we in the West still don't know what spiritual proof means.

But later on I needed a proof. I'd fallen victim to a severe addiction, and found the 12-step program of recovery from over 200 forms of addiction. The first step describes the addict as powerless over the addiction that he/she admits, and the second step resolves that we addicts "come to believe that a power greater than we, can restore us to sanity." The power will act to our benefit if we turn our will over to this higher power. In other words, if we admit we humans can't do anything, but there is a spiritual power which can.

I hope all the above does not lessen any interest in my story. I'm going to discuss such matters as managing inventories, or traffic, or schools, or health. But philosophers like to start with what they believe is most important in human life and managing, in my case, God. This is an old-age conviction on my part, but also a very old conviction of the human race.

How? How does one "come to believe?" I remembered the book that Russ Ackoff and I had written (*Psychologistics*), and how we had defined "belief." Suppose I changed my actions so that my actions fit the definition of this specific belief in a God. Then I'd "believe" in a God who would "restore me to sanity." So I tried it. I wrote out the conditions for believing that God exists and what He can do to remove my cravings. And a "miracle" occurred. The cravings disappeared, and appear if I "slip" and act dangerously (opposite to the conditions of belief in God).

Hence, I now had a belief in God, and was ready to do the remaining steps. This is not the method which is widely accepted by most 12-steppers, who are not logicians.

But I also needed more than this sort of proof. And I did receive the more direct proof. I meditated in my cabin on a clear sunny day looking out of my front door southwest across the Pacific ocean, one third of the way around the world, to Auckland, New Zealand. There was a "presence" which felt spiritual. I asked who it was, and there was a response, "I am here but not in any space or time, so that 'here' must be difficult to understand." So I asked about the spirit's qualities, mentioning some readings I'd made. The response was "all you need to know is that I am 'Infinite Kindness,' and I am going to teach you what that means over the coming years." That experience happened nine years ago, and the lessons go on, at first in the absolute silence of my sea-side cabin at 5:30am, then in the noisier and wetter shower. I "have" a God. I think, but I also have my old mind which believes in something called "scientific method." I've called myself a "philosopher of science."

The struggle to be kind applies to my self as well as others. I should point out that my behavior is not infinite kindness but tries off and on to initiate kind acts.

In the first draft of this autobiographical essay, I tried to tell the story from beginning to end, starting with the first statement of my life's managerial problem. The trouble is that I lost my audience, because that statement was made by a 17-year old who desperately needed some information from college and beyond. Hence I decided to make use of the opportunity any autobiographer has; he can order his life in time any way he wants. So I'll start with the end.

I'm an 84 year old man, somewhat cranky because I'm troubled, but also fiercely optimistic, surely egoistic, but terribly caring of this huge creature called "everybody."

I believe that not long after the end of the second millennium of the AD part of human history, there is a real possibility that human history as we know it will come to an end. That story of our race may very well not be "science fiction."

I was on the University of California at Berkeley campus for about a half century. I've learned that graduate students here and elsewhere know how to build an atom bomb. There is considerable disagreement about the availability of materials. Especially for a small or medium-size group. Since Hiroshima and Nagasaki there have been several millions who are Dooms Day people. They believe that not far away in the coming millennium there will be "nuclear winter." If not that, then super-AIDS, a "better" disease that spreads faster. Or an end of safe air, or water. Or any other evil triumph of applied science over the health of people of the millennium.

Those thoughts are "doom" thoughts. The thoughts are real, all over the world. What happens to you if you own them, and they are really quite cheap, is an unknown. Since they are acceptable to a lot of us, a lot of us own them. When you have them you may also have a disease called depression.

Or not.

And there it is—the possible story of human history. It's a management story, because the obvious question of the story is, first, "is the threat real and what form will its disasters take?" Second, "Can we humans do something about it or are we doing it already?" Third, "If we do something about it, how do we guarantee that what we do is sound, for example, better than the past?" Or, "We've found, over and over, that a war may end one threatened disaster, but the subsequent peace grows into another monster." Did all the wars I've been through create a better world?

Or, should we first look at the managing God? I don't know. But I believe we should look at the question early; "we" are in that class of humans who are living in the dooms-day possibility.

We have learned something in this century. World War I was the result of an incredible management policy of running Europe by alliances. World War II was apparently based on another policy of central government based on military nationalistic power.

When I wrote the first draft of this autobiography, I left out references to my friends and enemies, probably because I didn't relate such people to the topic of management. But of course they belong, except that very few of them were explicitly chosen by me to become friends or enemies. Many of them in my life were my teachers or students, swimming in the same pond, and then in a two-person pool. The first such friend, Mr. Bathgate, convinced me I had the ability to study a topic, in my case "fruits of the world," a 1,000 word essay in the 7th grade. It was a magic transformation of the mind-spirit from a student into a scholar, from a what-when temporary curiosity to a why-forever. Mr. Bathgate was replaced by Mr. Domincovitch (Mr. Domi) and the topic was "what good is it?"

Later I read a book called *Ten Sixty-six And All That*, which told the history of the world with comments on mankind's behavior by saying, "and that was a good (or bad) thing." I recognized that Mr. Domi did just that when he described some historical events, and it sounded just right to me. And I never reported him. Later on we became friends, where he took the role of ethical guide. I'd describe our relation as intense, based on my curiosity, that is, desire to learn. Later, before I graduated, it became mutual, as I contributed ideas he hadn't considered.

The story continued in college (University of Pennsylvania) and beyond. I'll be telling the story of Tom Cowan, which continued after I'd met Edgar Singer. Singer, one of William James's favorite students, gave a three-year seminar he called "The Analysis of Concepts," which was a study of the ideas of the sciences. It followed a plan of the sciences first suggested by Auguste Comte, a French philosopher who lived 1798-1857. Comte started with logic, went through the physical sciences, and ended with sociology.

Singer began, not with the "simplest" problem of science as John Locke had done, but with a fairly complicated problem ("the distance between two points on the surface of the earth at a moment of time") and showed what areas of science and their ideas are needed to make endless progress in responding to the question. Singer accepted as a postulate of all science that science's statements are imperatives: "the distance measured should be taken as falling in a range $\chi \pm \varepsilon$," where the "ε" is based on statistical theory. I learned from this teaching that all science is a branch of ethics; because science's sentences are given in the mood of uncertainty (with a measure of the uncertainty), and therefore take the form of an imperative.

My conclusion was that ethics is the main guide of science. We scientists don't go from the "is" to the "ought" because we're always in the "ought."

This is a point the positivists of my time missed (and still do). They assume that some sentences gained from experience can be made with certainty, but apparently never tried to measure an object along a scale. Had they done so, they'd surely be familiar with the uncertainty one feels in trying to line up two points on separate bodies, for example, a ruler and a piece of ground. There have also been attempts by positivists to argue that science is "ethics free," that is, that science makes no ethical assertions, which is absurd, or should be taken as absurd ethically.

Singer offers the image of a measurer who adds on the new ideas he needs in order to gain higher precision and generality. Eventually, the scientist has to use more than one observer and even later has to manage a lot of observers performing the same measurements in different times and places. So science, even precise science, requires a theory of management in order to measure anything, and often fails in its management. One of my tasks in WWII was to visit over a dozen plants to check manufacturing measurements made on ammunition to make sure the managers were managing correctly, that is, were manufacturing so that the bullets, in well-made guns, would work.

Thus Singer had a management model for all science, and the associated task of displaying the ideas that must be defined to make the system work. In effect, science as an activity requires a systems theory. The task of constructing the theory of science as a system became familiar to my students and many others. Something like this was being proposed in other places. Some system analysts used circles and other figures with arrows to picture the management of the research system. But the arrows were never explained, even though they were terribly important. Mathematical equations helped somewhat, but not completely. Suppose the link between two parts is based on trust, as between two states of the United States or two nation-groups. Just look at the United States and the Near East today. How do you invent a diagram of the interactions?

In my life, I've tried to build a mutual gratitude between myself and my colleagues in and outside of my department. Gratitude is the fertile ground for developing trust and love, the necessary links that hold friendship solid in cooperative work. So over the years I obtained extraordinary help from many people from many different scientific disciplines and other organizations in the world. Gratitude is like a beautiful plant which grows its branches to entwine other plants so that the entanglements produce beautiful flowers, fruits, vegetables.

But (a marvelous verbal interruption) I also was an angry man at times and allowed (encouraged) hate and anger to come in and start kicking that sweetness all over the place.

There are situations in the process of measurement when the observer must concentrate when he or she is using the sensory apparatus, and must try to eliminate his own preferences. The human mind is often called upon to make a comparison, for example, between a moving point and a line. This is a crucial judgment and may be done incorrectly. So there is a human judgment which is constantly needed and is based on the senses and judgment. If one compares two laboratories both of which are measuring cholesterol, one will often find differences in the judgments. The only solution is management, which determines how disagreements are to be resolved.

I've gone into some detail about measurement to show that management in science permeates deeply into every aspect of the scientific methods, and, like all management, error is a constant companion; thus management is needed to control it. Nature has not provided the human being with a sensory apparatus which gives observers perfect accuracy. We can reduce the importance of the human at times but often only by increasing time and expense, and the increases then become management choices. Of course, a lot of measurement can be automated, but judgment is still required when critical judgment becomes essential.

I need to go back now to the ambition part of my life. The story of my ambitions can start with age 17, an age that for me has always appeared so deeply important. It's April 1931, and I'm about to graduate from my school (Germantown Friends School, Philadelphia, PA). I'm also going to a dentist, who has decided I needed 32 fillings. He tells me he doesn't believe in Novocain, because he needs the patient's pain as a guide for the placement of his drill. Hence, I've had the experience of pain in the form of a drill near the nerve in the front teeth, the most intense pain I've ever had. So we're not close friends, this 40-year old dentist and 17-year old boy.

Before I leave him forever he asks me what I'm planning to do when I graduate. "I'm not sure, specifically," I say, "but in general I'd like to devote my life to helping humanity." He steps back a pace, his drill in hand, looks at me for a moment, and declares, "You'll never get anywhere with that idea."

So this guy, who definitely left an impression on my teeth, is also trying to make an impression on my soul at age 17. I don't remember that I said anything, but the story has stayed deeply fixed in the ground of my memory for almost seventy years. I think I was angry. But most of all I was impressed—not by his remark, but by the overwhelming conviction that I'd been right in what I told him.

Nowadays, at age 84, I'd answer him somewhat differently by saying something like, "I'd like to learn more about how humans can better their lives through management." At age 17, I didn't know much at all about management as a human activity and how it was connected to human suffering and joy.

But, otherwise, it was a good response to his question, and that's what I did do, with some times off, for the rest of my life. I didn't know whether I made any net gain in helping humanity, but I sometimes think I really tried.

I believe I made my first critique of management when I was five-years old. I was born in Philadelphia in August 1913, almost exactly one year before one of humankind's most stupid wars, World War I. I couldn't figure out what was going on, but I did realize that it was very serious and lots of people were dying.

At last I asked my mother, and she said, "It's the Kaiser in Germany, and he's an evil man. He eats babies." At that point I did make my first managerial critique: I didn't think that kaisers, or kings, or presidents should ever eat babies. I was slightly biased, no doubt.

And nowadays "we" don't eat babies, but "we" allow 35,000 babies to die of poverty every day in the world. And, as a philosopher, I don't think that such a world policy is ethically correct. But I don't have a Kaiser to blame or to fight a war over. An astonishing number say "it's just as well, and there's no need to do anything about it."

President Clinton has mentioned it once that I know of, and Bush and Reagan never. My managerial question is "global:" Who in the world should do something about baby starvation in a world that has enough food to feed everyone?

World starvation was only one of my many managerial criticisms as a child and young man. All my childhood through the teens I learned how the world was managed—badly. Africa had been torn asunder in attempts to use its resources and enslave its humans. Labor in America had gradually asserted its rights to negotiate pay and work conditions and had been threatened and shot (e.g., in the Pullman strike of the 1890s).

The class distinctions I observed were ethically outrageous. I found that the Churchman family in Philadelphia was "upper class" and our names were in the "Social Register" which identifies those girls who are to be debutantes and the boys who will go to their parties. We were so honored because there was a teenage Churchman who came over from England with William Penn in the 1690's.

When I was 17 I wrote the Social Register to tell them to take my name out, because I didn't approve of what they did, that is, how they managed. They assumed that the "social register" identified the "best" families in the city, when it was clear to me that they were not best, and there was no "best."

I was still a teenager when the 1929 crash of the stockmarket occurred, and I discovered that U.S. citizens gambled with the assets of corporations and companies. That seemed unethical to me, but I wasn't sure why.

My freshman year at the University of Pennsylvania was a marvelous eye-opener. I still have the journal I kept to evaluate my courses in terms of my future career. Some professors were completely irrelevant or even worse. The guy who taught the history of the English language had taught it too long, and succeeded in making a fascinating topic boring.

Generally I had a grand time as a freshman, and the most useful and overwhelming was an ethics course taught by a man who later became one of my best friends, Thomas A. Cowan. He also became a well-known jurisprude (theorist of law).

Tom decided we needed epistemology as well as ethics. He took us on a philosophical trip. First, we all became solid advocates of the empiricist (positivist) school, which declared that all knowledge comes from experience (with the help of logic). Then he gave us a turn at criticizing, and we could see that an empiricist has to say that we humans can know very little about the future because you can't see, hear or feel future events.

Consequently, we turned into rationalists, who believed in reason as their guide to truth. Thus a geometer can describe all triangles, for all time, by his reasoning. But reason alone sees nothing. Real triangles have to be seen. So before the term was over, we all adopted Kant who made a theory of knowledge that uses both sensation and reason. We ended his course thoroughly confused, but we also learned that confusion is the essence of education. If you're not confused by an idea, you're probably not learning very much about it.

I was utterly fascinated by the question, "What is good?" Some said the good is the sensation of pleasure, and pain is evil. Some (e.g., Kant) said the good is the practice of one moral law (the categorical imperative). Others said that the good is love. Others that it's the voice of conscience. The smart alecks said you can't know, and it's up to each of us to decide. And, then, there is God (more later).

I hated (literally had a feeling of disgust) with the ethical skeptics. Ethics is a tough topic, for me the toughest of all. My Quaker School education convinced me that all wars, no matter who starts them, are human evils. Believing that some wars are good (e.g., the American Revolution or Civil War) is an erroneous belief, I thought, because wars hurt and kill, and never gain world net benefit. There must be a better way to settle the differences between humans and their nations.

But total peace, I was told by the Quakers, meant world management. In 1918, Woodrow Wilson announced that World War I was to be the war to end all wars, and the League of Nations would keep the world at peace.

But, I thought, isn't an ethically sound government of a state obliged to conduct war when it is attacked by an enemy? To say "no" to this question seems ethically ridiculous.

How do you design a League where such attacks do not occur? At that point I was thinking hard about a global management. I was first introduced by my critics to the killer word "realistic." That word is used to kill idealism especially in the youth. "You have to be 'realistic'," I was told over and over. Furthermore, I was not patriotic. I realized that my idealism could be dangerous. I was also not a relativist, because I believed in non-trivial ethical obligations. Some of my critics told me I might end up in jail or dead. I've always had strong ethical managerial beliefs based on world peace, which have been the strongest beliefs I've held in my lifetime. They've gotten me in lots of trouble, partly because they sound to some like Socialism or Communism.

I also believed that some U.S. companies created U.S. wars in order to sustain their business ambitions, (e.g., United Fruit). I didn't know what Communism meant. I only wanted nations to stop fighting each other, and since they didn't seem capable of doing this, how about ending wars by a world management instead?

I still have a journal where I, as a teenager, described how a world management would work. The one thing my plan lacked was implementation: how do we convert a war-like human world into a one-management world, when "in fact" the likely leaders will have to use force in order to become global leaders? (In my boy's mind they would have to be men, since I didn't think of women as managers or soldiers.)

I was discovering gradually that one of the most important aspects of ethical management is implementation. "Of course" we humans should end all wars, and "of course" this takes a collective will to create one world management, but by what process can that hope be realized? And don't tell me that I'm not realistic, damn it all.

Do you like this kid? I did. I liked myself a lot. Was that good for me?

The story I just told is about a teenage mind while it looks for the first time at the whole world of human political affairs. It was helped by a Quaker education, which apparently never discouraged my looking as broadly as possible as a young human (age 17).

I did devote the rest of my life to the philosophy of managing of human affairs, in education specifically, but also in health, politics, business, arts, science and philosophy. I wrote books, taught classes, went out and tried to do good in the real world of business, war, government and education, and especially science, a seriously mismanaged industry, with its inept policy of subdividing its efforts into disciplines.

The motive was always the same: How could I learn more about how humans can help humans to better their lives, not just economically, but ethically? And "management science" is the name for that learning process. There is now a "science of management," a neglected branch of human inquiry for a species which is seriously weak in its knowledge of what to investigate. As a species, the perfectly sensible question, "which is better for humans in the Twentieth Century, abolishing poverty or investigating Mars?" is answered in the United States: "Mars."

Because I like to write, and am reasonably coherent in doing it, I'd like to say more on the adventure that will last until I can't hold a fountain pen or punch keys any more. If an old man feels that way, I should also explain how he feels about adventuring. My *Random House Dictionary* says that adventure may be "dangerous, but also exciting." It doesn't mention "enthusiastic" to describe the adventurer, but that's what I've been.

The question I've had is this simple: Is it possible for human beings to improve the lives of human beings, hers or his and others? This way of putting the question is just one of many, and a part of my story consists in describing the variations.

Management is not a very good word for what I really mean. It's inadequate, because in my country and my time (the twentieth century), "management" often tends to include the control of enterprises devoted to increasing wealth and power for a few people. I do intend that "management" include medical doctors, teachers, city administrators, road builders, farmers, priests, artists, comedians, and, hopefully, the unemployed.

My *Random House Dictionary* used a definer who didn't like managers and included words like "contrive" in the definition. I mean something very broad, that is, "teleological behavior," or "actions to attain goals" and even "strivings towards distant goals or ideals." The study of management is partially the history of past human struggles, but mainly for this young philosopher, it was the study of how humans should strive to create an ethically better world.

So let the topic be Global Ethical Management, and begin with "Global." This is just an open speculative type of comment—as free of con-

straints as the executive of any mind will let us go—on the subject of
global with special reference to humans in the future and the past—*and
with respect to caring*:

a.   a. What do I or we care about humans of the future?
a.   b. What do I or we care about humans of the present and past?

They seem to be radically different questions for humans who live
now and have similar minds like mine, because it seems obvious that
there's no way to care for the dead, and there ought to be a great deal
more caring for the present and the future, than there is.

But, of course, West knows that the "obvious" is a danger sign:
BEWARE: this is obvious and *therefore* probably wrong, seriously
wrong. Ambrose Bierce suggests that we define "self-evident" as "evident to oneself and oneself only."

So try this sort of reflection, that may be relevant for most boys who
love their mothers. Their mothers hope they'll be successful when they
grow up, fervently ("having great intensity of spirit!"). The boy catches
the spirit from his mom, and bases his career on it, even if his mom dies
long before his career has started.

Shakespeare expresses it well in *Julius Caesar*, as he has Octavius
carry out Caesar's ambitions in his speech after Brutus and company
have just slain Caesar; he serves his master's wishes elegantly even
when his master is no longer capable of doing so.

Soldiers, sailors and marines willingly go to war for their country,
knowing full well that they may be dead before the war is over. They still
have the ambitions of their great, great grandfathers. In fact, it's all too
obvious that lots of humans pursue goals they know they will never enjoy.
And they know that their ancestors pursued similar goals before them.

Hence, if we humans today pursue these goals of our fathers and
mothers and our ancestors, then "we the people" must include them as
well as our progeny, and "global" includes the past as well as the future.
We talk to our past as well as ourselves, and our future progeny.

If another example is needed, think how careful we of the United
States are in preserving the aims of our Constitution; we have a Supreme
Court to make sure we don't add amendments which violate the original
spirit of our ancestors.

Hence "global" should include the past as strongly as the future; that's
our ethical obligation. It's another question to ask our hedonist friends:

does the "number" in the phrase "greatest pleasure of the greatest number," include past and future humans?

You bet, for this rationalist.

But if you do bet, look at the size of your bite: the whole human race! That takes courage. But we've done it to ourselves. The bite isn't so big, because we don't have to travel far to touch all "ourselves."

Do you think Internet is a fad that will pass in a few years? It's just an old fashioned crude way of talking to ourselves around the world, with a few of us in the "we." But the scary part is the potential, which at this point seems to have few constraints. "Soon" we'll all be involved in all our affairs, and we'll want to.

When I was 27 (1940), it looked as though the world was going to have another war. But many people in the United States thought we should avoid getting entangled in it, and should follow the "Monroe Doctrine" of the 1820s: no entanglements in "foreign affairs." How long can we avoid getting tangled in the affairs of all humans when there are opportunities of talking to a human in Egypt right now in a handy chatroom?

It may take a century to open up information to the point I'm talking about, when information does mean far more than "news." I don't see why I should be cautious at my age. Nations are rapidly becoming "out of date," meaning they don't serve their original purpose any more; they are much too expensive in money and safety. We'll soon know more than we old-fashioned listeners imagined about what it's really like to be a kid in Rwanda when the politicians get upset. They'll be "our" children then, just "down the street."

The "we" will really count, because fear will have to join in how we react to the Internet news. You'll be able to talk to that kid in Rwanda; will you want to? Do you think "we" should? Is that alarming? Does that mean we drop the quotes around we, around the world, over all time?

Try it. Your imagination is big and strong enough. A world without borders, with everyone having easy access to getting and providing help (and joy) all over the world, for all the times, past, present and future.

All that is an example how the optimist in me reacts on occasion. Internet tells me I can go to Rwanda if I want to, and it helps. I have an inside "committee room" where conversations like that are going on all the time. Of course, there's a pessimist who claims the previous paragraphs are pure crap. But my whole committee thinks the twenty-first century, third millennium will include more and more of the earth. And I included this kind of speculation when I was much younger. No nations. Not like we have now, the fighting nations that behave like kids at a camp who have one central idea: I'm more "powerful" than you are and, therefore, better than you are.

Sure Internet may have too much porn and other undesirables. But right now you can take better sit-at-home trips and see starvation and living misery everywhere. Will that mean better management everywhere? I don't know but I can hope.

The main philosophical interest in my life have been the connection between management and science. Sometimes philosophers play a game with two concepts, to gain a better understanding: try x of x, and x of y. So, try management of management, and science of science, both of which are helpful, but "management of science and the science of management" could be the title of my intellectual life.

I first came across the idea when I was a Junior at Penn and chose Plato as my major topic, and especially the Plato of the early dialogues. The Greek academics of Plato's day had an intense interest in what we philosophers today call ontology, the theory of reality: just what exists in the world we humans inhabit? Today, the topic is spread over a number of disciplines. Stephen Hawking began by writing books about "everything," but he meant masses and their motions; he now wants to talk about spiritual reality, or God, or the psyche, or even "mind."

I was more like Plato, who disagreed with the physicists of his time (5th Century BC), and instead of making reality such things as air, water, earth and fire, claimed that the real reality is ideas. The material reality is simply a copy of the fundamental ideas. In his *Republic* he describes a pyramid, made up of ideas not stones. The ideas at the bottom of the pyramid refer to specific things like furniture, roads, trees, etc. The ideas further up are ideas of classes of entities. The ideas above are more and more general, and eventually become ideas like beauty, truth and the good.

Plato's big question was what idea sits at the top of the pyramid, and his answer was the good. For everything there is always the central question: what good is it? Not how true is it, or how powerful, because, says Plato, we should always be asking for any idea, what is the good of using the idea in our lives? Even love, dear hearts, may be terribly important in all your life, dominating everything you do, but when you reflect on why love is so important an idea, it's because love is the best thing around, and "best" is the highest peak of the good.

I'd translate that Platonic insight into managerial language. Every manager must ask "what are we trying to do in this organization we're supposed to be managing?" If we don't ask that question over and over, every day, every hour, we're in trouble. The right way to formulate the question is, "What good is what we're trying to do?" If you can't answer the question, you should. Says Plato. And that question is the fundamental question of ethics: what good is it?

The truth is secondary for Plato, and should be for all managers. They may not agree on what good means, but they'd better try to lead their organization toward what they believe is the good. I became a thorough Platonist in my Junior year in college, and still am. When I was a middle-aged philosopher of science, I heard my positivist friends claim that science does not contain any ethical statements because science only describes, and never judges. Did they mean that science needs no ethical management? How absurd.

The true is of great value in human lives, but only because the values are ethical. What good does it do to learn the truth? The only suitable answer is that we learn to manage better by acquiring true information relevant to our managerial concerns.

This piece of philosophy about the often hidden MIND of managers is quite old, and was first suggested by Immanuel Kant in the 1780s. He applied it to the mystery of how human beings are able to have meaningful experiences, so meaningful that they can make sensible decisions.

Hence, for this young man, ethics was the essential ingredient in all management, the pinnacle question in understanding how to manage well. All management information contains ethical assumptions, but the assumptions are often hidden.

It looks as though ethics, and especially the topic of hidden ethical assumptions, should also be the fundamental course in all management curricula, doesn't it?

As well as the fundamental course in all science curricula?

Is it? No. Neither in science departments nor business schools. All business firms seek to maximize the value of their stock or some other financial measure of the firm's existence. Are these good, that is, is it a good idea to maximize such measures?

At Berkeley, where I taught, the Business School puts ethics at a low point on the scale of importance because the Business School rarely asks whether the legal pursuit of wealth is a good idea.

What if the firm is criminal? What if it sells alcohol, tobacco, drugs, pornography, ways of cheating people, pollutes the environment by oil spillage, makes work boring, dangerous, insecure. In other words, "bad"?

Isn't there a real danger that companies, and corporations, will turn out to be evil? While I was asking myself these questions in college, the year was 1934, and the United States was in the middle of its greatest depression; Roosevelt was trying to use the government in ways that threatened the usual management of corporations, my parents were Republican and hated FDR, and I was a starry-eyed Platonist.

My mother thought I'd gone wild. She tended to drink too much, and when she did her anger increased; when she found out I was voting for Roosevelt for his second term, she called the Federal Bureau of Investigation (FBI) and told them I was a Communist. That act was going to haunt me later in life, because the FBI never ignored such information and the stains of such a report can never be wiped out. The FBI's MIND believed I was a Communist. Actually, I never was a Communist because I didn't favor using force to do anything, and I was a Platonist; which so far has not even tried to form a political party.

MODELS AND HUMANS

The end of WW II revealed to me that other scientists were also working on aspects of military management. Some worked on what the military called "operations," the planning of a campaign. The research for this part of the military was called "operations research" (OR). I didn't know of operations research teams at the time, but after the war Philip Morse and George Kimball put out a book on WW II OR experience and started an association. That book inspired one of the officers of the laboratory where I worked to start a peace-time OR group at Case Institute of Technology in Cleveland. Case asked me if I'd be interested in starting the group. So Ackoff and I went to Case, in its Business School; and I landed where I belonged.

We started courses in OR, and began inventing a curriculum in OR applied to business. This was not new, though it was new to business schools. The earliest writings I can find of a sophisticated mathematics applied to business were by Cournot in the 1830s, "sophisticated" in the sense that they went beyond arithmetic and elementary algebra; and used the calculus to identify maxima and minima.

Hence, it turned out that some managerial mathematical work had been done before the war, some was easy to do that hadn't been done before, and a huge area opened up, called "mathematical programming." Here's the idea. Suppose we could find a measure of a business firm that accurately and approximately describes how "well" the firm is doing over time and space. Suppose, too, that we could relate this "measure of performance" to the various parts of the company. Finally, suppose there is a group of executives who could control the variables by funding, for example, by hiring humans who could successfully manufacture so many items of a product every hour.

Then we should be able to figure out how many of each product to make so as to maximize the measure of performance, provided we were realistic, that is, paid attention to the capacities of the machines, accidents and breakdowns, and added on various kinds of overhead. Then we should be able to calculate the product mix, that is, how many of each product to make. For some companies this kind of calculation may involve a couple of million variables and thousands of constraint inequations. And this task is realistic because of computers.

One byproduct of this development has been the production of Ph.D.s, a human product who discovers new "models" that instruct the computer how to "solve" a set of inequations and equations with computer effort, which is much more efficient than human effort.

Thus at least a part of some large companies is now run by a MIND, but not just the minds of the executives.

I'll describe the use of mathematical programming in this manner. There is a "MIND" that runs a large manufacturing canned food plant. It decides what foods will be put in different sized cans and bottles, how the canned foods are to be advertised, priced and displayed. Not long ago, the MIND was a lot of minds—a collection of human minds. The MIND decided that some old products are to be discontinued and new ones introduced, old stores to be shut down, and new ones to be started. It decided where each product is to be made and its local price. There is a set of data containing costs and demands.

Finally, the MIND decides when to hire and when to fire personnel, etc., for each section. From all that data, the MIND, made up of several minds, decides on prices at each location at any given time and place. Often the MIND made up of human minds will suddenly reduce the human labor force, not because of any rational or empirical information, but because of a wholly human uneasiness.

Now suppose there's a way to design a MIND to calculate the "correct optimal," a MIND that determines the rational production schedule for all the products, each identified by what's in the can (e.g., 32 oz. of peas in water). The MIND determines the prices and when and where, in such a way that the measurement of the company's performance is maximized. And now welcome to the Twentieth Century! Now the MIND is made up of computer electronics and human operators, but not human managers.

Does that sound fantastic? And if we decide to increase or decrease advertising, or add or subtract a new or old product, the MIND has an answer if you ask it. Some existing MINDS have two million variables with 35,000 constraint equations, (probably more since my information comes from several years ago). But the MIND is a machine + the data collection + constraints + whatever. And if the managers want to add "good will," they'd better do it somehow.

There are difficulties. Consider this. A customer comes into a store, nicely dressed, and says he wants a 32 oz. can of peas, but the store has run out. There's a loss—to the store and the food company, the loss of the profit on the can of peas, plus the disappointment of the customer. Can you quantify the last? Your accounting department can't tell you, and probably the marketing department can't either. Food stuff has a tendency to let in all kinds of dangerous bugs. How can you guarantee yours won't? Your canned goods should have a high reputation. How do you gain it? By having your chief executive officer go on TV and announce "I guarantee it!"

So the MIND is probably not perfect. But isn't it better than any human brain, which can't maximize anything except by a set of guesses? Don't worry about whether computers can think; recently a computer defeated the chess champion of the world.

Every company has a MIND. Most of the managers are not even aware they have one. A lot of them construct the MIND by negotiations and votes and a lot of experience. Only God knows how that MIND works. I've listened to thousands of complaints about the models which are created by smart young mathematicians; there's a frequent claim that their models are "unrealistic."

But the critic doesn't realize that he joins a team that somehow shares a common teleology, and that prior to the firm's introduction to models, it had created its own model and its own data collection. The question is which MIND is "better" and what does "better" mean? We're back to ethics.

To me, a philosopher trained to study how humans acquire knowledge, as well as ignorance, the experience with OR was often amazing. I heard plenty about how unrealistic OR models are, but not even a peep about how unrealistic the previous managers' models were. My startling conclusion was that many managers had never made a comprehensive model of their operations, nor had they even made an evaluation of their own model. If I asked a production manager how many defective items he could tolerate, his answer was "none," at any price.

Consider the ghost story we just described: opportunity costs, for example, the customer who asks for an item you don't have on the shelf. That's what he wants, you don't have it, and the customer leaves. Forever. No record. He's gone, dead to you and your store, never noted by your accountants. The disappointed customer may never return, and some of his friends may never come to your store.

Nevertheless, he matters, especially if that ghost, in other guises, keeps reappearing. So you'd better stock up. Keep plenty of cans or shirts of all sizes. Now you can look with pride at your well stocked store. But that's the word that describes your store—"well stocked." The MIND that runs your store also harms you. A shirt that sits on a shelf for weeks takes up space, takes away your cash to buy inventory, but doesn't increase your income very much.

And furthermore, we OR smart alecks can often tell you what you pay to keep items available. And even if you don't run a shop, just take a walk around a city and begin counting the inventory you'll see in the windows, everywhere, just sitting. No, not quite. Sitting and getting older (like food) or sitting and getting obsolete (like computers) or sitting and getting dangerous.

There are models for inventory; they've been known and used by some companies since before WW I. Lots of companies use them. All you do is let x be the unknown amount of inventory you should have at the beginning of each period, t, and calculate the cost to the company, for each product, of (x,t) and what value (x,t) minimizes this cost. There are possible difficulties in actual practice, but the business principle is there.

Hence, the test of the usefulness of a model is just like the test of anything that claims to help you run an organization: test it, for example, mathematically. All you need is a pencil, a piece of paper and perhaps a mathematician, and he or she can be your high school son or daughter.

Of course, if you've been using your experiences and brilliances for a long time, and this computer kid with a 175 IQ comes along and wants to replace you, you get angry. And sensitive. And the old human MIND gets upset. It's time for a dose of conflict resolution. Maybe. It is the case that many manufacturing companies have been hit hard by computers that really don't care how you feel. Think of how the chess champion of the world felt when he was defeated by a computer. Why the next thing you know a computer will run for President!

But don't forget, computers don't care. Are you sure?

My question is this: are mathematical models, as now used by companies, sound? And should managers use them? The answer is that they all use opportunity costs, and we have no sound ways to estimate them. Hence, until we do have sound ways, modeling management operates partially in the dark. Is that bad? Not necessarily. Engineering, which uses science extensively, also operates in the dark when it applies current knowledge (science) to risky areas like buildings, health and transportation. For example, usually there is no sound way to estimate the cost of pain or death for a human being or animal.

My feeling is that all management today is deep in risk, but that "advances" should be judged in terms of the risks, which are probably better understood when models are used.

But I do have to explain that last sentence, because in matters of ethics and politics, the sentence describing someone as a follower of some ethical doctrine is usually ambiguous or merely suggestive. Both in the east (Asia) and west (Europe and America) differing ideas about ethics have been expressed, and there is as yet no solid method for resolving the differences.

Here are the differences:

1. *Hedonism or Utilitarianism*. This mainly European and American idea starts with the "accepted" fact that all humans experience both pleasures and pains, and that all pleasures are desirable (we all want them to occur) and all pains are undesirable (we don't want them to occur). The hedonists take the next step and assume that pleasures are good and pains are evil. Of course, that's not enough, because some pleasures (a rich dinner, for example) may eventually cause a lot of pain, or, more disastrous, watching an enemy dunked in boiling oil may be pleasurable by some humans. More seriously, companies fire their employees, and firing hurts the worker. Hence hedonism needs a lot of refinement.

The easiest way to refine it is to introduce the concept of utility, for example, money, which can be calculated for each plan of action by calculating the value of the action in money terms and its costs. The ethical rule then says we should maximize the money return of certain actions minus their costs.

There are plenty of criticisms of this method of defining ethics. It is the basis that a lot of American businessmen use to manage their firms and many congressmen use in voting for laws. But, as many people point out, it has a lot of unanswered problems.

The most obvious difficulty of using monetary cost, is the dollar value of a life. Countries deciding on whether to go to war against another country do not use cost-benefit analysis. Nor do you in deciding to rescue someone who's in a very dangerous place. But, with a few exceptions, most of us who try to practice operations research used some form of utilitarianism in defining the optimum choice of action among a class of options and often had to invent a way to estimate the cost of a life. I often did, but I recognized that great care should be taken because there was a higher ethical principle where utilitarianism doesn't work. See my *Prediction and Optimal Decision* (1970), which is superseded in some critical ways in *The Systems Approach and Its Enemies* and *Thought and Wisdom*.

2. *Morality.* This is also a very popular idea about ethics; in fact many people equate ethics and morality. Morality uses rules of behavior, like "Thou shall not lie, or kill," regardless of the results. Hedonism or utilitarianism depend on "I want," whereas morality is similar to the law: do this whether you like it or not. Too many parents teach their kids ethics by moral laws. Moses found that he was losing managerial control of his tribe as they sought the Promised Land after leaving Egypt. He goes up the mountain to consult God, and returns with a set of management principles that we call the Ten Commandments. They say "don't kill," "tell the truth," and "don't steal." One of these tells you not to fiddle around sexually. Another to worship the right god (in other words, since the Commandments were given to Moses by a "god," to obey God's moral principles).

One difficulty of moral laws as a basis for ethical actions is found very early in the lives of little kids who find that lying or stealing are useful or pleasurable. They ask their parents who tell them to stop. "Why?" The parents, if they are not careful, will find they are pushed down the narrow passageway of "Why's" until they have to say, "Because I told you so."

Immanuel Kant realized this when he claimed that there was but one moral law that could be verified by one explanation: any moral law must hold for all humans in all places and times, at all ages. For Kant this was the moral law: So act that the underlying principle of your action can be generalized into a universal law of morality. This is the way that mathematics works, in algebra, geometry and logic.

Kant's idea doesn't seem to work for a lot of young people, I've found. It's like mathematical induction. Less than half the class understands it, that is, the majority never reach a point where they can judge its truth or falsity. Kant's moral law was beautifully clear to Kant, and I believe he could never understand why anyone doubted it, or failed to apply it. How many people ask themselves, when they had a difficult decision to make, what was the ethical justification for an act they were thinking of choosing, and if the act fell under a universal moral law as an example?

It's plain unnatural to do so.

Kant (in the 1780s) was understandably naive psychologically, since the western study of the human psyche was yet to occur. Very often, our minds do not use what the designer thinks is a very reasonable process. In Kant's case it is not easy at all to see what the principle behind your proposed action really is, and whether your proposed action fits under that principle. For some minds Kant's test is impossible.

Furthermore, it's so easy to disobey any proposed moral law, especially when it becomes difficult to obey it. You are driving down a street and the traffic light turns red at the next corner. You're in a big hurry. So? Stop? But you want to hurry; you really need to hurry. But the law says you should stop. Those stupid lawyers! The hell with them. There are no cars in the cross street. No cops either. Go Ahead. Oops!

I never realized the force of Kant's categorical imperative until I studied the 12-step recovery program. The moral law is "don't slip," and you must follow it no matter what, even if you're convinced that a small slip "won't matter very much." The force of no exceptions is crucial, even if you apply it "one day at a time." The point is "absolutely no exceptions." And that's what Kant meant by "categorical." He contrasts categorical imperatives with "hypothetical," the imperative that uses "if:" "If you feel very good, why not a small slip?" Recovery in this case is to live without an "if." If you relax the categorical you run into the real danger of relaxing everything; and become fatally wrong.

A third alternative to find out what you should do: "Ask God." This ethical theory uses some authority that can be consulted and acts like a guide for all the major decisions of our lives: Always and everywhere. It's not like the captain of a ship or your boss, who govern you in some places or times and are human. God is your universal guide.

To people who believe in this ethical theory it feels as though they can talk to God, or at least listen to God, whose voice is "inner," and often is as much feeling as articulated sentences, and carries the tone or implication of divinity, a divine spirit. To a lot of other people, the claim of speaking and listening to God seems absurd. My son seems worried about how God can talk to billions of people. The obvious answer is that the laws of space and time don't apply in the spiritual world. In the west, we've pushed spiritualism out of reality in most universities, and ethics courses. The "good" plays second fiddle to the true in a world of intelligent beings who desperately need to find serenity.

To sum up all that lesson, we academics should admit we are made *intellectually* powerless by our specialization of knowledge, because our intellects alone are powerless to improve the essence of human life, and we have no other powers.

Imagine that after centuries of intellectual freedom, when humans are free to ask questions about any belief system, we have invented an organized global inquiring system that is miserably managed. We impoverish our babies to death at the rate of 35,000 a day in a world of food abundance and are not even curious about the slaughter. Could the financial question be this: Which is a better use of our resources, to investigate the surfaces of the desert planet Mars or feed our babies? "Sorry, West, those problems belong in different departments of our science effort, one in astronomy, the other in nutrition. Funds have already been allocated and can't be reallocated (no matter how many babies die)."

Of course, if a world war was being threatened, the answer might be different. It may be relevant to count the number of military personnel missing or killed per day in World War II, about 7,500, less than a quarter of the babies lost in our war against infancy.

I had to admit that our management of science was seriously at fault. There needs to be an ethics which helps every human. If we are the only species which has enough intelligence to ask questions about our survival, and we believe in the ethical principle that our children should survive, why don't we do better in that regard, no matter what the discipline?

There are other schools of ethics, some of them very strange, some obscure, some dominated by a leader. We are in the primitive period of world ethics, as long as we humans manage our affairs by splitting up into nations. Nationalism is just one form of tribalism, which is a local management, dangerously primitive.

Russ Ackoff and I started one of the first OR departments in the world and it (all of us) wrote the first text. We announced we would accept contracts to help business firms and other organizations. I'd like to describe one where my opposition to current management came out most clearly.

It's rather amazing to me how long and hard I resisted what is now the central idea of my autobiography, namely management. The real reason for resisting was a growing dislike of the philosophy of those people I called managers, the managers of business. At my school, the University of Pennsylvania, the teachers of management resided in the Wharton school. My grandmother (my father's mother) was born a Wharton, my father was called Wharton, and my grandmother was the first cousin of Joseph Wharton who founded the school in the 1890s, often described itself as the first such school.

But I didn't like the school, it was called a "business school," and I thought the purpose of the school was to make its students rich by its MBA programs. When you went to Wharton you got your MBA and then climbed the corporate ladder. Only one out of several dozen ever made it to the very top. Whatever happened to the disappointed? At one point, I and others started a small society dedicated to the problems of the failure in the climb up management mountains.

But, one of history's big "buts," a huge event happened which changed drastically the story of my life, the start of World War II.

I thought I'd help the war effort. I joined the research laboratory at the Frankfort Arsenal in Philadelphia even before the United States went to War in 1941. I was given the job of assessing the current inspection of small arms ammunition for misfires, which consisted of testing 100 and if they all went off, then accepted the lot of over 20,000 primers (at the ignition end of a bullet). Probability theory proved this was a poor test, and army ordnance experience over the centuries showed that misfires could be deadly, especially in a war.

I made a guess that there was some other weapon similar to a gun and I looked at a lot of similarities. At last I found that insect spray to kill bugs when tested over the whole range of concentrations from total failure to almost total kill (never 100%). This was a sound approach to inspection. It was easy to adapt the bug spray method to bullet firing and I did. That gave us a sound basis to test for a "nearly all" firing point (5 in 10 million).

But I then found that to get my method adopted I had to convince 50 colonels and generals in the Pentagon where the Army kept some of their top people. It took about two years of the War to do it. The delay was caused by a belief that everyone seemed to have that killing bugs is entirely different from killing humans, because bugs and humans belong to different disciplines. Bug spray manufacturers know that you can easily purchase something called log normal graph paper that makes the data about misfires easy to use to predict where there is almost 100% fires. One can then show the evidence that "all" the shots the GIs try will fire.

This experience was one of many which showed me how badly managed science was; in applied science it is vital that the disciplinary borders should be ignored. I've never seen an applied problem which can be confined to one discipline, economics, medicine, psychology, ethics.

Hence, once again, I had found that the management of science was badly designed. Why should we divide knowledge into arbitrary pieces? We didn't before the nineteenth century so it's not too late to change back especially when we know that the coming science of the third millennium will find more and more applications.

I found a somewhat similar story when I looked at the measurement of the hardness of steel, another crucial topic during the war when we used steel tanks to fight battles. There were a lot of laboratories using the Rockwell hardware test to see if the tank was safe against bullets. Were the testers "consistent?" Statisticians had found a way of testing statistical consistency. When we applied their method to the steel laboratories, we found consistency within the laboratories but occasional inconsistency between. Some laboratories claimed that the same piece of steel was almost as soft as lead and others that it was harder than any known steel. To give some comfort to the reader, this result is also common in blood testing. Something happens in a laboratory (probably through leadership techniques) that results in consistency within, but also inconsistency between laboratories.

I spent some time in DC3 planes during WW II making sure that the laboratories tested properly; that is, consistently.

I know I shouldn't put people and things together, but the way we test students in our educational system suffers the same defects. My experience has been with SATs, LSATs, MCATs, etc. There is a reasonably good correlation between a student's grades in classes and his or her scores in these tests. There is often no relationship between the test scores and later performances in the "real life" of the professional, in law, teaching, medicine, etc.

So I went to Princeton and talked to the people who designed the tests. They explained to me that they designed the tests to please the associations of faculty of the various disciplines. Thus human society splits humans into segments which don't communicate and molds students to fit their teachers' criteria of excellence and not the students' practice in the real world. Philosophers love to teach ontology, the theory of what is real and what is not. So there's an application. Is a student who does well on LSAT guaranteed to become a *really* good lawyer? No way.

My experience in the land of health was somewhat different. I began to get students from public health in my classes, and that led to my serving on masters and Ph.D.'s from the public health department. This led to a critique of health education, and that led to my running for dean. Imagine that. A philosopher running for dean of the school of public health! I said I thought the dean should run a seminar devoted to designing an education in public health better than the current one, the design of the education I had in mind would occupy most of the dean's time, so I'd have an administrative vice-dean to manage funds, class schedules, etc. The school, under some considerable opposition, voted me in as their candidate. But the top dogs of the university vetoed the idea "because Churchman has his head up in the clouds." But I thought "I am a cloud, raining good ideas about health education." I did believe that better health education was almost a necessity in my world. But my personal security side was glad I escaped.

I had a similar experience with architecture and city planning. But I was told that the dean would have to fire some dead beats, and obviously I couldn't fire anyone unless he or she had a satisfactory place to go.

The management of science is not the same as "scientific method." The positivists never realized there was a difference. "How should science fit into the social world?" is an ethical question, and positivism wanted to separate science from ethics. I thought a philosophy of science should study how science should implement good ideas in human society. What is ethics? It's the study of how to make good ideas turn real. That's the objective of philosophy: to ask relevant questions. And that remark takes me back to the title. What quality of life describes "ethical?" What design of human life is "good?" What is the best life a child should expect to live? With a huge income? The maximum honors? Or frame? Or kindness?

I reviewed ways to describe real ethical improvements, and used readings, discussions and arguments. I also used a dialectical process, of comparing opposite views. Finally, I talked to God in meditation. God suggested an idea. The reply was that humans might learn to manage with "infinite kindness" as a guide (St. Paul's "Love" might do, but it's so overused). Kindness also has another root meaning: the kind of animal we are. Only there's a marvelous secret we should begin to tell our children of future generations: We humans can *change* the definition of the human race through management. An evolutionary kindness management. (My education was Christian and I'd choose *Matthew* 25 and Paul's letters to explain, but there are thousands of other texts.)

I once wrote a paper called "The Piddling and the Grand," where I complained about the academic tendency to write dull, accurate, respectable piddling papers that Ph.D. candidates are forced to read and cite. So, because this is one of my last, here's a grand ending:

The human race can be defined by its evolution. It will evolve in kindness and capability, so some centuries or millennia from now it will understand how to manage with superb kindness, and also will know how to travel to the habitable planets which a future Hubble will find, so that intelligent kindness will people the universe.

So back to my kindness question, which I'd now like to pose this way: Will the human race need a belief in a God of Infinite Kindness in order to realize such a hope? If so, won't our progeny love to find what that means?

I've told enough stories to illustrate the philosophy I described in the theme I introduced at the beginning: The search for the truth with a God, a God of "infinite kindness," that is, a science with a God. It's a God who can make sense of "global," a world togetherness attained by the goal of mutual kindness among all humans.

It happened when Russ Ackoff and I started the first OR group, based on the idea that the study of management should be as broad as our imagination and intuition could lead us. We had no single discipline to guide us in the beginning, but we did see that we were all trying to improve the science of management. We were guided by our past but inspired by our ignorance. One part of our group later described our behavior as a modern Camelot, knights inspired by a new science, which allowed good-and-evil and true-and-false to mix. We were confused, and let the confusion lead. Leadership consisted of the guidance of enthusiasm.

The same thing happened at Berkeley, except that there the group was engaged in studying how to define NASA's missions. NASA stands for National Aeronautical Space Administration, which was formed when the Russians sent the first "Sputnik" into space. Here again we were to study how to study, so that people would matter. We gathered together as an antidisciplinary group who didn't know we were antidisciplinary.

Our first meetings were disasters. The economists loved mathematical models and the sociologists hated them. After the meetings the economists walked together complaining about the looseness of the sociologists, while the sociologists complained about the generalities of the economists. Then someone suggested that because both "sides" were criticizing the other "side's" methods, we might look at ourselves.

We did, and a miracle occurred. We began seeing ourselves, with our background painting of our self-portraits. We began dropping our disciplinary clothes and we adopted an antidisciplinary approach. We even began to describe our own approach: Space exploration needed a social science, economic, psychological view of man's first space exploration. And how about a space theology. What is the role of God in man's further exploration of space?

My question to myself was what does a research "leader" try to do? Crudely put, the answer is "don't let any discipline win." I'd begun to realize that on the campus the disciplines battle each other for students and dollars. But the exploration of space was interdisciplinary in the long run. So we saw it that way. What's the point of landing humans on the moon? To establish a human colony? Or what? Which discipline decides? That question is like asking which citizen decides in a democracy. Answer—all. A well-managed science should be managed by all. With kindness by all for the sake of all. Our final inspiration. Because the significant meaning of "power" is kindness, and because some people my age sit all day in chairs powerless, perhaps the God-given enthusiasm I've had would help them.

One final inspiration. Because the significant meaning of "power" is kindness, and because some people my age sit all day in chairs powerless, perhaps the God-given enthusiasm I've had would help them.

I've suggested in the title a label for the philosophy of this paper. Singer called it experimentation; his teacher William James called it pragmatism, and someday it'll get baptized properly.

POSTSCRIPT

Postscripts are often written by people who admire an author and want to explain why. But I'm using it to explain why I wrote this essay by providing the reader with my credo, and therefore why I'm so concerned about my life's habitat, the earth. I believe that humanity's habitat and the way humanity manages it is, at the end of the second millennium, in critical danger of total destruction or less, where the "less" is still disastrous. Second, such an end of the human habitat is not inevitable, because humanity has an ability to prevent it, called management. Third, management can be expanded so that its benefits will apply to "all" humanity, i.e., to everybody.

The ethical symbol of third millennium, I believe, should be a world for everybody. The word "for" needs to be sacred, applicable to all in the same manner. There are a lot of "no's": no poverty, no diseases, no great dangers, no wars, no rapes, no cruelities, no robberies, etc.

There are a lot of "yeses": joys, love, caring, dances, games, explorations, poetry, design, music, nursing, sharing, etc. All the above is about "ideals." But I do believe, as so many of my forbearers have, that ideals exist. They stand for all those benefits that we today hope for our progeny no matter how far they may be in the future. In that sense, the future should never be discounted. I live in a time and place were human hope is declining. That is tragic, because the mood influences caring, the very difficult task of caring for generations to come. They're not here to see and hear and enjoy. But they are real, very real, and without our hope they may not even exist:

> So live that your grandchildren to the nth grand will enjoy life enthusiastically.

C. West Churchman
June 1998

NB: "We" are on the Internet. The gem (global ethnical management) home page is http://Haas.Berkeley.Edu/~gem and my e-mail is westc@webtv.net.

PUBLICATIONS

1938

On finite and infinite modal systems. *Journal of Symbolic Logic, 3*(2), June, 77-82.

1940

Elements of logic and formal science. New York: J. B. Lippincott Co.

1941

With E.F. Flower. Philosophy. *The American year book 1940* (pp. 867-872). New York: Thomas Nelson & Sons.

1942

With E.F. Flower. Philosophy. *The American year book 1941* (pp. 833-840). New York: Thomas Nelson & Sons.

Towards a general logic of propositions. *Philosophical essays in honor of Edgar Arthur Singer, Jr.* (pp. 46-68). Philadelphia: University of Pennsylvania Press.

1943

Method of analyzing primer sensitivity. *Primer Information Committee Bulletin No. 5.* Philadelphia: Frankford Arsenal.

Method of taking copper indent measurements. *Primer Information Committee Bulletin No. 1.* Philadelphia: Frankford Arsenal.

With E.F. Flower. Philosophy. *The American year book 1942* (pp. 823-826). New York: Thomas Nelson & Sons.

The die test of primers. *Primer Information Committee Bulletin No. 7.* Philadelphia: Frankford Arsenal, September 10.

The effect of changes in mass of the falling ball on the sensitivity of primes. *Primer Information Committee Bulletin No. 6.* Philadelphia: Frankford Arsenal, September 6.

A sensitivity test for primer compositions. *Primer Information Committee Bulletin No. 10.* Philadelphia: Frankford Arsenal, October 9.

1944

With E.F. Flower. Philosophy. *The American year book 1943* (pp. 829-832). New York: Thomas Nelson & Sons.

Firing pin blows in small arms weapons. *Primer Information Committee Bulletin No. 22.* Philadelphia: Frankford Arsenal, March 3.

On a method of determining significant differences in primer sensitivity. *Primer Information Committee Bulletin No. 21.* Philadelphia: Frankford Arsenal.

On the statistics of sensitivity data. *Annals of Mathematics and Statistics.*

With B. Epstein. Statistics of sensitivity data. *Annals of Mathematical Statistics,* XV.

1945

With T.A. Cowan. A challenge. *Philosophy of Science,* 12.

Effect of modification of the radius of the firing pin of the cal...50 Browning machine gun on primer sensitivity. *Primer Information Committee Bulletin No. 40* (Memorandum Report MR-249). Philadelphia: Frankford Arsenal, November 1.

On the methodology for determination of composition of chemical compounds by analysis to a given degree of confidence. *Statistical Memorandum No. 2.* Philadelphia: Frankford Arsenal, January.

Probability theory. *Philosophy of Science, 12*(3) (July). I. Background, 147-157; II. Postulates of Experimental Method, 158-164; III. Non-Mechanical Concepts, 165-173.

1946

Carnap's "On inductive logic." (Discussion) *Philosophy of Science, XIII, 4,* October, 339-342.

The dialectic of modern philosophy. *Journal of Philosophy, XLIII*(5), February, 113-124.

With T.A. Cowan. A discussion of Dewey and Berkeley's "postulations." *Journal of Philosophy, XLIII*(8), April, 217-219.

With S. Ensor, M. Stevens, & R. M. Sigmond. Methods of making experimental observations. *Statistical Memorandum No. 4.* Frankford Arsenal, Philadelphia.

Most economic sampling for chemical analysis. *Industrial and Engineering Chemistry* [Analytical Ed.], *18*(April), 267-268.

With T.A. Cowan. On the meaningfulness of questions. *Philosophy of Science, XIII*(1), January, 20-24.

Philosophical aspect of statistical theory. *The Philosophical Review, 55*(January), 81-86.

With R.L. Ackoff. *Psychologistics.* Philadelphia: University of Pennsylvania Press.

With B. Epstein. Tests of increased severity. *Journal of the American Statistical Association, 41*(December), 567-590.
With R.L. Ackoff. Varieties of unification. *Philosophy of Science, 13*(4), October, 287-300.

1947

The consumer and his interests. In. C. W. Churchman, R. L. Ackoff & M. Wax (Eds.). *Measurement of consumer interest.* Philadelphia: University of Pennsylvania Press.
Discussion of symposium papers. *Analytical Chemistry, 19,* 957.
With R. L. Ackoff. Ethics and science. *Philosophy of Science, 14*(3), 269-271.
With R. L. Ackoff. An experimental measure of personality. *Philosophy of Science, 14*(4), October, 304-332.
With R. L. Ackoff. Footnote to "Logic of statistical tests." *Bulletin of the Institute of Experimental Method, 1*(4), 21.
Introduction. In C.W. Churchman, R.L. Ackoff, & M. Max (Eds.), *Measurement of consumer interest* (p. 17). Philadelphia: University of Pennsylvania Press.
Logic of statistical tests. *Bulletin of the Institute of Experimental Method.* University of Pennsylvania, Philadelphia, *1*(3), 12.
Much ado about probability. *Philosophy of Science, 14*(2), 176-178.
With R.L. Ackoff. Operational defining. *Bulletin of the Institute of Experimental Method,* University of Pennsylvania, *1*(5) , 43-49.
[Review of *Critical thinking*]. *Journal of Philosophy, 44,* 361-362.
Statistical inference. *Lecture Notes in Philosophy of Science, Part 1* (mimeographed). Philadelphia: University of Pennsylvania Press.
With R.L. Ackoff. Towards an experimental measure of personality. *Psychological Review, 54*(1), January, 41-51.

1948

Definitional models for belief, opinion, and attitude. *International Journal of Opinion and Attitude Research, 2*(2), Summer, 151-168.
In memoriam: Dr. William M. Malisoff. *Philosophy of Science, 15*(1), 2-3.
Methods of making experimental inference. Washington, DC: United States Department of Commerce.

The missing link—A post-mortem. *International Journal of Opinion and Attitude Research, 2*(4), Winter, 489-493.

[Review of *George Berkeley's philosophy re-examined*]. *Journal of Philosophy, 45,* 271-272.

[Review of *Basic problems of philosophy*]. *Journal of Philosophy, 45,* 415-416.

Risks associated with experimental inferences from data. *Statistical Memorandum No. 5.* Philadelphia: Pitman-Dunn Laboratory, Frankford Arsenal, March.

With R.L. Ackoff. Scientific method. *American Peoples' Encyclopedia.* Statistics, pragmatics and induction. *Philosophy of Science, 15*(3), 249-268.

Theory of experimental inference. New York: The Macmillan Co.

1949

The democratization of philosophy. *Science and Society, XIII,* 329-339.

A materialist theory of measurement. In R.W. Sellars et al. (Eds.), *Philosophy for the future* (pp. 476-494). New York: The Macmillan Co.

The relation of history to the theory of defining. *Papers of the Michigan Academy of Science, Arts, and Letters, XXXV,* published 1951, 369-375.

[Review of: American Catholic Philosophical Association *Proceedings, 22*]. 'The Absolute and the Relative,' Dec. 29-30, 1947. *Journal of Philosophy, 46,* 568-569.

[Review of: *In search of a way of life*]. *Journal of Philosophy, 46,* 791-796.

[Review of: *Theories of learning*]. *Journal of Philosophy 46,* 626-627.

1950

Basic research in marketing. In R. Cox & W. Anderson (Eds.), *Theory in marketing* (pp. 3-17). Chicago: R. D. Irwin, Inc.

Logical reconstructionism. *Philosophy of Science, 17*(2), 164-166.

With R.L. Ackoff. *Methods of inquiry, an introduction to philosophy and scientific method.* St. Louis, MO: Educational Publishers, Inc.

With R. L. Ackoff. Purposive behavior and cybernetics. *Social Forces, 29*(1), 32-39.

[Review of: *The idea of progress: A collection of readings*]. *Philosophy of Science, 17*(4), 362.

[Review of: *The limits of science: Outline of logic and the methodology of the exact sciences*]. *Journal of Philosophy, XLVII, 7*(March 30), 186-190.

[Review of: *The principles of scientific research*]. Washington, DC: Public Affairs Press; *American Statistical Association Journal,* (June 1951), 261.

[Review of: *Philosophy of nature*]. (Translated by A. V. Zeppelin, edited by W. Hollitscher & J. Rauscher). *Journal of Philosophy, 47,* 644.

With R.L. Ackoff. Some immediate and long-run prospects for value research. *First Report of the Committee on Cooperative Research in Values* (pp. 5-7). Detroit, MI: Wayne State University.

When do we start value research? *Journal of Social Issues, 6*(4), 61-63.

1951

Measuring effectiveness in operations analysis and research. *Second Conference on industrial experimentation.* New York: Columbia University Press.

[Review of: *Albert Einstein*]. *Journal of Philosophy, 48,* 222.

Some methods of operations research. *Proceedings of the First Seminar on OR* (pp. 31-37). Cleveland, OH: Case Institute of Technology.

Statistical manual: Methods of making experimental inferences. Philadelphia: Pittman-Dun Laboratory, Frankford Arsenal.

1952

Can scientific sampling techniques be used in railroad accounting? *Railway Age,* (June 9), 61-64.

Ethics, ideals, and dissatisfaction. *Ethics, LXIII(1),* 64-65.

[Review of: *Symbolic logic.*] *Philosophy of Science, 19*(2),180.

1953

Concepts without primitives. *Philosophy of Science, 20*(4), 257-265.

A critique of scientific critiques. *Review of Metaphysics, VII*(1), 89-97.

Operations research and market research. *Proceedings of the Conference on Operations research in marketing* (pp. 29-31, 79). Cleveland, OH: Case Institute of Technology.

Phases of operations research. *Research Operations in Industry, Proceedings of the Third Annual Conference on Industrial Research, Columbia University* (pp. 337-334). New York: King's Crown Press.

Prospect for railroad operations research. *Proceedings, Railway Systems and Procedures Association*, (Winter), 71-86.

Research and responsibility. *Industrial Laboratories, 4*(4), April, 1-4.

[Review of *The Anatomy of Mathematics*]. *Philosophy of Science, 20*(1), 81.

1954

With R.L. Ackoff. An approximate measure of value. *Journal of the Operations Research Society of America, 2*(2), 172-187.

History and prospects for operations research. *Proceedings of the Symposium on operations research in business and industry* (p. 110). Kansas City, MO: Midwest Research Institute, April.

Introduction. *Proceedings of the Conference on operations research in production and inventory control* (pp. 7-9). Cleveland, OH: Case Institute of Technology, January, 20-22.

Notes on a pragmatic theory of induction. *The Scientific Monthly, 79*(3), 149-151.

Operations research: An evaluation. *Management Faces New Problems*, Proceedings of the 1953 Fall Management Conference, Society for Advancement of Management, New York, 1953 and *Advanced Management, 19*(4), 15-18.

With others. Panel discussion on 'Administration of operations research.' *Proceedings of operations research conference*, New York Society for Advancement of Management, Sec. 15, January.

The philosophy of experimentation. In O. Kempthorne, T.A. Bancroft, J.W. Gowen, & J.L. Lush (Eds.), *Statistics and mathematics in biology* (pp. 159-172). Ames: Iowa State College Press.

Policy statement for management science. *Science, 1*(1).

[Review of: *Survey methods and theory*]. *Operations Research, 2*(2), 220-221.

Summary of the conference. *Proceedings of the Conference on operations research in production and inventory control* (pp. 99-102). Cleveland, OH: Case Institute of Technology, January 20-22.

1955

The application of sampling to LCL interline settlements of accounts on American railroads. In W.G. Ireson & E.L. Grant (Eds.), *Handbook of industrial engineering and management* (pp. 1051-1057). Englewood Cliffs, NJ: Prentice-Hall.

Management science, the journal. *Management Science, 1*(2), 187-188.

With R.L. Ackoff. Operational accounting and operations research. *Journal of Accountancy, 99*(2), 33-39.

[Review of: *Operationism*]. *American Journal of Sociology*, c. 1955.

A survey of operations research accomplishment in industry. *Proceedings of the conference on what is operations research accomplishing in industry?* Sponsored by the Operations Research Group, Engineering Administration Department, Case Institute of Technology, April 5-7.

1956

Costs, utilities and values, sections I and II. Cleveland, OH: Case Institute of Technology Press.

Discussion: Science and decision making. *Philosophy of Science, 23*(3), 247-249.

How is planning possible. In J.F. McCloskey & J.M. Cappinger (Eds.), *Operations research for management, Vol. II* (pp. 401-413). Baltimore, MD: Johns Hopkins Press.

Management science—fact or theory. *Management Science, 2*(2), 185.

Operations research in the chemical industry. *Industrial and Engineering Chemistry, 48*(3), 393.

Organizing operations research in the company. *Proceedings of the conference on case studies in operations research: A cross section of applications in business and industry* (pp. 60-62). Cleveland, OH: Case Institute of Technology.

Problems of value measurement for a theory of induction and decision. *Proceedings of the third Berkeley symposium on mathe-*

matical statistics and probability, V. Econometrics, industrial research, and psychometry (pp. 53-59). Berkeley: University of California Press.

[Review of: Foundations of Statistics]. Operations Research, 4(2), 254-258.

1957

Cost accounting and operations research. Operations Research, Record of the 1956-57 Operations Research Seminar (pp. 125-134). Ann Arbor: University of Michigan.

With R.L. Ackoff, & E.L. Arnoff. Introduction to operations research. New York: John Wiley & Sons.

The relevance of measurement to management science. Management Science, 3(2), 202 (abstract).

Summary. Proceedings of the conference on operations research, computer and management decisions (pp. 93-94). Sponsored by the Operations Research Group, Department of Engineering Administration, Case Institute of Technology, January 30, 31, and February 1. Cleveland, OH: Case Institute of Technology.

A summing up. Proceedings of the first international conference on operations research (pp. 514-520). Baltimore, MD: Operations Research Society of America.

1958

The development of the management sciences. Ekonomen, 5(March), 8-14.

Some concepts of theory. Rough draft, University of California, School of Business Administration, Berkeley, 1958. [Published copy torn from its source, which is undated and unidentified except for the page numbers 309-316.]

1959

Introduction. In C.W. Churchman (Ed.), Experience and reflection (pp. vii-xv). Philadelphia: University of Pennsylvania Press.

Science and morality. In A.M. Austin (Ed.), Low-level irradiation (pp. 129-131). Washington, DC: American Association for the Advancement of Science.

With P. Ratoosh (Eds.). *Measurement: Definitions and theories.* New York: Wiley.

1960

Case histories five years after. *Operations Research Journal,* (March-April), 254-263.
With P. Ratoosh. Innovation in group behavior. *Proceedings of the second international conference on operations research* (pp. 122-128). London: English Universities Press.
Management sciences. *Encyclopedia Britannica.* U.S.A.: Encyclopedia Britannica, 1960, 1971, 747-750.
On a potential customer for an intelligent technician. *Proceedings of the Western joint computer conference,* pp. 283-284.
Operations research and values. *Operations Research Handbook.*
Organizations and goal revisions. In J. Benbury & J. Maitland (Eds.), *Proceedings of the second international conference on operations research* (pp. 6-11). London: English Universities Press.
Preface. *Management Technology, 1*(2), 1.
Sampling and persuasion. *Operations Research, 8*(2), 254-259.
A scientific evaluation of goals. *Proceedings: 6th annual conference of the advertising research foundation. Management challenges and research responses* (pp. 19-23). New York: Advertising Research Foundation, October 4-5.

1961

Decision and value theory. In R. Ackoff (Ed.), *Progress in operations research, Volume 1* (pp. 34-64. New York: John Wiley and Sons.
Prediction and optimal decision: Philosophical issues of a science of values. Englewood Cliffs, NJ: Prentice-Hall.
With others. Realism in management science: A report. *Management Technology, 3* (Proceedings of TIMS Methodology Symposium), December, 63.

1962

An inventory of values and research. In Q. Wright, W. Evan, & M. Deutsch (Eds.), *Preventing world war III* (pp. 273-277). New York: Simon & Schuster.

On rational decision making. *Management Technology, 2*(2), 71-76.

On the intercomparison of utilities [Sur l'Intercomparaison des Utilités]. *Économie appliquée, archives de l'I.S.E.A.* (pp. 191-208). Vendôme, France.

Research at system development corporation. *The Proceedings of the Military Operations Research Symposia, 2*(2)1, 139-144.

[Review of: *Logic, methodology and philosophy*]. Paper presented at the International Congress for Logic, Methodology, and Philosophy of Science, Stanford University, 1960; published in *Proceedings. Econometrica.*

[Review of: *Studies in item analysis and prediction*]. *Technology and culture.* Stanford, CA: Stanford University Press.

1963

An analysis of the concept of simulation. In A.C. Hoggatt & F.E. Balderston (Eds.), *Symposium on simulation models: Methodology and applications to the behavioral sciences* (pp. 1-12). Cincinnati, OH: South-Western Publishing.

Freedom, fairness, and planning in marketing. In H.W. Huegy (Ed.), *The conceptual framework for a science of marketing* (pp. 44-50). Marketing Symposium. Urbana: University of Illinois Bulletin, October.

Introduction. *Research directorate report by the Research directorate staff, TM-530/006/00.* Santa Monica, CA: System Development Corp., January.

The X of X. *Management Science, 9*(3), 351-357.

1964

An approach to general systems theory. In M. Mesarovic (Ed.), *Views on general systems theory.* New York: John Wiley & Sons.

With H.B. Eisenberg. Deliberation and judgment. In M.W. Shelly, II & G.L. Bryan (Eds.), *Human judgments & optimality* (pp. 45-53). New York: John Wiley & Sons.

Knowledge and action. *Journal of the Operations Research Society of Japan, 6*(2).

Managerial acceptance of scientific recommendations. Report on further implementation experiments. *California Management Review,* (Fall), 31-38.

Marketing theory as marketing management. In R. Cox, W. Alderson, & S.J. Shapiro (Eds.), *Theory in marketing* (pp. 313-321). Second series. Homewood, IL: American Marketing Association/Richard D. Irwin.

On the simulation of group interaction. Abstract in *ORSA Bulletin, 12*(2).

Reality and systems. *Atomzeialter Information und Meinung*, "Forschung und Entscheidungsvorbereitung," *6*, June, 165-170. [Reprinted in: D. Riepe & J. Pustalinck (Eds.), *The Structure of Philosophy*. Totowa, NJ: Littlefield Publishers, 1966.]

1965

[Review of: *Behavior and the relative importance of value*]. A. Kaplan, *The conduct of inquiry: Methodology for behavioral science; Science, 147*(3655), 283-284.

With A.H. Schainblatt. Commentary on "The researcher and the manager: A dialectic of implementation," "Introduction," and "On mutual understandining." *Management Science, 12*(2), B-2, B-40-B-42.

Foreword. In A. Veinott (Ed.), *Mathematical studies in management sciences* (pp. vii-viii). New York: Macmillan Co.

Introduction. In M. K. Starr & A. F. Veinott, (Eds.), *Readings in management science*. New York: Macmillan.

On the design of educational systems. *Audiovisual Instruction, 10*(5), 361-365. Washington, DC: Department of Audiovisual Instruction, National Education Association of the United States.

Reliability of models in the social sciences. In P. Langhoff (Ed.), *Models, measurement and marketing* (pp. 23-38). Englewood Cliffs, NJ: Prentice-Hall.

[Review of: *A strategy of decision: Policy evaluation as a social process*]. *Operations Research, 13*(1), 159-161.

[Review of: *The new utopians: A study of system design and social change*]. Englewood Cliffs, NJ: Prentice-Hall.

[Review of: *Operational research in local government*]. *Management Science, 11*(9).

Toward a mathematics of social science. In F. Masserik & P. Ratoosh (Eds.), *Mathematical Explorations in Behavioral Science* (pp. 29-36). Homewood, IL: R. D. Irwin & The Dorsey Press.

1966

The ethics of large-scale systems. *Economic and Business Bulletin of the School of Business Administration, 18*(4), 30-40.
Increasing the productivity of business and economic research. In J.F. Kane (Ed.), *Proceedings, American Association of Collegiate Schools of Business Golden Jubilee Meeting* (April 25-29).
With F.E. Emery. On various approaches to the study of organizations. In J.R. Lawrence (Ed.), *Operational research and the social sciences* (pp. 77-84). London: Tavistock Publications.
Operations research in the forest products industry. *Proceedings, Seminar on OR in the forest products industry* (January 1-6). Los Angeles: International Business Machines Corp.
Perception and deception. *Science, 153*(3740), September 2.
[Review of: *ESP: A Scientific Evaluation*]. *Science*, 153.
With C.E. Kruytbosch, & P. Ratoosh. The role of the research administrator. In M. C. Yovits et al. (Eds.), *Research program effectiveness (N.Y.)* (pp. 425-440). New York: Gordon & Breach.

1967

With C.E. Kruytbosch & R.L. Hershey. Nourishing and managing industrial research. *California Management Review* (Summer).
On exponential change. In E. Reed (Ed.), *Center diary: 18* (pp. 52-55). Santa Barbara, CA: The Fund for the Republic, Inc. (May-June).
The paradox of reform. *The university: An environment for creativity?* Sponsored by the Common Ministry. Pullman, WA: Washington State University Press, (September).
Research on research. *Isenberg lectures*. East Lansing: Michigan State University Press.
Systems planning for implementation of change. In D.D. Bushnell, D.W. Allen, with Sara S. Hitter (Eds.), *The computer in American education* (pp. 44-48). New York: John Wiley & Sons.
Technology, formulation and implementation. In D.D. Bushnell, D.W. Allen, with Sara S. Hitter (Eds.), *The computer in American education. Commissioned by the Association for educational data systems* (pp. 44-48). New York: John Wiley.
The use of science in public affairs. *Governing urban society: New scientific approaches* (Monograph No. 7, May, pp. 29-48). Philadel-

phia, PA: Fels Institute, American Academy of Political and Social Science.

Guest Editorial. Wicked problems. *Management Science, 14*(4), B-141-B-142.

1968

The case against planning: The beloved community. *Management Decision, 2*(2), 74-77.

Challenge to reason. New York: McGraw-Hill.

The future of information systems. *Management 2000.* New York: American Marketing Association, The American Foundation for Management Research.

Humanizing education. *The Center Magazine, 1*(7), 90-93. [A publication of the Center for the Study of Democratic Institutions, Santa Barbara, CA]

New frontiers to conquer--The research challenge. In C.C. Ling (Ed.), E.W. Carter (Assoc. Ed.), *A seminar for new deans* (pp. 1-10). St. Louis, MO: American Association of Collegiate Schools of Business.

The prospects for social experimentation. *Science, 159*(1 March), 965-966.

Challenge to reason. New York: McGraw-Hill.

With C.E. Kruytbosch, & P. Ratoosh. Styles of administration in research and development organizations. In E. Glatt & M.W. Shelly (Eds.), *The research society* (pp. 345-356). New York: Gordon & Breach.

Whither the collaboration of management and science? University Park, PA: Center for Research of the College of Business Administration, The Pennsylvania State University.

Why do we seek technological growth? Paper prepared for broadcast on RIAS, University of the Air, West Berlin, Germany (August). [Published in the German journal *Universitas*].

[Review of: The prospects for social experimentation]. *Science, 159*(3818) (1 March), 965-966.

The systems approach. New York: Dell Publishing Co.

1969

Architecture and operational research: Is collaboration possible? *Architectural Design, 487*(September).

Real time systems and public information. *Proceedings, Fall Joint Computer Conference on Real Time Information Systems and the Public Interest*, 1968. San Francisco, 1969, 1467-1468.

With B.G. Buchanan. On the design of inductive systems: Some philosophical problems. *British Journal of the Philosophy of Science*, *20*(4), 311-323.

With A.H. Schainblatt. PPB: How can it be implemented? *Public Administration Review, XXIX* (2).

[Review of: The artificiality of science]. *Contemporary Psychology*, *15*(6).

Real time systems and public information. *Proceedings, Fall Joint Computer Conference on Real Time Information Systems and the Public Interest*, 1968. San Francisco, 1969, 1467-1468.

[Review of: *Scoring the university*]. *Science, 163*(3868), 14 February, 664-665.

1970

The artificiality of science. *Contemporary Psychology, 15*(6), 385-386.

Kant: A decision theorist? *Theory and Decision, I* (pp. 107-116). Dordrecht, Holland: D. Reidel Publishing.

Model building and management. *Proceedings of IBM Computer Science Symposium: Corporate Decision Making*. Japan: IBM, pp. 21-35 (English edition); 37-53 (Japanese edition).

Operations research as a profession. *Management Science, 17*(2), B-37-B53.

Preface. The undergraduate and the large university. *Management Science, 17*(2), B-1.

Preparation for management: An assessment. *Proceedings*, Fiftieth Anniversary of Queen's University, Kingston, Ontario, Canada.

R^2 on E: Some suggestions for research on the role of research in education. In B. Lawrence, G. Weathersby, & V.W. Patterson (Eds.), *Outputs of higher education, their identification, measurement, and evaluation*. Boulder, CO: Western Interstate Commission for Higher Education.

The role of weltanschauung in problem solving and inquiry. In R. Banerji & M.D. Mesarovic (Eds.), *Lecture notes in operations research and mathematical systems*. Berlin: Springer-Verlag.

Suggestive, predictive, decisive, and systemic measurements. *Journal of Safety Research, 2*(3), 131-136.

Ungewissheit, wahrscheinlichkeit, und risiko ("Uncertainty, probability, and risk"). In O.W. Haseloff (Ed.), *Planung und Entscheidung* (pp. 97-107). Forschung und Information Band 5. Berlin: Colloquium Verlag.

1971

The design of inquiring systems, basic concepts of systems and organization. New York: Basic Books.

Measuring social change. *Accounting Review, 46*(1), 30-35.

On the facility, felicity, and morality of measuring social change. *Accounting Review, XLVI*(1), 30-35.

On whole systems: The anatomy of goal seeking. In C.W. Churchman, *Design of inquiring systems, basic concepts of systems and organization* (pp. 4-78). New York: Basic Books, Inc., Publishers. Operations research prospects for libraries: The realities and ideals or strategies for operations research in libraries. In D.R. Swanson & A. Bookstein (Eds.), *Operations research: Implications for libraries* (pp. 6-14). Chicago: University of Chicago Press.

The past's future. In W.E. Stone (Ed.), *Foundations of accounting theory* (University of Florida Accounting Series No. 7). Gainesville: University of Florida Press.

Systems analysis and organization theory: A critique. Internal Working Paper 3, Social Applications of Resource Information, Space Sciences Laboratory, University of California, Berkeley, June.

The systems approach to measurement in business firms. In R.R. Sterling & W.F. Bentz (Eds.), *Accounting in perspective* (pp. 51-57). Cincinnati, OH: South-Western Publishing.

1972

Business education: Preparation for uncertainty. Management education: Preparation for uncertainty. *Organizational Dynamics*, (Summer), 12-20.

Epilogue. The past's future: Estimating trends by systems theory. In G.J. Klir (Ed.), *Trends in general systems theory*. New York. John Wiley & Sons.

Management and planning problems. In H. Sackman & H. Borko (Eds.), *Computers and the problems of society* (pp. 209-230). Montvale, NJ: AFIPS Press.

Managing research divisions. Management of Research and Development. Papers presented at a Seminar organized by the Scientific and Technical Research Council of Turkey, Istanbul, May 4-8. Paris: Organisation for Economic Co-operation and Development, 59-90.

Measurement: A systems approach. *Proceedings of the fifth University of Western Ontario philosophy colloquium,* 1969. [Also in J.J. Leach & R.E. Butts (Eds.), *Science, decision and value.* Dordrecht, Holland: D. Reidel, 1973, pp. 70-86]

Preface to the discussion of the ORSA guidelines. *Management Science, 18*(10), B-608-B-609.

[Review of: *An executive for all seasons*]. *The Future Executive. Fortune, LXXXVI*(1), 115-117.

[Review of: *Outline for social costs and benefits in business management*]. May 1.

[Review of: *Systems analysis and policy planning: Applications in defense*]. *Journal of Policy Sciences, 3*(1), 117-120.

[Review of: *Databanks in a free society; Computers, record-keeping, and privacy; Report*]. *Science, 166.*

1973

Basic concepts of operational control. In A.H. Rosenthal (Ed.), *Public science policy and administration* (pp. 160-176). Albuquerque: University of New Mexico Press.

Comparison and administration--Philosophical discourse. *Journal of Comparative Administration, 5*(1), 15-29.

A critique of the systems approach to social organizations. In R.F. Miles, Jr. (Ed.), *Systems concepts: Lectures on contemporary approaches to systems* (pp. 191-205). New York: John Wiley & Sons.

Die idee des fortschritts. *gdi topics*, Gottlieb Duttweiler-lnstituts, Thun/ Schweiz, 4(4), October, 15-22.

Morality as a value criterion. In J.L. Cochrane & M. Zeleny (Eds.), *Multiple criteria decision making* (pp. 3-8). Columbia: University of South Carolina Press.

On comparison and administration: A philosophical discourse. In A.P. Balutis (Ed.), *Journal of Comparative Administration (5)*1.

1974

Foreword. I.I. Mitroff, *The subjective side of science: A philosophical inquiry into the psychology of the Apollo Moon Scientists* (pp. ix-xii). Amsterdam: Elsevier Scientific Publishing Company.

Foreword. M.F. Nicosia, *Advertising, management, and society: A business point of view* (pp. xi-xii). A project of the Consumer Research Program. New York: McGraw-Hill.

Notes on the organization of an exoteric university. *American Behavioral Scientist, 18*(2), 190-200.

Perspectives of the systems approach. *Interfaces, 4*(114), 6-11.

Philosophical speculations on systems design. *OMEGA. The International Journal of Management Science, 2*(4).

1975

The new rationalism and its implications for understanding corporations. In E.M. Epstein & D. Votaw (Eds.), *Rationality, legitimacy, responsibility: The search for new directions in business and society* (pp. 52-68). Santa Monica, CA: Goodyear Press.

Editor. *Systems and management annual.* New York: Petrocelli/Charter.

With L. Auerbach, & S. Sadan. *Thinking for decisions. Deductive quantitative methods.* Chicago: Science Research Associates, Inc.

With L. Auerbach, & S. Sadan. *Thinking for decisions. Deductive quantitative methods. Solutions manual.* Chicago: Science Research Associates, Inc.

Towards a theory of application in systems science. Invited Paper, *Proceedings of the IEEE, Special Issue on Social Systems Engineering, 63*(3) 351-354.

What is information for policy making? In K. Manfred (Ed.), *Information for action: From knowledge to wisdom* (pp. 33-40). New York: Academic Press.

Willingness to pay and morality: A study of future values. In S.H. Smith & A.H. Rosenthal (Eds.), *Fish and wildlife resources evaluation.* First of a series of policy studies conducted by the U.S. Fish and Wildlife Service in the field of resources evaluation. Washington, DC: U.S. Fish and Wildlife Service (February).

1976

Epilogue to: Behavioral models for market analysis. In F.M. Francesco & Y. Wind (Eds.), *Foundations for marketing action* (pp. 182-914). Hinsdale, IL: Dryden Press.

Management science and human values: A retrospect. In T.J. Kastelein, S.K. Kuipers, W.A. Nijenhuis, & G.R. Wagenaar (Eds.), *25 Years of economic theory, retrospect and prospect* (pp. 87-101). Leiden: Martinus Nijhoff.

Morality and planning. In C.W. Churchman (Guest Ed.), *Design methods and theories, Journal of the DMG and DRS*, 10(3), 165-181. [Design Methods Group, Design Research Society]

The niggling and the grand: An assessment of world modeling. In C.W. Churchman & R.0. Mason (Eds.), *World modeling: A dialogue* (pp. 159-163). New York: North-Holland/American Elsevier, North-Holland/ TIMS Studies in the Management Sciences, 2.

Towards a holistic approach. *Proceedings, American Association for the Advancement of Science Conference on Adapting Science to Social Needs*. Washington, DC: American Association for the Advancement of Science Office of Special Programs (May 5-8, pp. 11-24).

1977

A philosophy for complexity. In H.A. Linstone & W.H. Clive Simmonds (Eds.), *Futures research: New directions*. Reading, MA: Addison-Wesley.

With H.G. Nelson, & K. Eacret. Value distribution assessment of geothermal development in Lake County, CA. LBL-6875, Energy and Environment Division, Lawrence Berkeley Laboratory University of California, Berkeley, Oct. 1977. UC-66, TID-4500-R66. [Prepared for the U.S. Department of Energy under Contract No. W-7405 ENG-48. Copies available from: National Technical Information Service, U.S. Department of Commerce, 5285 Port Royal Road, Springfield, VA 22161]

Values goals and prophecies in large organizations. In M. Marois (Ed.), *Proceedings of the world conference, Towards a plan of actions for mankind, Volume 4: Design of global systems models and their limitations* (pp. 161-168). Oxford and New York: Pergamon Press.

1978

Foreword. J.P. van Gigch, *Applied general systems theory* (2nd ed., pp. ix-x). New York: Harper & Row.

A sense of life: Perspectives of wildlife policies regarding endangered species. In S.H. Smith & A.H. Rosenthal (Eds.), *Concepts and practices in fish and wildlife administration* (pp. 4-7). [Second of a series of policy studies conducted by the U.S. Fish and Wildlife Service in the field of resource policies and evaluation]. Washington, DC: Department of the Interior, U.S. Fish and Wildlife Service, May.

1979

The dog that belonged to himself, or on the nature of the mind that believes the real world, it is essentially cybernetic. In K. Krippendorff (Ed.), *Communication and Control in Society* (pp. 31-36). London: Gordon and Breach.

Paradise regained: A hope for the future of systems design education. In B.A. Bayraktar, H. Müller-Merbach, J.E. Roberts, & M.G. Simpson (Eds.), *Education in Systems Science* (pp. 17-22). London: Taylor & Francis Ltd.

The systems approach. New York: Dell Publishing Company. (Revised and updated)

The systems approach and its enemies. New York: Basic Books, Inc.

Systems science. In P.W. Hemily & M.N. Özdas (Eds.), *Science and future choice* (pp. 218-231). Oxford: Oxford University Press, Clarendon Press.

1980

Intuition and information. In H.P. Holzer (Ed.), *Management accounting 1980, Proceedings of the University of Illinois management accounting symposium* (pp. 167-176). Urbana-Champaign: University of Illinois Press.

The safety profession's image of humanity. In R.C. Schwing & W.A. Albers, Jr. (Eds.), *Societal risk assessment. How safe is safe enough?* (pp. 343-346). Proceedings of the General Motors Symposium on Societal Risk Assessment. New York: Plenum Press.

Systems thinking. In G.P. Wood & A.T. Mosher (Eds.), *Readings in agricultural administration* (pp. 6-10). New York: Agricultural Development Council.

1981

Counterpoint to Christenson's critique—A dialogue. *JEM, Journal of Enterprise Management, 3*(2), 200-202.

Gown and town: Planning our lives. In A. White (Ed.), *New directions for teaching and learning: Interdisciplinary teaching, No. 8.* San Francisco: Jossey-Bass.

The measurement of mood and the mood of measurement. In R.O. Mason & E.B. Swanson (Eds.), *Measurement for management decision* (pp. 152-159). Menlo Park, CA: Addison-Wesley.

On dictionaries. *Synthese* (46, pp. 449-454). Dordrecht/Boston: D. Reidel Publishing Co.

[Review of: *Systems thinking, Systems practice.* New York: John Wiley & Sons, 1981.] *European Journal of Operational Research* (December). Amsterdam, Netherlands: North-Holland Publishing Co.

Self images of the professional. In S.H. Smith & A.H. Rosenthal (Eds.), *Emerging patterns and problems in natural resource administration* (pp. 4-7). [Fourth of a series of policy studies conducted by the U.S.Fish and Wildlife Service the field of resource policies and evaluation.] Washington, DC: Department of the Interior, U.S. Fish and Wildlife Service, February.

Trends by systems theory. In R.O. Mason, Richard & E.B. Swanson (Eds.), *Measurement for management decision* (pp. 152-159). Reading, MA: Addison-Wesley.

1982

An interdisciplinary look at science policy in an age of decreased funding. In D.I. Phillips & B.S.P. Shen (Eds.), *Research in the age of the steady-state university* (pp. 109-113). Boulder, CO: Westview.

Reply to M. C. Jackson. *Journal of Applied Systems Analysis, 9*(35).

Success of failure. In S.H. Smith & A.H. Rosenthal (Eds.), *The natural resource agency—Its people and organization* (pp. 5-8). Washington, DC: Department of the Interior, U.S. Fish and Wildlife Service, June.

Thought and wisdom. Seaside, CA: Intersystems Press.

Who should decide about Locke? (pp. 19-21). Pamphlet published by
   the California Council for the Humanities, San Francisco, CA.

1983

The case against central planning research. In R.M. Thrall, R.G.
   Thompson, & M.L. Holloway (Eds.), *Large-scale energy models,
   prospects and potential* (pp. 25-27). Boulder, CO: Westview.

1984

With A.A. Rosenthal, & S.H. Smith (Eds.), *Natural resource administration: Introducing a new methodology for management development.* CO: Westview.

1989

Churchman's conversations. *Systems Research, 6*(1), 1ff.

1990

Ackoff comes of age. *Systems Practice, 3*(2), 125ff.

1994

Guest editorial: What is philosophy of science? *Philosophy of Science,
   61*(1), 132 ff.
Management science: Science of managing and managing of science.
   Interfaces, 24(4), 99 ff.
With I.I. Mitroff. The management of science and the mismanagement
   of the world. *Knowledge and Policy, 7*(2), 64 ff.

1997

With N. Verma. The theory of the firm: An epistemological analysis.
   Systems Practice, 10(6), 657-676.

A SURPRISED ACADEMIC: LEARNING FROM OTHERS WHILE WALKING ON THIN ICE

DAVID J. HICKSON

So I became an academic researcher. I suppose that I must be some kind of empiricist. The kind that wants organizational research to originate in empirically usable theory, then try to conjure revised ideas out of the far end of the empirical process, for unexpected concepts are exciting. Which is why I might call myself an empiricist, but do not easily accept others giving me that label when they mean by it someone with no interest in theory.

I suppose, too, that I have become some kind of positivist in the way that I do research. A puzzled positivist, enticed by both the artistic and the scientistic. Enthralled by the insights of Shakespeare, yet impressed by the mass of teachable prose on organizational phenomena that makes my bookshelves sag. Which is why I might call myself a positivist, but do not easily accept others giving me that label when they mean by it someone for whom positivism is the only way.

Yes, I did become these things, but it was not always so, nor even conceivably so.

Management Laureates, Volume 5, pages 93-128.
Copyright © 1998 by JAI Press Inc.
All rights of reproduction in any form reserved.
ISBN: 0-7623-0178-3

AN ENGLISH ACCIDENT

I am a surprised academic. Academia was over my head, and sometimes it still is. No member of my family had ever stepped inside a college or university, or been to a secondary school (as we British call high school). I myself never "went to university"—as we British say, unless we say we went "up" to it, which pushes home the social status of it having been Cambridge or Oxford—it is never called "going to school". True, my father caused me to be born middle class, by himself taking such advantage of the then newly universal free primary education that he achieved a white-collar job, no less, and even a professional administrative qualification by correspondence course. Spheres academic, however, were remote and unknown.

So here I am, accidentally academic, and as an English Brit already revealing the fine awareness of social gradations that we are said to have.

My problem is that I do not know how to write a biography. I never read biographies, and don't often read books. Academically, I have always got by with reading what was needed for the purposes of whatever research I was currently involved in, and not a lot else. There never seems to be time for it. I always fancy reading widely and at last becoming learned, but I suppose I must be a "doer" more than a reader.

Perhaps, too, this bent is because I must have a narrow mind, if I recognize that in myself aright. I know the psychologists have a word for it. For myself it means that as the traffic rushes by on academia's information highways my mind shuts out the noise and focuses. It simplifies and clarifies for itself. So do we all, but I must be towards one rim of the bell-shaped curve. Hence, in all the din from roads and bells, I think that such contributions I have been able to make to the team research I have been involved in usually have been by discerning simplifying patterns and categories. I just couldn't abide complexity. I wonder if that is how my team-mates see it?

So not knowing how to write a biography, even an auto one, I wondered how to begin. Surely the interesting bits should be at the beginning, to grab attention? Surely it did not have to be in time-worn chronological order? Surely I could tangle it somehow to make it more enticing? Yet I see now that I have actually begun, and that my mind could not tolerate tangled complexity anyhow.

Therefore let me do the familiar thing, simplify and categorize. I see behind me a series of phases in this bio-processual analysis. A formative phase, a traditionalistic phase and, in academia, five phases, behavioral, structural, power-fu<u>ll</u>, decisional and cross-cultural.

A FORMATIVE WAR

I share my birthday, 20 April, with my friend of longstanding, Cornelis Lammers, doyen of Dutch organizational sociologists, and to our mutual chagrin with another better known European, Adolf Hitler. I am the least old of this trio, my year being 1931, and the only one born in Birmingham, England. It was not long before Adolf affected both the others, a one-way causal arrow that as far as I know did not return to him. He instilled into the youthful Cor in occupied Amsterdam a subsequent curiosity about the sociology of military occupation, and he displaced me into coast and countryside. My father had moved from my Birmingham birthplace to a better job in Bristol, but this folded up shortly after war came and his wartime job was outside the city. So we missed much of Adolf's bombing, though I do remember crouching in the cupboard under the stairs of our city house during the first night raids, and the fun of picking up pieces of bombs and anti-aircraft shells when walking to school next morning.

It was formative in another way not to be in the thick of it. One night as I lay in bed listening to the distant sound of the German bombers droning towards Bristol, I thought of those people way up above me. What on earth did they think they were doing? Moreover, whatever they thought, they could still drop a leftover bomb on me to lighten the plane for the getaway. But I was not wanting to do anything to them. I did not dislike them. I did not know them, nor they me. It seemed silly. I became what I can best term a confused doubting pacifist, never quite sure but thereabouts.

Several years later this developed into an antipathy towards the nation state, when I read a book on the militarism inherent in sovereign entities. Yes, I did get time for a few books in my young days. That attitude lies behind my Euro-federalism as a means of diminishing national sovereignty, which is not the same as diminishing societies and cultures. It lay behind my taking part in the founding of EGOS, the European Group (it's now an extensive network) for Organizational Studies, and accept-

ing the founding Editorship of the Euro- based but supranational journal
Organization Studies. It has spurred my cross-cultural writing.

But all that was still decades ahead. The other formative wartime
eventuality was that I got severe teenage asthma, probably due to where
we were living. In those days you just lay in bed struggling for breath,
week after week and sometimes month after month, with little or no aid
from bottles of medicine. Indeed, I remember how quickly I once got
better when one bottle of foul pink stuff was taken away. I grew out of
it, except for one recurrence in late years. At the time, however, conva-
lescence meant weeks strengthening body and independence of spirit
wandering woods and beaches alone, and it meant dropping back a
whole year at school. This galvanized me. Okay, if I were weakened
physically, then I would compete the other way, by concentrated hard
work. And so I did, then and since. Although isn't that what only son
achievers tend to do anyway?

Altogether, Adolf had a greater effect on the orientation and the quantity of my academic work in the decades to come than did the comprehensive scholarship of Cor. Regrettable, isn't it?

TRADITIONALISM WITHOUT MAX WEBER

Traditionalistically, I joined the family business. Ferocious swotting had
caught me up two thirds of a school year, and got me unexpectedly good
school-leaving grades. However, as no one seemed able to tell me what
a university did, or what sort of a job it led to, I left school and "went
into the office." With hindsight, I am glad I did not go on to a degree. I
might have had a humdrum life in English or History, my favorites,
rather than the excitements of research in the then unthought of organizational analysis.

I "went into the office," too, because my father was for some years in
and out of sanatoria with tuberculosis. My mother, who had secretarial
skills, helped keep the job open for his return, and so did I.

"The office" was the administrative support for Bristol Stock
Exchange. No, not a stockbrokers, but the administration of the institution itself. There was a Secretary with capital S (my father), an assistant
(me), and a typist (sometimes my mother). It was not really a family
business, but did rather look like one. The saving grace was that it was
not a closed family group but a trio, each of whom was constantly chat-

ting to and working with numerous brokers and their staffs and walking around their offices nearby (interacting I would say now).

It was a training in respectfulness and repartee, respect for one's betters and cheerful chit-chat for all and sundry. Because it was traditionalism without Max Weber. No one had ever heard of the likes of him, or of his types of authority—charismatic, traditionalistic and bureaucratic. They had all heard of Karl Marx, but whatever they may have heard was not at all to their taste.

Traditionalistically, I addressed the stockbrokers as Mister X (there were no women, but there was a Mr. Stock!), and said "Yes, sir," "Certainly, sir." There were legal formalities to be insured, but no formalism. No written, or even stated, office rules. You just got on with it. Everyone trusted everyone. The motto of the Stock Exchange then, and I believe still, was "My Word is My Bond." Stockbrokers bought and sold in the beautiful mahogany and leather dealing room by word of mouth.

Max would have loved it as a case study of traditionalism. Implicit hierarchy, customary ways of working, familistic and patriarchal. Moreover, it was secure, warmhearted and friendly, pleasant to work in. One of the last small local stock exchanges.

Marjorie and I, too, were and are traditionalistic. We met in a traditional way at a New Year's Eve dance, in the last moments of 1949. She was the traditional uneducated country girl making good in the big city, training as a children's nurse. In later years that led to further qualifications for her, including a mid-life social studies degree, and then into social work, a future cut short when she lost much of her sight. She found fresh outlets in voluntary work. We delayed marriage, as tradition required, until I had completed qualifying professionally as a Chartered Secretary (a corporation administrator) by solitary study at home in evenings and weekends. Marjorie and I have the traditional one son and one daughter, Adrian and Luci, who appear to have traditional marriages; with Cheryl and Paul respectively. They have furthered a new family tradition by both graduating at university and marrying graduates they met there, Adrian going on to a future in electronic engineering and fathering, and Luci into marketing and mothering. Through them we have the superb grandchildren that tradition decrees for grandparents, Christopher, Jessica, Daniel, Nicholas, and Philip.

Yet Bristol Stock Exchange was not enough. I was a Young Liberal, a member of Britain's smaller third political party, and when Britain and France in connivance with Israel invaded Egypt at Suez in 1956, I stood on a box in the city's main thoroughfare and proclaimed to the unconcerned citizenry hurrying by, "Citizens of Bristol, you are at war." This sort of thing began to go too far. The Chairman of the Stock Exchange had a kindly chat with me about the responsibilities of a servant of a quasi-public institution. Perhaps I could have been discreetly right wing, who knows. But I saw that without a political outlet, all I had was a job that I already knew inside out, and that for the rest of my days.

I did get a position as a trainee financial journalist with a London investors' magazine, which certainly would never have led me into the pages of this book. Maybe I would have become wealthy instead. But the company's obligatory pension scheme turned me down before I had started because of my asthmatic history.

So I decided to go into the real world of industry, and out of the chimerical sphere of finance. I never did get there.

AMATEUR BEHAVIORALISM

That is not quite true, because I did spend time in blue-collar clothing standing over hot metal moulds pouring in molten lead by hand. This was in the Exide auto batteries factory near Manchester.

I arrived there via a year (1957/58) at UMIST, the University of Manchester Institute of Science and Technology. Coincidentally, the colleague I have worked with longest of all, Gill Sharpley, secretarial Gill-of-all-trades, was living opposite in the fire station where her father was chief. We did not meet for another fifteen years.

Stepping curiously into academe's groves for a personnel management course, I was bowled over by James Fraser's lectures on psychology. They were, well, bad. Rambling and meandering. Or so they seemed to me who knew nothing of what he was talking about. Yet he intrigued me—and whose teaching can achieve more? I had to do something about it so I read the three paperback Penguins, Hans Eysenck's *Sense and Nonsense in Psychology*, and his *Uses and Abuses of Psychology*, and J.A.C. Brown's *Social Psychology of Industry*. A new mental universe opened. It was possible to think about people. I had never thought of that.

I had quit on my employment with nothing to go to, and Marjorie was expecting our son Adrian, so (as usual) I worked ferociously hard. Hence I got the year's best grades. I had not realized how much easier full-time study can be compared to solitary evening study, and anyway the achievement was not as marvelous as it sounds since the graduates on the course were taking it casually as an easy topping off to their degrees, whereas I took it seriously.

It got me on to the factory floor for the first and last time. For my grades did not get me a personnel management job. Come August, with my fellow students long gone off to work, I was still uncomfortably unemployed because at my age, 27, employers demanded relevant work experience. Mine was relevant only to a text on Weberian ideal types. Then the head of department, Reg Revans, a mathematical physicist believed to be Britain's first Professor (capital P) of management, looked around for someone to study the incentive payment system, as he conceived of the research, at Exide. He saw me, achiever of the best grades. Wonderful. I was offered the job for two years, a great surprise, which shows that in research terms he did not know what he was doing either. Perhaps he thought he did.

I got a research assistant's pittance. It was much more money than we had ever had. We celebrated with a week at Blackpool, a Coney Island cum Virginia Beach except that it faces the Atlantic the other way around. I was about to become an academic, to my surprise.

On Monday morning I began work. I did not know the word methodology. I just knew that when I had wanted to know what someone did, they showed me. So I asked to go into a workshop and find out. This took days to arrange, for I had been provided with a managerial white coat but now some soiled dungarees had to be found.

Eventually I found myself pouring the molten lead from a ladle, picking hot spittles from the holes they made in my bare arms. What those Northern workmates thought of a pale middle-class young man with a pale Southern accent, I never knew. Fortunately the genial repartee I had acquired in my own former work life stood me in good stead.

I ended up with my only degree, a "Masters Degree by Research" on work-group norms. No exams, you understand, though the exam-less British thesis is not the pushover that some North Americans imagine when they come to attempt one as a soft option.

When the appointed supervisor, a lecturer in trade union affairs, dropped out because he knew even less about research than I did, which is difficult to believe but true, James Fraser generously helped me unofficially with a kindly professionalism to which I owe much. As a psychologist he did know what methodology meant, in his particular way. In him I first saw the standards of honesty and openness we academics should expect of one another, though we transgress them sometimes in the competition to overstate our work so as to catch attention. Through him I learned from an article by Enid Mumford, from the flourishing Liverpool industrial sociology group, that pouring molten metal and chatting was not, well, pouring molten metal and chatting, but participant observation.

A couple of years later this led, with the encouragement of Derek Pugh, to my first two academic papers, in the journal *Occupational Psychology*. The first of these attempts at amateur social psychology on worker groups appeared alongside papers on The Assessment of Quality in Kippers, and Intelligence and Wastage of Student Mental Nurses. Did the fish really smell so bad, and was intelligence really so debilitating? Perhaps my resounding truism that on the shopfloor Social Man "links arms" with Economic Man did merit its page space after all.

STRUCTURALISM WITH WEBER ET AL.

I met Derek Pugh (who appears in Volume 4 of this series) because in 1960 I returned to my birthplace, Birmingham. A friend told me of a Research Fellow post advertized in the Industrial Administration Department of its municipal technical college, which was being upgraded into a CAT, College of Advanced Technology, and later became the University of Aston. I applied, and surprisingly got it. I was amazed and proud. Now I was a real academic. Not until years afterwards did I find that far from crushing the competition, I was the only serious applicant for a long-vacant post. So was I humbled.

Derek was already there, but I did not know it. I dreamed of the great work I was about to do, pioneering research in this teaching-only institution. I helped out with my own first ever teaching, training trade union officers in public speaking skills. Then one day Derek met me in the corridor. As he says in his biography (1996, p. 247):

> I don't remember when I first met David—though it was as momentous for me as Oliver Hardy first clapping eyes on Stan Laurel. But I still do remember very clearly the look on his face when I told him…that we were going to set up a research unit.…*He had not been told.*

(Please note that I am the skinny one, Stan, as well as a few months younger). As I wrote in my "Reminiscences of Aston" in the festschrift volume marking Derek's retirement (Clark, ed., 1997, p. 12):

Yes, I was aghast. It was a complete surprise. I had thought that here I alone led the way in research. Why had no one told me what was afoot?....Who was going behind my back...? Which way now, flight or fight?

Trusting that my being kept in the dark was inadvertent rather than Machiavellian, I chose fight. I joined. Was I right! I had everything to learn from working with others. I had no formal research training, just one solo factory study. Derek, an outstanding mentor then and since, was far ahead of me and I don't think I have ever caught up. But he led intellectually, never domineeringly. To me he was ever patient, ever willing to listen, ever ready to explain, as I floundered in an academic group much of whose conversation left me behind. He even grasped that now and again an innocent query from me opened up a fresh thought about what was until then taken for granted.

Over the years we, together with Marjorie and Natalie, have become firm friends. We still write together.

Our first and still continuing authorship collaboration was in writing *Writers on Organizations*. This began when Derek was asked by the Administrative Staff College, near London, to revise its leaflet on leading management writers. Derek, always groupy in nature, asked Bob Hinings and myself to work on it with him. By the time three academics finished revising the leaflet it had become a book. It was first published in 1964. With the fifth edition by Penguin in 1996 (in the United States by Sage, 1997) it must be about the longest running book in this field, and in Britain a best seller. American students seem slower than the British to grab an easy exam aid. For that is what it is, just unembellished short summaries of the main work of the best known writers and researchers. Reissuing it every few years is an entertaining hatchet job, removing those on the down grade and adding summaries of those on the up. There is a fat omnibus edition, *Great Writers on Organizations* (1993), which includes all those who were in the first four editions. So it never dates and Derek fantasizes about it going on after we have gone on.

Bob Hinings had joined us as the third member of the impending Aston team. His friendship and scholarship have helped me through academia ever since. Whereas Derek had his origins in psychology, Bob brought us a profound sociology. He brought as well an ability to type, which he had learned whilst conscripted (the British don't say drafted) into the Air Force, plus an ability to fire a rifle for which he had been paid an extra sixpence per day. We never needed the latter skill, and had there been an enemy he would probably have been more effective hurling the typewriter at it.

Aston and the Astonians

The Aston team, the Aston group, the Aston unit, the Aston school, the Aston program, as it is variously called, embraced several generations of members. As well as Derek, Bob and myself, these included Chris Turner, Keith McDonald, and Theo Nichols, all from sociology, Graham Harding, Kerr Inkson, and Roy Payne, from social psychology, Diana Pheysey, a mongrel like myself, John Child bringing a hint of history and economics, and in a variety of assisting and administering capacities, Rita Austin, Pat Clark, Cindy Fazey, Ruth Goodkin, and Will McQuillan.

Aston could have been called the Pugh Program. But early on Derek put forward the principle that "everyone goes on everything unless they don't want to." I have always tried to follow that since. So each of us knew we would get a full share of naming on publications, without having to claim it, irrespective of what part of the work we did. This all but removed intra-group competition. And we wanted to be known, should we be known at all, by an impersonal term (Aston, it became) above any one of us.

How then was it that our first four publications in the very new *Administrative Science Quarterly* (ASQ) began with Pugh and Pugh and Pugh and Pugh? This was merited by Derek's massive input but, just as much, we talked over what to do and agreed that unknowns as we were needed a brand name that would stick. It must be Pugh. Editorially, *ASQ* swallowed hard over the then unusually long lists of other authors that followed the brand label.

We clung to another principle of common commitment promulgated by Derek. No individual rooms. No pretentious names on blank closed doors. All desks together in one room. Casual conversations prompted by proximity were the stimulus to ideas, Derek argued. Individual thought occurred in the bath, in bed, on the train, wherever. Real work was done at home. Personally, I have worked this way ever since. Not a single sentence even of this bio was composed in a university room.

We set out to study workers, because that was what the funding brought by Tom Lupton, head of department, was for. Moreover, because of my research with workers, it was what I thought all research

was about. In our first home in the basement of a condemned and otherwise uninhabited office building, our ivory tower in a basement, we
scrawled on the right hand side of our blackboard "worker behavior." or
some such. To the left we began to list factors that might influence that.
Technology, ownership, size. Crucially, the day came when Derek clat-
tered down the bare wooden stairs and said, "Where's management?"

We were never the same again. It led to *ASQ*. Obviously, management
affected workers, but what was management? How could it be concep-
tualized? How could you get at it empirically? No one seemed to have
done anything comparatively, across different sorts of organizations,
though a couple of years later we found that over the water Dick Hall
was using questionnaires to compare bureaucratization in American
organizations. We became excited by the challenge.

Little by little, "management" for us dissembled into features usually
thought of as structural. They themselves demanded explanation, and
"worker behavior" was pushed off the board, to be returned to one
day—ultimately we never had time. So were conceived what we named:

- Specialization
- Formalization
- Standardization
- Centralization, and
- Configuration

This was the nearest I ever came to co-authorship of poetry.

We were purists. Concepts had to be defined and operationalized in
terms of the research aims, whatever casual lay categories there might
be. Specialization, for example, was a count of the number of activities
specialized out of a list of defined possible activities, not a count of
departmental titles. There were scales, and even factor analysis, novel-
ties in this field then. I struggled along. "Please, who is Max Weber?"
What does unidimensional mean?" "Where is orthogonal?"

I also learned that studying many requires numbers, that this is a matter of sample size and not, or should not be, a matter of belief for or
against. Yet although our scales were constructed from years of case
originated interviewing, before long we were suspected by some of
being mindless mono-causal numericalists. We have even been classified as size theorists! Good grief. The clearest outcome was a multivari-
ate explanation of structure, in which size was one among several

factors, albeit for some structural features the most influential. Still, better be misunderstood than ignored, so thanks to all who misunderstood.

No correlation coefficients were 1.0, of course. Neither they nor our view of them were "determinist," though that too was often asserted. It was John Child who subsequently put into print what had been unthought out and implicit, that all structural features are subject to some degree of choice and can work both ways "causally." He came to work with Derek in a repeat study of structure on contrasting samples.

We did not study structure only. We went on to look at what we thought of as Group-level phenomena. I worked with Kerr Inkson on a questionnaire survey of managers' roles, and Roy Payne joined Diana Pheysey in two in-depth case studies, projects that we knew amongst ourselves as Shallow-G and Deep-G. Kerr and I never published much. I was worried by peculiarities in the questionnaire results. Had there been today's pressure to "publish or perish" we would probably have been more reckless.

I had hoped that our efforts would lead us to perceive some hitherto unknown form of organization lurking in the back streets of Birmingham where no researcher had ever set foot. I was disappointed that we saw no such thing. The research produced empirically well-founded variations on bureaucratic and traditional forms, and seemed to become known for its methods more than anything. I find it strange, though explicable in terms of the contemporary demand for fast new findings, that no one has gone on to do something similarly substantial aiming at improving the concepts and methods. Aston is treated as if monumental. Yet it was no more than a first attempt, pending the next.

It made me into whatever kind of positivist I am, thinking in variables, independent and dependent. It convinced me that whether these or other words are used for it, research should be explanatory, trying to explain to some extent some things by some other things, however we may conceive of them.

By now I had obtained a lectureship (equivalent to a tenured assistant professor) with a low teaching load so that I might continue in the research team. This was a milestone. It was at last a permanency, confirming me in an academic career and giving Marjorie and I security after eight years of short contracts. I went into the most expensive store in Birmingham and asked for their largest box of chocolates. It had a handle that revolved a tray of chocs beneath a window in the lid. Wow!

POWER-FULL CANADA

One day in 1967 I opened a letter on my desk in the collective room. It had a Canadian stamp, but I knew no one there for I had hardly left England, let alone flown to North America. The letter offered me a full professorship at the University of Alberta, a place I had never thought of. I was astonished. The greatest surprise yet. I realized they must read *ASQ*.

I replied cautiously, asking whether there were funds and posts for a research team. There were, ample. Years later I was to write a piece on "Munificence and Scarcity" (in Bryman, ed., 1987), contrasting Alberta as a supportive research environment with subsequent struggles back in England.

I did not want to leave Aston. I had no plans to do so. But Alberta was extremely tempting. Moreover, Derek and I shared a sneaky feeling that research groups had a limited life, so better for me to move away voluntarily rather than calamitously, with the hope that we could engineer a coming together again "after the break". We didn't. Derek went to London Business School and I returned not to Aston but to Bradford Management Centre.

For Alberta, a research team had to be assembled. As a team colleague, Bob Hinings excels, and fortunately I was able to entice him and Mary to join in the adventure. This was momentous for them because long afterwards it led to them and their daughters settling there permanently. I wrote around, and Cor Lammers recommended Hans Pennings (now of the Wharton School). Already in residence were our Canadian member, Rodney Schneck and the Texan reason for it all, Charles Lee, who had written the fateful letter to me. We were a stimulating diversity of American, Canadian, Dutch, and English.

Crossing the Atlantic for the first time in the following year, 1968, Marjorie and I with Adrian, now 9, and Lucy, 7, had an unearthly landing in the New World. We had only known people speaking with a North American intonation on the pictures—sorry, movies. Now we were in a continuous wrap around film set where everyone was putting on a convincing act all of the time. When would they revert to normal speech?

More than that, we were suddenly Lilliputian in scale. There were giant cars—sorry, autos—giant corn flakes, and soon, a giant house with a giant fridge and, yes, a giant salary.

Most wonderfully, we were beginning two fabulous years visiting fabled places. As I write even now I have still bristling on my desk a small cactus which I wrested with my bare hands from a Montana hillside, the first Wild West cactus we had ever seen. Here in England it must be an illegal immigrant, and nowadays I would frown on ecological defoliation.

Working Against Time

I had agreed to go for two years, 1968 to 1970. I reckoned that was the absolute minimum time needed for a worthwhile piece of research. Minus holidays, we had only 22 months. We drove ourselves hard.

With hindsight, I have always been glad we made the effort. What resulted was a textbook example of positivist research design. It was an attempt to advance explicit theory, tested under specified semi-controlled conditions. It could only have been achieved with the utter concentration we were able to give to it. Though Charles and Rodney had the usual departmental responsibilities, Bob and Hans and I were free of administrative and political distractions and had no more than a little teaching to keep our hands in. There is a message here for those who imagine that academics can produce quality research when they have no quality time.

Of our two *Administrative Science Quarterly* papers in 1971 and 1974, the lead theory paper, "A Strategic Contingencies Theory of Intraorganizational Power," became a Citation Classic (see Hickson, 1989) beyond even the levels achieved by the main Aston papers. Asked to explain why, I wrote in 1989 that it was hard for an author to know, but:

> I do have a personal opinion. It is that the paper draws together the intuitively obvious in a usable, readily comprehensible, way. In social science there do not seem to be "discoveries." Rather the achievement is the expression of ideas that have been around anyway, in a form that enables others to recognize and remember them better than before. This paper has something of that quality. (p. 20)

We began by thinking about power and influence, working from a single common room in which were our desks, Aston fashion. I had proposed beforehand that we do something of the kind. I did so because an intriguing footnote lingered in my mind. It was on p. 175 of *Formal Organizations* by Peter Blau and Dick Scott, which we at Aston had hailed as the first textbook in our new subject. It said that Michel Crozier was soon to publish a book (it was his well-known *The Bureaucratic Phenomenon*) suggesting that power accrues to those who can control areas of uncertainty.

We developed this footnote into a theory that used ideas from Crozier, Joan Woodward and David Mechanic of Wisconsin, a nice mix of French, English and American. The theory tried to develop from their ideas an integrated explanation of why some departments, sections, units or whichever, in organizations have more say (or less) than do others. The organizational pecking order. When we tested it on small breweries and packaging manufacturers, selected so that specific conditions were controlled for, it worked.

One of my regrets is never having been able to take it further. When I arrived at Bradford I felt new people needed ownership of a new challenge, not the development of another team's work. I wonder?

Once I was back in the comparatively leftist UK milieu, Stewart Clegg, the first Ph.D. candidate I supervised (conversely I was his first Ph.D. supervisor!), contended that the theory was alright in itself, but trivial. It only explained maneuverings in power arenas the boundaries of which were pre- fixed by hierarchical capitalist institutions. Hm? I have said that I supervised Stewart. More accurately, I endeavored to. I think he won. His thesis, so removed from my style, was given a publishing contract before it was finished. We taught each other more than anything a tolerance of differing approaches any or all of which may have something to offer. I took from Stewart as much as from Mao Tsetung that one hundred flowers should bloom.

It is an oddity of my past that the first handful of final year degree-level students whom I taught when the Birmingham College became the University of Aston included Lex Donaldson. His, too, has become a name to conjure with in organization theory, but at the far end of the spectrum from Stewart. In the debates of the day, Lex's defenses of contingency theory often speak for me better than I could myself. Whereas Stewart keeps me on my toes.

An even greater oddity is that both Stewart and Lex have ended up in the same city, Sydney, Australia. Of course, the three of us know each other remarkably well. After all, Stewart, too, gained his first degree at Aston, and Lex's Ph.D. supervisor at London Business School was Derek Pugh!

Yes, I returned to England from Canada as intended at the end of two creative instructive years. Canada was and is very attractive to me. I find it a relatively open and considerate society, despite being politically fractured, to which I owe a great deal. But the émigré Brits there despaired of "the old country" and their attitude, far from persuading me to quit on it, reinforced my intention to return and play my small part in this grey-green island of small grey people, as they appeared from afar. Anyway, Marjorie and I felt culturally very English.

Halfway through my time at the University of Alberta I was very surprised to be flown home to be interviewed for a Chair at Bradford Management Centre. I was successful, even though the interviewing panel unexpectedly included Vic Vroom, of Yale and psychological fame. I owe this in part to Derek, who had been asked what potential candidates were around and suggested my name among others. Never had the thought of such an appointment crossed my mind. I had no career plan. Chairs especially were remote, except as furniture. In Britain and continental Europe, they carried the prestige title Professor (capital P) which lesser folk could not use. It is still mostly so, though rightly the rarity and prestige are diminishing.

So we went to Yorkshire for the first time, to a history of wool textiles and the Brontë sisters' novels, and the scenery of the Yorkshire dales.

DECISIONS, DECISIONS, DECISIONS

On the bookshelves beside me is a yellowing Christmas card sent me from Bradford by Gill and the others at a time when I was in Holland. "Decisions, Decisions, Decisions" is all it says, with a picture of three goofy guys on camels staring at a desert sky full of stars, unable to decide which one to follow. Those versed in Christian mythology will appreciate the joke. The card was sent because at Bradford we studied decisions.

The Chair in which I was ensconced had no such starting brief. It was entitled Behavioural Sciences, whatever that meant. For similarly political reasons it has at times since been entitled Organizational Analysis, International Management, and a Research Chair, but what I did went on much the same. The benefactor who funded the title Behavioural Sciences did so in the belief that this was unique. As a title it may well have been, but I wasn't. He also believed that his protégé might help solve Britain's industrial relations problems, but when I lunched with him in his stupendous apartment overlooking the Royal Palace in London, I imagine he was disappointed. I was hopelessly out of my social depth with a butler and variegated other domestics, and perhaps he was out of his academic depth. We were not made for each other.

Indeed, I was in a particularly egalitarian phase. Another room-in-common for researchers' desks and for my own was ready, I swapped my Professorial wine allowance for a collective tea kettle, and I declined to deliver a ceremonious Professorial Inaugural Lecture on the grounds that I would if everyone else at lower levels also did, but not if its function was to glorify Professors only. Some said I was chicken, but I was surprised to discover that the Vice-Chancellor (which is English English for President) was not displeased. I did not realize then that he was known nationally as "Red Ted."

I looked around for a group to fill the room. Richard Butler was attracted back to his native land from a Ph.D. at Northwestern University in Illinois. We shared an interest in powerlike things, and we set out as a partnership.

Our decisive recruit was Runo Axelsson from Sweden, for he pointed out that managerial power was manifest in the making of major decisions. Not routine ones, but the big ones, often called strategic, such as new product or service launches and takeovers and restructurings and the like.

David Wilson joined us with degrees from Leeds, and another stalwart throughout, Geoff Mallory, from industry and a subsequent Bradford undergraduate degree as a mature student.

We tried to think about how decisions were made. We groped for a couple of years, for whilst studies had been published of single cases, and there were brilliant insightful ideas about decisions like satisficing and incrementalism, there were absolutely no explicit concepts with which to empirically compare one decision-making process with another.

Graham Astley came into the team, another Englishman back from the States, and began to clarify for us the difference between political and technical elements. David Wilson took the lead in six exploratory in-depth case studies. We began to move uncertainly towards our eventual total of 150 cases of decisions.

To me, we were always pushing uphill, compared to my previous research experiences. Many of our peers were skeptical. Andrew Pettigrew's work had revivified the British taste for deep case studies, and we

seemed unable to convey to others that our uniquely large sample was
also case based, and not just a survey. Further, only we ourselves
seemed to think that it was possible to study *process* comparatively
across large numbers. Process seemed indissolubly linked with one-off
case studies. Conceptually groping as we still were, we failed to portray
sufficient confidence to the Social Science Research Council to obtain
from them any long-term funding so that we could concentrate on the
task. It was a nice instance of the conundrum that you may not get
funded to do it until after you have done it and so can express yourself
confidently. Richard and I were forced to give more attention to getting
money bit by bit from the Council for the others' salaries than we gave
to the research itself.

We lurched from grant to grant at six monthly and twelve monthly
intervals. David and Geoff heroically continued to contribute even
whilst on the dole. Graham Astley, his pay precarious, could endure it
no longer and returned to the States to make a name for himself, before
dying tragically young, a loss to us all of a penetrating mind. I had to
learn that hierarchy was always hierarchy and was compelled by the
many other distractions of a Professor to retreat from the research room
behind my own door. Mistakenly fearing to push myself and my own
views too much on a group that needed to think afresh, I think that I
failed the other way by not putting sufficient into my share of the leadership.

Into crisis came the amiable unsuspecting David Cray, a product of
Mike Aiken at Wisconsin, to replace Graham. We deliberately sought an
American, because I argued that we had no time to lose and an American, with longer and more methodological Ph.D. training than a Briton,
would get to work quicker.

David grasped what we were doing in no time at all. His cheery personality and research skills revitalized the group. We moved forward
with renewed energy.

By the mid 1980s we did indeed demonstrate that processes, decision-
making processes, could be compared. We had formulated variables that
would do it. We did discern three general types of process—Sporadic,
Fluid and Constricted—and did explain how they ensued primarily from
the complexity and politicality of what was being decided. The work
took nearly a decade.

Then for me came paradise. We needed to write a book. I had earlier
turned aside an invitation to spend a year at the Netherlands Institute for

Advanced Studies in the Social Sciences and Humanities (NIAS) at Wassenaar, near The Hague, because I did not want to be diverted from the research effort. Providentially the invitation now came once more. Geoff Mallory took over my teaching, and with the unswerving support of the Management Centre's Director (or Dean), Chris Higgins, I went.

1982/83 at NIAS, an equivalent to the "think-tank" at Stanford University, was the nearest a researcher like me can come to heaven. No phone, no administration, no politics, no teaching, just Dutch coffee and a quiet room overlooking the garden. There I wrote most of *Top Decisions*, published in 1986 in our joint names.

For Marjorie, it was not such a pleasure. She had newly lost a good deal of her sight, and life in strange surroundings was a strain for her. Nor did she have any equivalent to my scholarly aim to make it all worthwhile. Still, we both loved Dutch tidiness, Dutch apple pie with cream, and the traffic-free paths of the coastal dunes.

The team that accomplished the Bradford studies of decision-making processes dispersed, Geoff Mallory and Davids Cray and Wilson in different directions. Judith Hyde, whose indomitable flying fingers typed through our data, had long gone. Richard and I continued on, Richard to work on investment decisions and on joint ventures. In 1988 I negotiated a personal deal with the University relieving me of administration and teaching in return for a drop in income, so that I could resume research which I saw being squeezed out by the mounting overload.

Then the Wilsonian David, now at Warwick, reminded me that we had not looked beyond the juncture when decisions are reached, which is usually formally marked by a management board authorization. We had been too exhausted in money and energy to go further than that. Anyway, most of the decisions in our cases had not been implemented when we collected our data. But by now they had.

So we applied to the Research Council for a grant to follow up cases from our data bank to see what happened when decisions came to be carried out, and to try and explain why they succeeded or failed. Again, no money was forthcoming.

Then out of the darkness came the American cavalry! In modern dress, of course. Someone in the Pentagon or related edifice had seen and liked our *Top Decisions* book, and ordered the troops to target Hickson. Milton Katz of the US Army Research Institute (Social Science Program) office in London found me, and I was asked what research I needed funding. I did not need time to think.

Eight years later, David and Sue Miller and I are working enthusiasti-
cally on getting the results of the research fully published. Sue achieved
a pioneering Doctorate on decision implementation, supervised by me,
and then as Research Assistant she led the way in our fresh data collection. She is now at Durham Business School, David again at Warwick
Business School after a period at Aston.

This most patient and genuinely understanding of funding agencies,
more so than almost any other I have known, has kept faith in us through
this long haul. We have used its budget to overcome geographical separation by the peculiar expedient of daylong working sessions in a room
in a sometime down at heel hotel in the small town of Chesterfield.
Chesterfield has a church with a crooked steeple, a candy factory ("Ah,
mints on the breeze today"), and is exactly midway for the three of us.

In that phoneless room, and in Ivy's café opposite, we have found that
there are "routes" in the management of implementation which make
success more likely, that there is both coupling and decoupling between
the processes of deciding and implementing, and that certain organizational strategies are the most risky. As I have said, we are writing that
alongside my writing this.

Of course, military money is a trifle awkward for any degree of pacifist, even a confused doubtful pacifist. I console myself that there have
been absolutely no strings or pressures, and that our results are publicly
available to militarist and pacifist alike, in any case. I suppose we all
have our price.

HOW NOT TO DO IT

Money does talk, and can talk politically. Soon after arriving at Bradford
I had found it impossible in terms of university politics to turn aside a
proffered grant from the national government's Department of Health
and Social Security to study family health clinics. Most attractively, this
was secure and long-term, for five years. Yet it entrapped me in all the
things I knew not to do.

Because I was already committed in my own mind to the work that
became the studies of decision-making, I could be involved only peripherally in the research on clinics. The research staff, Gerald Beales, Judy
Etheridge, David Field and Michael Wheeler, regarded the project in a
different way to myself from the start, and I could not put in the time to
try and think out with them a constructive integration. Yet unless senior

figures as I was are fully involved in all stages of a project, data collection included, then team underachievement is likely. Such senior figures do not know what they themselves are talking about and team performance suffers.

Even worse, the initial impetus was managerial, how to improve clinic performance. There was no academic, scholarly, idea. Yet the most useful research begins in theory, whether intuitive or explicitly stated. That gives the best chance of a result which flows into teaching and in the long run influences practice. There is too great a contemporary emphasis on designing research for instantly applicable results, to agendas set by managerial needs. The pursuit of short-term gain in the field of organizational analysis foreshadows long-term loss.

Hence, for us, the consequence for the study of clinics was an ineffectual report to the funding department, and little more. By the time it was sent in, all those who had been interested had moved elsewhere, and it evoked no response. Not even a postcard. I fear that was fitting.

CULTURE, CULTURE, CULTURE

The "decisions, decisions, decisions" Christmas card symbolized the culture from whence I come, and Canada had taught Marjorie and I how English we are within that broad culture. Even before these promptings, my attention had been caught when a small side project at Aston, in collaboration with Joe Schwitter of Ohio State University, showed that firms around Birmingham in England were less formalized than those in Ohio. Aha!, we had said, here in Britain is a society in which control relies on a common cultural traditionalism and requires less formalization. So it does, as has often been reaffirmed since. But after a while John Child and others began to criticize the fragility of this primitive kind of comparison, which jumps to conclusions about societal culture without ever defining or operationalizing what that is. It was Monir Tayeb who splendidly showed how to do better by tracing culture independently of what it might predict in the workplace, for a thesis under John's supervision comparing English and Indian factories. The External Examiner from another university was none other than myself.

And then there was Charley McMillan. A Canadian, he was hired from the MBA Program at Alberta to sit in the corner of our research room there and do odd jobs whilst the real researchers got on with "A Strategic Contingencies Theory etc." But Charley was no mere odd-job-ber. He seized the opportunity to launch research that he made his own, first an Aston-type comparison which added Canada to what we already had on Britain and the United States, then moving with me to Bradford to mastermind a more wide-ranging comparison of firms in Britain, Japan and Sweden. This was well-designed and executed, but I have always felt that we, mostly I, underperformed on it. My cupboard still holds the partially written book that we never finished. Still, it sent Charley on his way as an academic and consultant, and indeed personal advisor to the then Canadian Prime Minister, Brian Mulroney. The project brought into my life Koya Azumi, Japanese American, and Dezso Horvath, an escapee Hungarian in Sweden who eventually moved on to Toronto. Most significantly, it heightened my interest in societal culture.

By the mid 1970s I was teaching a cobbled together cross-national elective course to Bradford MBAs. I called it "Comparative Organizations," and hardly anyone came. I taught precisely the same, called it "International Management," and had to close the books.

I have always hoped my teaching would help to raise awareness, don't we all. But my heart was in the cross-national stuff as never before. Here I had an ulterior motive that went right back to that formative experience as a boy during the European War. These management students would never dream of knowingly touching social science, but perhaps I could open for them a wider perspective in this International Management guise. In return, they opened for me an interest in all things religious as I tried to understand the underlying viewpoints behind the several races, many nationalities, and many cultures in each year's group.

But the syllabus was patchy, lacking coherence. Then arrived Geert Hofstede (who, like Derek Pugh, appears in Volume 4 of this series). He came to me via his compatriot Cor Lammers who entered my story again by inviting me to help him edit a cross-national and cross-institutional book *Organizations Alike and Unlike* (1979). Chapter 6 was by Geert, on "Power Distance." Poor second-hand questionnaire material, it seemed. Then gradually the meaningfulness of his oft-played quartet Power Distance, Individualism/Collectivism, Uncertainty Avoidance and Masculinity/Femininity began to dawn on me. They were a landmark. Here was an integrating conceptual framework on which teaching could be built. Never mind what detractors said about its flimsy operationalization, it was derived from a remarkably controlled and huge sample, and above all it rang true.

Much else flowed from this interest of mine. A meeting in Paris in 1973 of a dozen or so Europeans gave rise to EGOS, the Euro association I mentioned earlier. It was instigated not by a European but by Mike Aiken, also mentioned earlier, an American who whilst working in Belgium was taken aback by the mutual isolation of West Europeans. So much do the Europeans owe to the Americans.

A triumvirate, Franco Ferraresi of Turin, Jean-Claude Thoenig of Paris, and I were deputed to do something about this situation. The outcome now is a flourishing Euro-network, becoming formalized as an institution, whose colloquia (conferences) are ever lively.

Every group wants to see itself reflected in a magazine. I feared that EGOS would want to. It did. As a non-reader, the last thing I wanted was more paper on shelves. More not to read. Then in a room in a hotel in Speyer on the Rhine, in 1977 some conspirators cornered me and surprised me by asking if I would edit a brand-new Euro-based journal. I suppose I was asked because I had some years' experience as a non-American oddity on the editorial board of the *Administrative Science Quarterly*. Again, so much do the Europeans owe to Americans.

After prolonged thought, I had a go. I have recounted what happened in "Inside Story: The Bedroom Scene" in the first issue of *Organization Studies* (*OS*) in 1980, and in "Pristine Pages: Institutionalizing and Editing a New Research Journal" (in Cummings & Frost, 1985).

I would never have contemplated the burdens of editing but for this one-off opportunity to fulfil my personal Euro-puzzled-pacifism. *OS* is wholly supranational, not a between nations international collaboration but a venture beyond nation. Its mission is to open publishing to those for whom publishing in English would otherwise be culturally and linguistically out of reach. The work was overloading, responsible, enriching, as it was too for Pam Waterhouse who ran the office. Luckily for me, I had the calm judgment and deep scholarship of Alfred Kieser as first Co-Editor. It was a wrench to let go in 1990, but after a dozen years a fresh impulse was desirable.

I had already enjoyed receiving a Swedish Honorary Doctorate at Umea, which officially made me a little more Continental and slightly less an islander. I was crowned with a wreath of laurel leaves like Roman Emperors once were. This made me look not so much like Julius Caesar as like the sinister "lean and hungry" Cassius of Shakespeare's play. So much for laurels on Stan Laurel.

Turning 180 degrees, I took a trip Westwards and learned hugely from accompanying Beto Oliveira, known in Brazil by another selection of his numerous names as Carlos Arruda, interviewing Brazilian managers on their decisions. I experienced Brazilian cordiality, and Brazilian urgency in action, mingled confusingly for an Anglo like me with a pliable clock. Suzana Rodrigues, who did her own doctoral research on decisions in the Northern English rain and wind rather than the dripping Brazilian heat, was the origin of this and of our friendships with both families.

The culmination of my long-evolving personal commitment was the writing of *Management Worldwide* (1995) in which—guess who—Derek collaborated, and its companion reader *Exploring Management* (1997). They attempt an introductory global spin within the cosy embrace of paper Penguins.

A SURPRISING FINISH

I am surprised to finish this tale. Have I really written so much so quickly? I see now why I have always been so tense. Whilst I learned from others I was always walking on thin intellectual ice myself, always just about to go under. Sorry if that icy metaphor clicks only with readers way up in the Northern hemisphere, or a few far South (which tempts me to be funny about penguins again).

In addition to all those from whom I have learned most because I worked with them, and the huge number I have learned from at a distance, there are three Continental Europeans who must be mentioned once more. German, French and Dutch respectively, they are Max Weber, Michel Crozier and Geert Hofstede. The first fathered posthumously the line of research in which I work. The others I am proud to know personally, the first instigating my interest in power and decisions, the second framing my interest in societal cultures. I skid about on the ice guided by their thoughts.

Thoughts are what research is about. Whether or not there is a philosophical real world out there beyond what we see, what we see is real enough for me. Yet thoughts are not enough to make empirical research happen. This needs, too, research entrepreneurs who get things going—perhaps I have been one of these—and providers of money and jobs who determine what is possible. Looking back, I see that all three—thinkers, entrepreneurs and providers—are essential.

None of the three can do without the others. Without each, nothing would happen.

Looking back, I see also that it has been a surprisingly good life to be mixed up in all this. It still is. Others meanwhile have had less rewarding occupations. Some, indeed, have poured molten lead. Lives hemmed in by the routineness of it all, lives paying for my life. So, yes, of course I would do it all again, not least the gardening and hiking in the hills, which have kept me in Yorkshire in preference to London or North America. Even more so if next time I could be absolutely sure rather than just hopeful of its benefit to society as well as to myself. What I would beg for would be 48 hour days so that I had time for the fun of being a socio-linguist as well. Wherever did all those words come from?

PUBLICATIONS

1961

Motives of workpeople who restrict their output. *Occupational Psychology, 35*(3), 111-121. [Translated and republished by *Forfa-briefe, 3*, 62. Germany: Braunschweig]

1963

Worker choice of payment system. *Occupational Psychology, 37*(2), 93-100.

Financial incentives and group interests. *Management International, 3*(3/4), 136-142.

With D.S. Pugh, C.R. Hinings, K.M. Macdonald, C. Turner, & T. Lupton. A conceptual scheme for organizational analysis. *Administrative Science Quarterly, 8*(3), 289-315.

1964

With K.M. Macdonald. A Scheme for the Empirical Study of Organizational Behavior, *International Journal of Production Research, 3*, 1, 29-34.

With D.S. Pugh, & C.R. Hinings. *Writers on organizations*. London: Hutchinson.

1965

With D.S. Pugh. Organizational theory: The facts about "bureaucracy."
The Manager, (December), 37-40.

1966

Do big organizations have most paperwork? *The Chartered Secretary*,
VI(10), 451-454.
A convergence in organization theory. *Administrative Science Quar-
terly*, *11*(2), 224-237.

1967

With C.R. Hinings, D.S. Pugh, & C. Turner. An approach to the study
of bureaucracy. *Sociology*, *1*(1), 61-72.
With R.L. Payne. Measuring the ghost in the organizational machine.
European Business, *13*(May), 1967.

1968

With D.S. Pugh. The comparative study of organizations. In D. Pym
(Ed.), *Industrial society: Social sciences in management*. London:
Penguin Books.
With D.S. Pugh, C.R. Hinings, & C. Turner. Dimensions of organization
structure. *Administrative Science Quarterly*, *13*(1), 65-105.

1969

With C.R. Hinings & R.L. Payne. A dimensional analysis of organization structure: Some results. *Transactions of the Sixth World Congress of the International Sociological Association*, Evian, France,
1966.
With J.M. Pennings, C.R. Hinings, C.A. Lee, & R.E. Schneck. Uncertainty and power in organizations: A model of sub-unit functioning. *Mens en Maatschappiz*, *44*(5), 418-433. ["Man and Society,"
The Netherlands]
With D.S. Pugh. A dimensional analysis of bureaucratic structures. In R.
Mayntz (Ed.) (Free University of Berlin), *Burokratische organizations*. Kiepenheuer & Witsch.

With D.S. Pugh, & C.R. Hinings. An empirical taxonomy of structures of work organizations, *Administrative Science Quarterly, 14*(1), 115-126.

With D.S. Pugh, & D.C. Pheysey. Operations technology and organization structure: An empirical reappraisal. *Administrative Science Quarterly, 14*(3), 378-397.

With D.S. Pugh, C.R. Hinings, & C. Turner. The context of organization structures. *Administrative Science Quarterly, 14*(1), 91-114.

With M.W. Thomas. Professionalization in Britain: A preliminary measurement. *Sociology, 1*(3), 37-54.

1970

With J.H.K. Inkson,& D.S. Pugh. Organization context and structure: An abbreviated replication. *Administrative Science Quarterly, 15*, 318-329.

With D.S. Pugh, & D.C. Pheysey. Organization: Is technology the key? *Personnel Management Magazine, 2*(2), 20-26.

1971

With C.R. Hinings, C.A. Lee, R.E. Schneck, & J.M. Pennings. A strategic contingencies theory of intraorganizational power. *Administrative Science Quarterly, 16*(2), 216-229.

With D.S. Pugh, & C.R. Hinings. *Writers on organizations* (2nd ed.). London: Penguin Books.

1972

With C.R. Hinings, J.M. Pennings, & R.E. Schneck. Contingencies and conditions in intraorganizational power. *Quarterly Journal of Management Development* (Special Issue, Summer). [Also in Comparative Administrative Research Institute Series, No 5, Kent State University].

With J.H.K. Inkson, J. Schwitter, & D.C. Pheysey. A comparison of organization structure and managerial roles: Ohio, USA, and the Midlands, England. *Journal of Management Studies, 7*(3), 347-363.

With D.C. Pheysey, C.R. Hinings, & D.S. Pugh. A research approach to organizational functioning. In W. Hill & D.M. Egan (Eds.), *Read-*

ings in organization theory: A behavioural approach (2nd ed.)
Boston: Allyn & Bacon.
With D.S. Pugh. Causal inference and the Aston studies. *Administrative Science Quarterly, 17*(2), 273-276.

1973

With A.E. McCullough. Power in organizations. Unit 3, 11-30, in Open
University text *People and organizations.*, Open University Press.
With C.J. McMillan, C.R. Hinings, & R.E. Schneck. The structure of
work organizations across societies, *Journal of Academy of Management, 16*(4), 555-569.

1974

With C.R. Hinings, J.M. Pennings, & R.E. Schneck. Structural conditions of intraorganizational power. *Administrative Science Quarterly, 19*(1), 22-44.
With C.J. McMillan, C.R. Hinings, & J. Schwitter. The culture-free context of organization structure: A tri-national comparison. *Sociology, 8*(1), 59-80. [Republished in T.D. Weinshall (Ed.), *Culture and management,* Penguin, 1977].

1975

With E.A. Holdaway, J.F. Newberry, & R.P. Heron. Dimensions of organizations in complex societies: The educational sector. *Administrative Science Quarterly, 20*(1), 37-58.

1976

The power project: Setting up a research program. In C. Brown, P.G. de Monthoux, & A. McCullough (Eds.), *The access casebook.* Stockholm: THS.
With D. Horvath, C.J. McMillan, & K. Azumi. The cultural context of organizational control: An international comparison. *International Studies of Management and Organization, VI*(3), 60-86.
With D.S. Pugh. *Organizational structure in its context: The Aston program, Vol I.* Saxon House/D.C. Heath.

1977

With R. Axelsson, R.J. Butler, & D.C. Wilson. Organizational power in organizational decision-making. In M. Warner (Ed.), *Organizational choice and constraint*. Saxon House.

With R.J. Butler, D.C. Wilson, & R. Axelsson. Organizational power, politicking and paralysis. *Organization and Administrative Sciences*, *8*(4), 45-60.

With C.J. McMillan. The cross-national context of organization theory and design. In H.C. Jain & R.N. Kanungo (Eds.), *Behavioural issues in management: The Canadian context*. McGraw-Hill Ryerson.

1978

With R.J. Butler, R. Axelsson, & D.C. Wilson. Decisive coalitions. In B. King, S. Streufert, & F.E. Fiedler (Eds.), *Managerial control and organizational democracy*. Wiley.

1979

Edited with C.J. Lammers. *Organizations alike and unlike*. (A book of original research papers commissioned from an international cross-section of authors). Routledge & Kegan Paul.

With C.J. McMillan, K. Azumi, & D. Horvath. The grounds for comparative organization theory: Quicksands or hard core? In C.J. Lammers & D.J. Hickson (Eds.) above.

1980

With W.G. Astley, R.J. Butler, G.R. Mallory, & D.C. Wilson. Strategic decision making: Concepts of content and process. *International Studies of Management and Organization*, *IX*(4), 5-36.

With B. Kuc, & C.J. McMillan. Centrally planned late development: A comparison of Polish factories with equivalents in Britain, Japan and Sweden. *Organization Studies*, *1*(3); (also published in Japanese in: *Organizational Science, 13*(4), 56-68, December 1979).

With G. Mallory. Scope for choice in strategic decision making and the trade union role. In A. Thompson & M. Warner (Eds.), *The behavioural sciences and industrial relations*. Gower Press.

1981

With W.G. Astley, R.J. Butler, & D.C. Wilson. Organization as power. In L. Cummings & B. Staw (Eds.), *Research in organizational behavior, Vol. 3*. JAI Press.

With D. Horvath, K. Azumi, & C.J. McMillan. Bureaucratic structures in cross-national perspectives: A study of British, Japanese and Swedish firms. In G. Dlugos & K. Weiermair (Eds.), *Management under differing value systems*. De Gruyter.

With C.J. McMillan. *Organization and nation: The Aston program, Vol. IV.* Saxon House/D.C. Heath.

1982

Operations technology. *Citation Classic in Current Contents,* 14, 32, 20. Philadelphia: Institute for Scientific Information.

With W.G. Astley, R.Axelsson, R.J. Butler, & D.C. Wilson. Complexity and cleavage: Dual explanations of strategic decision-making. *Journal of Management Studies, 19*(4), 357-375.

With D.C. Wilson, R.J. Butler, D. Cray, & G.R. Mallory. The limits of trade union power in organizational decision making. *British Journal of Industrial Relations, XX*(3), 322-341.

1983

With G.R. Mallory, R.J. Butler, D. Cray, & D.C. Wilson. Implanted decision-making: American owned firms in Britain. *Journal of Management Studies, 20*(2), 191-211.

With D.S. Pugh, & C.R. Hinings. *Writers on organizations* (3rd ed.). London: Penguin Books.

1985

Pristine pages: Institutionalizing and editing a new research journal. In P. Frost & L. Cummings (Eds.), *Publishing in the organizational sciences*. Irwin.

With K. Azumi, D. Horvath, & C.J. McMillan. Structural uniformity and cultural diversity in organizations: A comparative study of factories in Britain, Japan and Sweden. In K. Sato & Y. Hoshino (Eds.), *The anatomy of Japanese business.* Sharpe.

With R.J. Butler, D. Cray, G.R. Mallory, & D.C. Wilson. Comparing one hundred and fifty decision processes. In J.M. Pennings (Ed.), *Organizational strategy and change.* San Francisco: Jossey Bass. [Reprinted in *Economia Aziendale*, Milano, 1/85]

1986

With R.J. Butler, D. Cray, G.R. Mallory, & D.C. Wilson. *Top decisions: Strategic decision-making in organizations.* Blackwell & Jossey-Bass (USA).

With R.J. Butler, D. Cray, G.R. Mallory, & D.C. Wilson. How long does it take to make a decision? *Management Research News, 9*(3), 2-7.

With R.J. Butler, D. Cray, G.R. Mallory, & D.C. Wilson. Governmental influence upon decision making in organizations in the private and public sectors in Britain. In R. Wolff (Ed.), *Organizing industrial development.* De Gruyter.

With D. Cray, R.J. Butler, G.R. Mallory, & D.C. Wilson. Proactive and reactive decision making. In V. Subramaniam (Ed.), *Problem recognition in public policy and business management.* New Delhi: Ashish Publishing.

With D.C. Wilson, R.J. Butler, D. Cray, & G.R. Mallory. Breaking the bounds of organization in strategic decision-making. *Human Relations, 39*(4), 309-332.

1987

Ruminations on munificence and scarcity in research. In A. Bryman (Ed.), *Doing research in organizations.* Routledge & Kegan Paul.

Decision-making at the top of organizations. *Annual Review of Sociology, 13*, 165-192.

With G.K. Kenny, R.J. Butler, D. Cray, G.R. Mallory, & D.C. Wilson. Strategic decision making: Influence patterns in public and private sector organizations. *Human Relations, 40*(9), 613-632.

1988

With D. Cray, G.R. Mallory, R.J. Butler, & D.C. Wilson. Sporadic, fluid
and constricted processes: Three empirical types of strategic decision-making in organizations. *Journal of Management Studies*,
25(1), 13-39.

1989

Power and uncertainty in organizations. *Citation Classic in Current
Contents 21*, 39, 12. Philadelphia: Institute for Scientific Informa-
tion.
With R.J. Butler, D. Cray, G.R. Mallory, & D.C. Wilson. Decision and
organization: Processes of strategic decision-making and their
explanation. *Public Administration*, *67*(4), 373-390. (Published in
Spanish as: Organizacion Y Decision in *Ciencia Y Sociedad*,
XV(4), 412-440, 1990, Dominican Republic.)
With D.S. Pugh. *Writers on organizations* (4th ed.). London: Penguin
Books & Newbury Park, CA: Sage.

1990

Politics permeate. In D.C. Wilson & R.H. Rosenfeld. *Managing organizations*. McGraw-Hill.

1991

With D. Cray, G.R. Mallory, R.J. Butler, & D.C. Wilson. Explaining
decision processes. *Journal of Management Studies*, *28*(3), 227-
251.

1992

Decision-making at the top in contrasting societies. In H. Mannari, H.K.
Nishio, J. Watanuki, & K. Azumi (Eds.), *Power shifts and value
changes in the post-cold war world*. Kibi International University
Press.

With S. Miller. Concepts of decision: Making and implementing strategic decisions in organizations. In F. Heller (Ed.), *Decision making and leadership.* Cambridge University Press.

1993

[Editor]. *Management in western Europe.* (A book of original chapters on twelve nations commissioned from an international selection of authors.) De Gruyter.

With D.S. Pugh. *Great writers on organizations: The omnibus edition.* Dartmouth.

1995

[Edited]. *Managerial decision making.* Dartmouth.

With D.S. Pugh. *Management worldwide: The impact of societal culture on organizations around the world.* Penguin.

With D.S. Pugh. Top of the pops among the gurus. *Competitiveness Review: An International Business Journal, 5*(2), 75-78.

With S.B. Rodrigues. Success in decision making: Different organizations, differing reasons for success. *Journal of Management Studies, 32*(5), 655-678.

1996

The ASQ years then and now through the eyes of a Euro-Brit. *Administrative Science Quarterly,* 40th Anniversary Issue, *41*(2), 217-228.

With C.A. Arruda. Sensitivity to societal culture in managerial decision making: An Anglo-British comparison. In P. Joynt & M. Warner (Eds.), *Managing across cultures: Issues and perspectives.* International Thomson.

With R.J. Butler, D. Cray, G. Mallory, & D.C. Wilson. Sifting the garbage: Conceptualizing and explaining processes of strategic decision making. In M. Warglien & M. Masuch (Eds.), *The logic of organizational disorder.* De Gruyter.

With S.J. Miller, & D.C. Wilson. Decision-making in organizations. In S. Clegg, C. Hardy, & W. Nord (Eds.), *Handbook of organization studies.* Sage.

With D.S. Pugh. Organizational convergence. In M. Warner (Ed.), *International encyclopedia of business and management*. Routledge.
With D.C. Wilson, & S. Miller. How organizations can overbalance: Decision overreach as a reason for failure. *American Behavioral Scientist, 39*(8), 995-1010.
With D.S. Pugh. *Writers on organizations* (5th ed.). London: Penguin Books & Newbury Park, CA: Sage.

1997

[Editor]. *Exploring management across the world: Selected readings.* Penguin.
The ivory tower in a basement: Reminiscences of Aston. In T. Clark (Ed.), *Advancement of organizational behavior.* Dartmouth Publishing.

THE LIFE AND TIMES OF
A PERENNIAL STUDENT

THOMAS A. MAHONEY

The invitation to contribute an autobiographical essay was flattering and rewarding. The challenge of responding, however, is intimidating. What, if anything, in one's life and career is worth study by others? As suggested by the example of George Strauss (1993), the answer for me likely lies in review of the evolution of my field of study, Human Resources, and not in my own personal evolution. An autobiographical review, however, provides the opportunity to recognize and pay tribute to the many people who influenced my personal as well as professional lives.

The challenge of responding also brought a realization of the differences of autobiographical and biographical analyses. Autobiographers write from the perspective of personal values and emotion and are ill-suited for analyzing the impact of their lives; that analysis is best left for the biographer. What the autobiographer can provide is a retrospective record of experienced events and reactions that others may find useful in explaining observed actions, events, and consequences. Thus I view this essay as a data source for any biographical analysis, however unlikely.

Management Laureates, Volume 5, pages 129-170.
Copyright © 1998 by JAI Press Inc.
ISBN: 0-7623-0178-3

A PERSONAL BEGINNING

The history of my life and career evidences in many ways the history of American society from 1930 until the present. The events that shaped my life were those that shaped many others as well during this period. Born in St. Louis in 1928 to A. Waite and Mildred Flood Mahoney, my earliest recollections are of an urban society living through the Great Depression. My father had been an office supervisor with American Telephone & Telegraph Company. With the advent of my birth and the expectation of a continuing career with "the telephone company," my parents moved from their city flat to a modest new home in an emerging suburb. The depression worsened, however; my father was terminated and began a succession of temporary jobs--Christmas salesclerk in a department store and policeman for the suburb in which we lived, among others. Having spent his childhood on a farm in northwestern Missouri, my father viewed farming as a more secure livelihood than employment in an industrialized economy; at least one could always grow one's own food. He also chafed at being dependent upon an arbitrary boss or supervisor. Thus began a search for an affordable agricultural investment.

We moved to a small dairy farm in northern Indiana in 1936, the family having expanded to include a brother 18 months younger than I, James, and an infant brother, Donald. While affordable, the farm was hardly promising as an enterprise—it included 8-10 scrub cattle, two horses (one almost blind), and a house without plumbing or heat. Over the next 30 years, my parents would transform it through strenuous work into a farm with registered Guernsey cattle and productive crop land. Over that time a variety of ventures were employed to maintain a cash flow--raising chickens for the sale of fryers and eggs, sheep for the sale of wool and lambs, bee-keeping for the production of honey, and hogs for butchering and sale, and, in the early years, my father working as a railway mail clerk and as a guard for an ordnance factory. We boys even ran a trapline hoping for muskrats and minks that might be skinned and the skins sold. The entire family pitched in including my mother who had charge of the chickens, tractor driving for hay making, and maintaining the breeding and milk records for the Guernsey herd being developed.

We boys went to a consolidated township school, two grades to each room. I had started school at mid-year in St. Louis, something unknown in Argos, Indiana. With our move, I was, in effect, advanced a half-year with students one to two-years older. In retrospect, this placement affected my development and experiences for the next 25 years--my peers were always 1-2 years more advanced than I in physical, emotional, and social development. I began to lie about my age to maintain my position among them.

Work obligations on the farm precluded other employment for years, although my first paid employment—$.50 a day—was driving teams of horses for neighbors during haying activities. With the advent of World War II, employment opportunities for young males opened. Lying about my age during the summer when I was 15, I joined my peers working as a section gang laborer on the Nickel Plate railroad; the work day was from 7 to 3, leaving time for another 4-5 hours of farm work. My outside income was a welcome addition to our family resources. The following summer I worked on the railway signal gang as my peers were being drafted into military service. Other jobs on the side included delivering ice in the summer to homes, bars, and retail establishments.

One major lesson learned growing up on a dairy farm relates to the role of personal discipline and order. Dairy cattle had to be milked morning and evening, seven days a week, rain or shine, and in sickness and in health. This regularity of milking was important for the comfort and health of the cows, as well as for the record of the herd being developed and the daily shipment of milk. Family vacations or trips of more than a day were impossible—someone always had to be there for the milking. I marvel at my father who, for many years, milked before dawn and after dusk regardless of anything else. His example of discipline set a model for us boys.

A second lesson learned from farming was the importance of patience. There was a time and season for everything and nothing was gained by trying to hurry things. Impatience, whether experienced while milking, haying, herding sheep, or even repairing broken machinery led more often than not to future disappointments, mistakes, and more delays. This lesson of patience was later to stand me in good stead when working with graduate students and conducting research.

School and learning were always fun. Although only my father had completed high school, education was always a priority of my parents. They were avid readers and we always had books to read. We boys grew up with a constant expectation that we would complete college, an uncommon expectation among our fellow students. There was always an expectation that we would work to "do our best" but no sense of competition against others. Thus there was a value to striving to one's limits, but not a value to achieving more than others. The farming experience was a model for striving to make the most of one's opportunities, rather than a model for out performing others as was more common among my peers living in town.

Nearing the end of high school, my peers were drafted and/or enlisted in service for World War II. Naturally I felt left behind and incapable of maintaining the relationships I had formed. I withdrew from high school at 17 in mid-year to enroll in engineering at Purdue University, already having qualified for graduation from high school. By mid-year I convinced my parents to let me enlist in a special army reserve program for engineering education. By the end of the year, although still only 17, I convinced them to permit me to transfer into the regular army. Such was the felt importance of maintaining membership with my peers.

Military service was a mixed bag. Immediately upon completing basic training, I was assigned to the training of other recruits. And that was how I spent much of my remaining service. This was my first experience at teaching, although un-welcomed at the time. That period also demonstrated to me the losses occasioned by personnel practices. Whereas one might celebrate the foresight of those who assigned me to training new recruits, I learned through later experiences that the army's manpower assignments were based upon need for headcount, rather than upon considerations of ability and interest. If 25 personnel were required for an assignment, the first 25 personnel files in a stack, however ordered, were those selected. My final assignment was hunt-and-peck typing of discharge papers at a demobilization station.

Returning home, I took an active role in the farm and began planning for my future education. I soon also obtained a job at the Studebaker plant in South Bend, 35 miles away, from 7-3 each day, permitting another 4-5 hours of farm work. My brother, James, having graduated from high school that spring, was selecting a college for his continued education. He had an interview scheduled at a college that was unknown to me, Wabash College. Several days before the interview, he cut his hand badly on a bandsaw and I drove him to the interview. That accidental occurrence was a major turning point in my life. While my brother was being interviewed by the admissions officer, I was entertained by the Dean of the Faculty, George Kendall. Dean Kendall taught Shakespeare, having been a touring performer of Shakespeare before the war;

he was also a member of General Douglas MacArthur's wartime staff. I was fascinated by George Kendall, his breath of knowledge, his fascination with scholarship, and his view of the liberally educated gentleman. No question for me! Wabash College would be my choice. Understandably, my brother James then settled upon Indiana University for his education. Having already completed a variety of college courses, I negotiated a mid-year entry and returned to my job at Studebaker, the farm life, and several evening courses at the Indiana University extension campus in South Bend, living during the week at the YMCA in South Bend and returning to the farm on weekends.

The Studebaker job was an aid in my development. It provided very needed funds that I saved for my college education. It also exposed me to an urban and an industrial society which I had not known. The factory and assembly-line culture is familiar to today's students largely through the writings of others. I was able to experience it at Studebaker and later in a summer job working the night shift at a General Motors Delco Remy factory. It was, in many respects, mind-numbing work, repeating the same activities over and over again by rote. It was also instructive to note and to participate in the many diversions, tricks, and games invented by the work force, both to relieve the tedium and to outwit supervisors and "the system". It was a competition unknown on the farm, yet a competition against "the system" and not an inter-personal competition. One example that I experienced resembles similar incidents recorded by Whyte, Dalton, Roy and others (1955).

In my case, two of us worked at a bench, moving transmissions from pallets to the bench for final assembly and greasing before hanging them on feeder lines to a larger assembly line. It was dirty and physically difficult work. The job description called for us to use small overhead cranes to transfer the transmissions to the bench, but we found it quicker to move them manually. We were paid on a piece-rate basis and would have earned more than the weekly standard set for the job if we were paid for the full number produced and required for final assembly. Time study engineers observed us performing as specified in the job description (using overhead cranes) and confirmed the piece-rate set, yet performance in that manner would not have provided the required output. The foreman found it more convenient to let us perform the job as we wished, turn in a production number acceptable to the engineers, and maintain a record of unreported production. We would then be scheduled for overtime work at time-and-a-half pay on Saturday when we would play cards or read books until we worked down the record of unreported production.

I came away with an appreciation for the role of human resources in an organization that could never have been acquired through formal study. Later as I would study the reports of William F. Whyte, and others, I would recognize these factory experiences within the larger context. I felt an advantage over fellow students, having experienced the events being described.

The years at Wabash greatly expanded my horizons. The focus there was upon learning and I plunged headlong into it. The course that most intrigued me was on the history of philosophy taught by Joseph Cotton. We ranged over all of the various schools of philosophy, pitting one against another, as we sought understanding. I considered majoring in philosophy, but rejected it as impractical for later employment. Instead I opted for economics, which I reasoned might have more relevance for some sort of employment.

Economics was taught by John Van Sickle, an unreconstructed Austrian-school, neo-classicist economist, a disciple of Ludwig von Mises and Friedrich Hayek. Although unintended, Van Sickle economics was quite a complement to Cotton philosophy. Micro-economics was taught as a system of logic, all propositions being derived from a set of basic assumptions, not unlike much of philosophy. The methods of analysis were common although the subjects of inquiry differed. Contrary to the curricular requirements of the school, I successfully petitioned to major in economics and to minor in philosophy, which seemed to me a perfect combination.

Micro-economics as taught by Van Sickle permitted little challenge from empirical evidence. Empirical evidence that seemed to counter the predictions of micro-economics was dismissed as the result of market imperfections or short-run adjustments, and thus was given little consideration. Yet much of what I had experienced both on the farm and in the factory contradicted the predictions of micro-economics. I yearned to argue with Van Sickle, and was forced to learn classical theory which was all he would admit as argument. Unknowingly I was learning the joint roles of theory and empirical observation and the importance of their blending. Certainly I learned the power and potential of theory, both in economics and in philosophy.

The Wabash experience, in retrospect, also taught me the value of multi- or inter-disciplinary approaches to issues. I was challenged by the differences in approaches—assumptions, priorities, and focuses—of philosophy and economics and struggled to enjoin them. Since then I have continued to be fascinated by the contributions of different disciplines to the understanding of a single issue and I strive to utilize as many disciplinary approaches as possible. This has been particularly useful in the study of industrial relations and human resources, subjects rarely understood completely from the viewpoint of a single discipline. Just as I learned from arguing with Van Sickle's reasoning, I continue to learn by fashioning arguments among disciplines addressing a common problem or issue.

Coming from a family of meager education, I had never heard of or considered graduate studies until my senior year when I faced the issue of "what next?" Benjamin Rogge, a young faculty member in economics sensed my plight and began to steer me to graduate study in labor economics. I viewed economic theory as fun, but sterile, whereas labor economics dealt with real issues and problems. Through his guidance, I applied to both the University of Wisconsin and the University of Minnesota, which I later entered. I was drawn to labor economics presumably because of my interest in real-world empirical observation and my focus upon problems of people at work, the things which I had experienced, and my attraction towards multi-disciplinary analytical methods.

At Minnesota I served as a Research Assistant (RA) with the Industrial Relations Center (IRC) while completing formal studies. The research experience with the IRC, rather than formal course work, was the initiation of my professional development, and a review of the remainder of my career parallels the development of the field of study known then as Industrial Relations.

EMERGENCE OF INDUSTRIAL RELATIONS

The IRC was the outgrowth of an Employment Stabilization Research Institute (ESRI) formed at the University of Minnesota in 1930. Funded by a grant from the Rockefeller Foundation, the institute was a reaction to the many varied problems occasioned by the depression and observed in the Twin Cities. Faculty members were drawn together from labor economics, industrial psychology, political science, sociology, and industrial engineering to research these problems. Little was known about the various problems occasioned by unemployment in an urban society, and an early focus was upon observation, assessment, and measurement. In consequence, the emergent IRC became known as *the* "dustbowl of empiricism" as efforts were directed towards measurement and assessment of employment, unemployment, labor mobility, workers' skills, education and training. Description was sought first with any prescription to follow later. Publication of a report of these early efforts, *The Local Labor Market* (Yoder & Paterson et. al., 1948) was one of the first intensive studies of this kind.

The ESRI evolved into the Industrial Relations Center in 1945 with the initiation of related research centers at several universities (e.g. Princeton, MIT, Chicago, Yale). While each center evolved individually, they maintained an informal coordination through the Labor Market Research Committee of the Social Science Research Council (SSRC), which met annually from 1945-1954 at the IRC in Minnesota. At these meetings, representatives such as Wight Bakke, Douglas MacGregor, Albert Rees, Charles Myers, John Dunlop, Lloyd Reynolds, George Schultz, William Whyte, Dale Yoder, and Donald Paterson would critique research efforts and debate directions for future research while we doctoral students would listen from the back of the room. The one issue upon which all agreed was the importance of empirical research. Beyond that, the prescriptions varied from participant-observer methods (Whyte) to survey methods (Yoder/Reynolds) and psychometric assessment (Paterson). Early issues that provoked disagreement were the relative degrees of attention to be devoted to education and to research, and the relative roles of theory and empirical research. The prevailing views were that research was necessary before considering education, and that "industrial relations studies could make only minor contributions to existing theory" (Nelson, 1955, p. 39). It also became apparent at the last meeting in 1955 that interests were being polarized into what were termed the "human relations approach" and "union-management studies;" differences in priorities, conceptual models, and research methods suggested that collaboration in some more unified approach would be impossible. In a sense, this marked the beginning of what is known today as Organizational Behavior, which, in time, emerged from the human relations approach. Also at that last meeting, one of the participants accidentally joined a conference of proctologists instead of the SSRC committee and, reportedly, only discovered his mistake after several hours.

Industrial relations at Minnesota was defined broadly as concerned with the development, allocation, and utilization of human resources in economic activity, something in between strict labor economics and human relations. Subjects encompassed collective bargaining, all aspects of personnel administration, and governmental and social efforts to prevent and alleviate unemployment, under-employment, and low wages. No single discipline was adequate to address all of these issues and the faculties of labor economics, psychology, sociology, and political science were joined in the IRC. Industrial relations existed as a topical area for research and application, not as a recognized discipline for academic study. Research assistants to perform the research projects of the Center were drawn from graduate students in the disciplines related through activities in the Center. Whereas we graduate students took formal course work in the traditional disciplines, much of our learning came from inter-disciplinary exchanges in the IRC as we contributed to the design and execution of different research projects. Lacking formal study of industrial relations, basic courses for students were courses in "labor problems" in economics (Dale Yoder) and "individual differences" in psychology (Donald Paterson).

The IRC was dominated in its early days by Yoder and Paterson, who jointly founded it and directed its activities. They secured funding through research grants to support activities ranging from development of skill and aptitude testing to employee attitude measurement and investigation of employment practices regarding retirement of older workers. Support from the professional community of employers and union leaders was sought through the offering of non-credit courses in supervision, a Workers' Education program, and annual joint conferences on topics of concern to both employers and unions. My first teaching was to experienced factory supervisors and union stewards. Exchanges in those classes continued my learning about the realities of industrial relations that had begun at the Studebaker plant. Three anecdotes illustrate the climate of those times.

- A supervisor on the loading dock of a trucking firm related in class how he had removed the doors to the washroom on the dock thus permitting him to monitor any loafing there from any location on the dock. The removal of the outside doors on the open loading dock given the cold Minnesota winters likewise discouraged loafing in the washroom.
- One business agent from an AFL union representing skilled craftsmen and wearing various gold and jeweled rings elicited reaction from a CIO union business agent representing unskilled and semi-skilled workers to the effect that he could not be elected

if he wore such ornamentation. The AFL leader replied that he could not have been elected without the ornamentation.

- A business agent of a large local union that had switched its affiliation from an alleged Communist dominated union to another, appeared to speak at an IRC conference flanked by three husky bodyguards who took up positions around the room while the business agent spoke. There was obvious tension throughout the audience.

Such were the realities of industrial relations in the 1950s.

The linkages with the professional community, employers and union leaders, provided the impetus and opportunity for my Master's thesis research, investigation of union membership participation in local unions. Various union leaders working with the IRC had voiced concern about lack of membership participation and asked for advice. Consistent with the empirical focus of the IRC, I proceeded without a conceptual model or logically derived hypotheses to identify examples of local unions with differing degrees of membership participation in local union meetings and then compared these samples for suggestions of differences. I interviewed business agents, attended union meetings, made observations of whatever variables occurred to me, and then made comparisons and drew conclusions. Although that exercise was adequate for the time and resulted in an early publication, I would certainly expect a more polished approach guided by a theoretical or conceptual model from a student today. The research approach of the IRC at that time was to identify a problem or concern, go out and look at it, count and measure whatever could be observed, and expect answers to emerge from those efforts. There was no real attempt to draw formally upon related theories in the design of research efforts; that occurred only as related theoretical orientations unconsciously shaped what the researcher observed.

Herbert G. Heneman, Jr. was instrumental in my early career development in numerous ways. It was he who actually conducted the work of the IRC, administering the research programs, guiding the work of the RAs, and challenging our talents. Because of him I was given assignments for which I was unprepared and then guided and assisted as I grew into meeting the challenges. And we learned from each other: Theodore Lindbom, Marvin Dunnette and George W.(Bill) England as doctoral students in Psychology, and Harland Fox, Earl Cheit, Einar Hardin and me in Economics. The conflicts between and blending of disciplines as we worked on issues continued the experiences of Wabash and thrilled me. The dust-bowl empiricism of the IRC provided an anchor in the real world which I had lacked at Wabash, while I also learned the valuable contributions of theory in shaping and guiding empirical work. I continue to benefit from the tensions among disciplinary orientations and between theory and empirical investigation.

EVOLUTION OF INDUSTRIAL RELATIONS

Industrial Relations (IR) began to evolve into a specialized field for academic study at Minnesota during the 1950s. This evolution from a set of issues for related disciplinary research to a form of separate profession capable of graduate study was a topic of concern to various universities with centers in Industrial Relations. Yoder, Paterson, and Heneman firmly believed that IR should be viewed as a distinct profession and drew many analogies with the profession of medicine. The research program of the IRC was at one point organized into so called "laboratories" (e.g. management development laboratory) reflecting this orientation. In 1953 the University established a master's degree in IR (MAIR) to provide this professional education and training. Clearly a professional model served at that time. Other universities—Cornell, Illinois, Michigan State—also began to offer specialized graduate study in IR about the same time, while still others—Harvard, MIT, Princeton—maintained the tradition of related but different disciplines contributing to the study of common issues, reflecting, in part, the disagreement within the SSRC committee concerning IR as a field for research or as a profession for education.

Industrial relations at Minnesota, both in research efforts and educational offerings, began shifting away from labor-market analysis and towards so called "manpower management" and labor relations, the practices impacting industrial relations within employing organizations. The two terms Personnel Administration and Industrial Relations were for a time merged in the acronym PAIR to characterize the Minnesota model of IR. The so-called "human relations" model was never a part of the Minnesota model. Related changes were also evolving in the broader professional community. The Industrial Relations Research Association (IRRA) was founded in 1947 as a society of scholars and professionals in the broadly defined field of IR. Although cast as a "research" association, much of the membership came from professionals engaged in labor relations, public policy, and labor union activities; scholars from psychology and professionals engaged in what was then termed "personnel administration" commonly were not members and many affiliated instead with the American Society of Personnel Administration (ASPA), now Society for Human Resource Management (SHRM). The Academy of Management established a division of Personnel in 1972 appealing to scholars at that end of the IR interest scale. What used to be included within the broad term Industrial Relations was clearly being sub-divided, both in practice and in academic institutions, the IRRA attracting academics and professionals interested in issues of labor relations, ASPA attracting professionals interested in personnel administration, and the Academy and Division 14 of the American Psychological Association attracting academics interested in issues of manpower management, increasingly labeled human resource management.

Many of the universities offering specialized degrees in IR also established programs of Workers Education for union leaders and stewards. The inclusion of Workers Education efforts in the missions of these IR programs distinguished them from traditional business school programs and served to justify separate departments (e.g. Minnesota) or schools (e.g. Cornell, Illinois) for IR. An early assignment of mine as a research assistant was to develop an initial curriculum for Workers Education at Minnesota, an assignment of which I was relieved as I was replaced by a more experienced director. With Yoder and Heneman opting to view IR as a unique profession, there was considerable tension between IR and the Minnesota business school. Part of this doubtless was the playing out of personal ambitions and power aspirations, but the consequence was isolation from the business school, characterized as a professional school serving employers, and the IR program, characterized as professional education for employers, union leaders, and political leaders. This conflict, at Minnesota, later led to efforts to characterize IR as a discipline rather than as a profession and thus warranting an identity separate from the business school. Interestingly, the Workers Education program with a clear professional orientation for union leaders was maintained, in part, as a pawn in the struggle with the business school; leaders of the labor movement were rallied periodically to resist politically any attempt to merge IR within the business school.

The tension experienced through viewing Industrial Relations as (1) a field for inter-disciplinary study, (2) a single discipline worthy of separate identification and academic orientation, and (3) a professional field of practice continued for years at Minnesota. Each view was adopted and pressed energetically by Yoder and Heneman as it served a unique purpose at a point in time. While the three views were merging in practice, Yoder and Heneman argued that they were incompatible and would adopt whichever view appeared more supportive of some specific end of theirs.

Another point of tension in the early IRC related to the felt contradiction of IR as a professional field and IR as an academic discipline was that posed by semi-consulting research and more traditional basic research. Whereas most yearned to conduct basic research into major issues of the day, funding for such research was not readily available. As a supplement, relatively broad research topics were elaborated (e.g., management development, employee attitudes) that permitted research at individual corporate sites and funded by those corporations, but which might conceivably be integrated into some broader research program. The tension posed by satisfying individual sponsors and maintaining the integrity of the broader research program often surfaced. Several major research efforts that were initiated during the 1950s and 1960s and which continued for some time include studies of the vocationally handicapped by Lloyd Lofquist and Rene Dawis, and Bill England's stream of research into the meaning of work. For whatever reason, my interests and efforts kept evolving over time (as will be noted later) and moved from labor-force participation of women through manager selection, training and motivation, into manpower planning, organizational assessment, and various topics within employee compensation.

My dissertation research in the mid-1950s utilized data collected earlier in a six-city study of labor mobility coordinated by the Labor Market Research Committee of the SSRC. In it I continued my debates with John Van Sickle of Wabash by exploring the links between voluntary mobility and wage differentials. Illustrating the diverse approaches of the IRC, I was at the same time engaged in research into aspects of leadership and management development. Being caught up in the research efforts of the IRC, I never considered seriously the prospect of leaving for another university upon completion of the PhD despite advice from some faculty that I should move to another environment for the initiation of my professional career. Thus I stayed on at the IRC, caught up in the exciting research efforts and in the emerging and growing program of academic studies. Bill England, graduating in Psychology, and I, graduating in Economics, both made the transition from research assistant/graduate students to research associate/faculty members at the same time and remained collaborators at the IRC for many years.

EXPANSION AND BROADENING

The 1960s began with a major effort sponsored by the Ford Foundation to change business management education. Reports by Frank Pierson (1959) and by Robert Gordon and James Howell (1959) were critical of existing education for business managers and recommended changes. Two of the major recommendations were for the introduction of the behavioral sciences and the introduction of advanced quantitative analysis into the curriculum. Remember that education programs in IR that included the behavioral sciences were distinguished from business management at that time. In retrospect, both of these recommendations impacted upon my developing career.

The first and most obvious impact occurred as I was accepted for a fellowship at a Ford Foundation institute conducted at the Harvard Business School to teach advanced mathematics for application to business to about 22 faculty members selected from schools of business around the country. The intent of the program was to qualify these faculty to introduce quantitative analysis into the curricula of their schools, and to imbue them with the evangelism required for that effort. That year at Harvard, under the tutelage of Howard Raiffa and a special faculty he had assembled, was fabulous. It enabled me to engage in my favorite occupation, that of learning. I sopped up everything available. In addition to the development provided by our faculty, I was introduced to fellow classmates from whom I learned and who went on to achieve fame in their respective fields; these were faculty members from about 22 different schools of business, faculty specializing in finance, economics, marketing, operations, and statistics. Not surprisingly, given the then current estrangement between industrial relations and business schools, I was the only faculty member specializing in industrial relations. In addition to basic mathematics, I learned what was going on in leading business schools and the interests of their faculties. It was a stimulating year! Influences upon my research efforts will be noted later.

During that year I also completed fine-tuning a book manuscript summarizing much of my earlier work on issues of management development, published as *Building the Management Team: A Guide to Management Development* (1961). As apparent from the title, I was already moving away from the IRC focus upon the individual and moving towards a more organizational focus. I recall reading March and Simon's *Organizations* (1958) during that year and noting with a shock that they had usurped my field of study. Almost all of the empirical work cited in the early chapters and from which they built later chapters came from work that I identified as *industrial relations*.

Publication of *Building the Management Team* opened another door at just that time. Fred Gracie of the National Development Foundation (NDF) of South Africa, then an association similar to the American Management Foundation, spotted the book, enjoyed it, and engaged me to present three one-week seminars, as well as a number of one-day presentations, based upon the book for senior managers throughout South Africa. I had become engaged to Ursula Burg after a five-year courtship and our tentatively planned marriage during the summer of 1961 was graciously postponed till winter to permit the South African venture. That was merely the first of a number of career-supportive efforts Ursula would make throughout our later marriage. The series of seminars began a long relationship with many South Africans and I have returned, on average, every 2-3 years for tours of duty. The early returns were for the NDF, then working with a consortium of the Van Leers Company, Greatermans department stores, and the South African Breweries company, later visiting appointments with the University of Witwatersrand and Stellenbosch University business schools, and assignments with Stellenbosch Farmers Winery and Standard Bank. Other linkages stemming from the South Africa visit will be introduced later.

A second impact of the year at Harvard relates to the academic linkages of IR and business schools. The Minnesota model, which was all I knew, called for strict separation of IR and business management. Their academic programs and students were considered quite different. The MAIR at Minnesota had developed into a strong program attracting and graduating highly qualified and motivated students who had no contact with the business school. At Harvard I became familiar through my fellow students with the curricula and research programs of leading business schools and gained respect for them. Further, I became convinced that MBA education, vitalized from the recent critiques and the growing interest in management education, would become a mini-boom industry over the next 10-20 years. I returned to Minnesota convinced that the IRC could benefit from closer integration with the business school. And I sought to convince my colleagues of the wisdom of this belief.

Suffice it to say that I was unsuccessful in that effort. And the wisdom of that outcome is irrelevant today. The IR program was successful in establishing a Ph.D. degree in IR, separate from Management, in 1964 and began to attract highly qualified students. Almost all of the doctoral students also held research assistantships at the IRC and this initiated a period of vital intellectual development for me, as well as stimulating new research efforts. During the period of transition to the PhD in IR, I was able to work with Stephen Carroll, Thomas Jerdee, and Donald Schwab as research assistants. Perhaps the most difficult to supervise, because of his rebellious, iconoclastic streak was Donald Schwab. I was, however, able to assist him informally with his dissertation research in a different relationship. That relationship contributed much to my personal development, however, and I have continued to rely upon Don's stimulation in the years since.

During my studies relating to management development, I had unconsciously begun shifting my attention from the individual as the focus of analysis to the organization. That continued as an interest when I returned from Harvard. With the introduction of the Ph.D. in IR, there was a felt need to structure concentrations for study within the IR field. Based upon the interests of the associated faculty and work elsewhere within the field, it was relatively easy to identify four areas of concentration—labor markets, collective bargaining, employment staffing, and motivation and rewards. I successfully argued for a fifth as well, organization studies. Thus was IR defined at Minnesota and continues as such today.

Following this interest in organization studies, I approached the subject within the research traditions of the IRC, that of dust-bowl empiricism. What was needed, I reasoned, was a criterion of organizational effectiveness. Whereas others had approached this task with logic and propositions, I sought to identify those criteria employed by managers in assessing the effectiveness of their subordinate organizations. I was joined in this effort by William Weitzel, newly recruited to the faculty. Bill and I collaborated in this effort for some time before each veered away to pursue other interests. We have continued to collaborate over the years, although that collaboration has been assisting one or the other with individually initiated work rather than jointly developing some work of equal interest to both.

It is interesting to note the shifts in the focus of IR studies over the years. Early on, the primary focus was upon labor market operations and collective bargaining. The concerns of industrial psychology began expanding, concerns such as selection, attitudes, and training. And the individual increasingly became the unit of analysis. Some interest began shifting to the organization as the appropriate unit of analysis, as witnessed in the work mentioned above. A stark example of this was the shift from employee attitudes as indicators of morale to organization climate. This shift occasioned considerable concern, both conceptually and methodologically. Although the concept of morale had a collective work-force base, not necessarily accommodated in surveys of attitudes of individual employees, that distinction had been ignored and attitude surveys were employed as measures of work force morale. Organization climate, however, was conceptually distinct from morale and considerable attention was focused upon both conceptualizing and measuring of morale as a construct. Meanwhile the individual continued as a predominant unit of analysis. It has only been in recent years that attention has shifted again to the organizational level of analysis, as particularly evidenced in research into the impact of different HR policies and programs.

Another area of interest emerged for me with attempts to utilize the quantitative methods learned during the year at Harvard. One of the outcomes was an attempt to apply Markovian models in manpower planning and in analyzing internal labor market structures. This effort, using years of computerized personnel records from several cooperating companies, involved various doctoral students who worked with me in developing and testing various models with company records. Three notable student collaborators who went on to successful academic careers were David Dimick, George Milkovich, and Paul Nystrom. George joined the Minnesota faculty upon graduation and we continued our collaboration in the development of a computerized manpower simulation model. He is currently on the faculty of the ILR school at Cornell University.

Computer simulation models used as management games for instruction were relatively common at that time. Typically, however, those models focused upon issues of inventory management, production scheduling, pricing and distribution decisions, and financial decisions.

All made very simplistic assumptions about the role of human resources and typically permitted only decisions limited to headcount management. We set out to develop a simulation encompassing the entire range of human resource management decisions. We sought to incorporate the best available knowledge concerning the effects of headcount decisions, employee training, wage structure and wage level decisions, and supervision upon organizational performance in the assumptions of the model. Because this was prior to subsequent research into the utility of HRM programs and the empirical estimation of organizational effects of HRM activities, we relied upon our judgements utilizing available theory, empirical research, and logic in formulating the assumptions to be incorporated into the simulation model.

We sought an organizational setting within which we could argue that human resource decisions were the primary determinants of performance. Fortunately, I had been retained for some years (and would continue until 1982) as consultant to the regional office of State Farm Insurance. In that role I spent one-half day a week at the regional office, participating in staff meetings and counseling individually with employees ranging from the resident Vice-President through underwriters, claims representatives, and agents. I had come to know the organization well and could argue that sales and servicing performance were primary in overall performance. Given state regulation of rates, pricing was not a major factor in competition and neither was raw material and inventory management; productivity in product delivery and service were central. Sales were lost through lack of contact with customers and delays in delivery of policies and, since many sales are renewals, through inadequate servicing of claims. Thus we developed Minnesota Home Group, our manpower simulation model. Key to this development were David Dimick, and Frank Krzystofiak, doctoral students at that time who have gone on to productive academic careers of their own. They helped us to develop the assumptions of the model and then to incorporate them into a computer framework. The model was used extensively for some years in graduate courses and in executive education. Interestingly, in retrospect, one of the lessons learned in those seminars was a preview of industry learning during the 1990s, the importance of controlling headcount while manipulating other HR efforts; too often decision makers in the simulation responded to lost sales and/or low profits by hiring and terminating employees. The most successful decision makers utilized more often the levers of training and motivation while controlling headcount. Unfortunately, this observation was not the result of rigorous research in which we might have had confidence.

COLLABORATION WITH STUDENTS

During the 1960s and 1970s I was blessed with a number of challenging and stimulating doctoral students, many of whom also worked with me as research assistants. More and more my research shifted to reflect joint interests with these students. Since I taught primarily in the concentrations of motivation and reward and of organization studies, these research efforts spanned those topics. Just as I delighted in the confrontation of different disciplines and models in the analysis of a single topic or issue, so I encouraged these students to engage in the same exercise. Thus it is not surprising that there was considerable variety in their research projects or that our joint works were published in journals as diverse as *Personnel Psychology, Administrative Science Quarterly* (ASQ), *Academy of Management Journal* (AMJ), *Organizational Behavior and Human Decision Processes, Journal of Applied Psychology,* and *Industrial and Labor Relations Review.* Because I viewed Industrial Relations, contrary to Yoder and Heneman, as a broad range of issues that served as a battleground for different disciplines, all of the research topics and the professional journal outlets appeared to me as quite consistent with my approach.

Roy Richardson was the first to graduate with a PhD in IR at Minnesota. Taking my favorite course in motivation and rewards, he was excited by the seemingly contradictory conceptualizations of equity and rewards proposed by J. Stacy Adams (1965) and Elliot Jaques (1961), the one based upon social comparison and the other based upon internal standards applied to time-span of discretion of jobs. And he set out to contrast the two in a study of "fair pay." Prior to that time Jaques was relatively unknown in the United States, although well known and accepted in the U.K. and Commonwealth; even today his model receives but little acceptance in the United States, despite the support of Richardson's research.

Paul Nystrom and George Milkovich followed soon after Roy with empirical investigations of the internal labor market model, elaborating work that we had conducted earlier in the application of Markov models to manpower planning and simulation. In the same vein, David Dimick examined pay policies and their impact upon payroll costs and employee performance elaborating upon the manpower simulation model we developed. Blanchard (Bud) Smith was interested in the decision-making approach taught by Kepner-Tregoe and set out to analyze and compare individual and group problem-solving in a field experiment setting; he later joined with Kepner-Tregoe and Associates.

Marc Wallace was disturbed by the lack of attention given seemingly important variables in the investigations into executive compensation levels at that time, and focused upon the effects of two such variables, type of control (owner v. manager) and industry concentration. His finding that owner-controlled firms paid less, other things being equal, than manager-controlled firms has since been replicated numerous times. Ed Locke's goal setting experiments intrigued Peter Frost who questioned their generalizability to experimental settings with relatively complex tasks and to variations in level of goals; he set out to investigate this with some relatively ingenious laboratory manipulations. Jerry Newman and Norman (Fred) Crandall joined Peter in the application of laboratory experiments, although they focused upon various different aspects of individual decision making. Linda Krefting rejected the archival methods of Wallace and the laboratory methods of Frost, Newman and Crandall, her peers, and opted for field research even before selecting a topic. The topic she selected, a just-noticeable increase in pay, was difficult to conduct in the field although field methods probably are more appropriate than laboratory methods for investigation of this topic.

It was interesting and beneficial to my own learning to watch and participate in the natural groups of doctoral students that formed during their studies. The group of Wallace, Frost, Krefting, Newman, and Crandall was particularly exciting. They came from different backgrounds in English, economics, business and psychology and brought those disciplinary backgrounds and interests with them. They interacted constantly as peer students and RAs, displaying mutual support and controlled competition at the same time. They stimulated each other and me with constant interplay of ideas as we confronted and argued about industrial relations issues. It was an exciting time.

David Pierson was interested in reward issues but, coming from an engineering and not psychology background, was less interested in motivation concerns. Instead, he opted to examine the existence of and influences upon the phenomenon of "wage clusters" identified earlier by John Dunlop in the industrial sector; he hypothesized the same phenomenon would appear in the public sector and proposed environmental and institutional determinants of clusters. Benjamin Lowenberg also studied reward structures, and opted to examine the generalizability of findings about compensation of industrial executives to the compensation of labor union executives. Ben suffered kidney failure towards the end of his research, yet he struggled on valiantly and was able to complete his research before his death. His devotion to completion in the face of certain death was a model to all of us associated with him.

Frederick Hills and Nanette Weiner opted for research into organization studies, although both were interested and qualified in reward issues; both went on to publish later on compensation and rewards topics. In both instances, their dissertation research was motivated by what they viewed as faulty prior investigations by others, and they sought to improve that research with improved conceptual models and improved analytical methods. Kenneth Wheeler, about the same time, conducted laboratory research into Victor Vroom's VIE model as applied to occupational preference and choices. And Charles Cambridge investigated influences upon employee voting behavior in union representation elections. This range of interests from organizational theory to motivation and occupational choices and to union representation and collective bargaining, and the subsequent publication of their research in *ASQ, AMJ* and *Journal of Vocational Behavior* demonstrate the spectrum encompassed by IR and my interests at that time at Minnesota.

Industrial relations at Minnesota at that time was far more than Tom Mahoney. In addition, there were students working with Herb Heneman on assorted issues, usually related to human resource management, students working with George Seltzer and Mahmood Zaidi on issues of labor-market analysis, students working with Bill England and Rene Dawis on issues of managerial values, the meaning of work, and vocational rehabilitation, and students working with Mario Bognanno on issues of labor relations. Faculty associates Marvin Dunnette and John Campbell from Psychology also had active research programs going with students in the IR program. The decades of the 60s and the 70s were exciting in terms of research and teaching, with a variety of active and supportive colleagues and a variety of challenging and stimulating students.

John Deckop, the last doctoral student who worked with me at Minnesota, revisited the determination of executive compensation, employing a far more sophisticated model and more advanced analytical techniques than previous work. I recall mentioning to John as he was exploring topics that it was about time someone revisited executive compensation given the changes in compensation and in analytical methods over the years. This is a research issue that likely will continue to be revisited again and again in future years.

Working with Peter Frost as a doctoral student was a result of my continuing link with South Africa. Having made contact with Peter in South Africa, he came to the IRC for the MAIR, was caught up in the intellectual excitement of his peers, and stayed on for the Ph.D. Peter has since gone on to a very productive and rewarding career of scholarship in what might be called organization studies, but which was definitely within the purview of IR at Minnesota when he was there. Another student from South Africa was Hilton Blake, who stopped with the MAIR, returned to a research post in South Africa, and now practices in industry. Continuing contact with Hilton has always been stimulating and enriching. John Fossum, later to become director of the IRC, also worked with me as he completed the MAIR; he then went on for the Ph.D. at Michigan State, and returned to the IR faculty at Minnesota.

The students with whom I have worked have gone on to a variety of careers—teaching, research, and consulting with a variety of focuses—organization studies, negotiation strategies, executive compensation, organization development, collective bargaining, workforce diversity and equity, and assessment of HR strategies. No single model captures all of them or their careers. Their variety of interests and abilities stimulated and challenged me. What I sought to develop in each of them was expansion of their conceptual frameworks and an ability to think creatively about issues utilizing a variety of models and approaches. As they developed, so did I, and I am indebted to all of them for the stimulation and challenge they provided to me.

TEACHING AND PUBLICATION

A short time ago, invited to reflect upon the joint roles of research and teaching in my career, I came to the realization that research and teaching, instead of competing, have been complementary influences in my career, a career of learning (Andre & Frost, 1996). I have always enjoyed learning and continue to seek opportunities for learning. And I find that my learning occurs through seeking answers and resolutions to puzzles and contradictions. Probably reflecting my learning experiences at Wabash and at Minnesota, I find the seeming contradictions of different disciplines as they address a common phenomenon a particular stimulus to learning. For example, economics tends to analyze wage phenomena as dependent variables, variables which are the consequence of worker behavior in a free labor market. Psychology, on the other hand, tends to view wage phenomena as independent variables which shape and determine employee behavior. Seeking to join these seemingly contradictory paradigms in the joint explanation of both wage and behavior phenomena was an early challenge from which I have learned much.

Quite naturally I approached teaching as a learning experience for both students and myself, and I sought to engage students in the cross-disciplinary examinations of phenomena in which I was interested. Consistent with the beliefs of the early days of industrial relations, I accepted that there was no single, over-arching theory or model of industrial relations or human resources. Rather, one accomplished more through the confrontation of relevant disciplinary theories and models to develop one's way of thinking about a particular phenomenon. In retrospect, I realize that I sought to develop in students their familiarity with associated disciplinary paradigms and their abilities to utilize these paradigms in developing their own understanding and ways of thinking about relevant phenomena. I believed, as I still believe, that there is no one right way to approach, analyze, and resolve issues of human resource management for all time. Rather than providing answers to students, I sought to engage them in debates and examinations of conflicting analyses, and to develop their interest in and ability to seek insights into whatever issues they confronted. I had enjoyed this as a student, enjoyed it as a teacher, and sought to develop students' enjoyment in the action as well. I always thrilled when a student developed insights and analyses not considered before. One favorite course, for example, utilized essentially the same final examination year after year. Questions were distributed to the class several weeks before the examination and they were encouraged to engage in group study and debate about the questions. Analogous to the old joke about the final examination in economics in which the questions never changed—the answers changed—I thrilled when students were able to develop new and improved answers over the years.

During this time I published a book, *Compensation and Reward Perspectives,* which I regarded as the fruition of many years of teaching. One of my favorite courses addressed theory of employment compensation. Books regarding employment compensation at that time, however, were "how to do it" texts prescribing methods for wage surveys and job evaluation and rules of thumb developed through practice; there was virtually no theory or logical rationale presented. Given my orientation and interests, I sought to develop in students some conceptual foundation for the analysis of compensation and reward issues. My interest in disciplinary paradigm confrontation led me to collect conceptual models from various disciplines as they related to issues of motivation and rewards, and to encourage students to confront the apparent contradictions and to formulate their own resolutions. The confrontation of disciplinary models was accomplished by assembling readings around specific issues of wage level, wage structure, equity considerations, incentive compensation, and the like. Readings were drawn from theory and empirical research in labor economics, industrial and motivational psychology, and sociology. Essays from the different disciplines were organized around topical issues in such a way as to offer what appeared to be competing analyses or explanations. Readers (students) were challenged to find ways of merging these analyses and explanations exactly as I taught the course. It exemplifies my approach to the definition of IR and the unique aspects of IR which fascinated and challenged me. Although the book was never a money maker, it received quite favorable reviews and remains an accomplishment of which I am proud.

That course, illustrated in the book, probably was my most successful attempt to engage the minds and conceptual abilities of students. Perhaps more than any other area of human resource management, motivation and reward systems provide an ideal focus for the confrontation of related disciplines and the development of cross-disciplinary models. It has been particularly rewarding to observe its impact in the later publication of some of the major texts in employment compensation by students from the course: *Compensation* by Milkovich and Newman (1984), *Compensation Theory and Practice* by Wallace and Fay (1983), *Compensation Decision Making* by Hills (1987), and *The Management of Compensation* by Nash and Carroll (1975). All of these books seek to incorporate relevant theory and conceptual models with descriptions of practice, a characteristic that was absent from earlier texts in the field.

ACADEMY OF MANAGEMENT

About 1981 I was invited to become editor of the *Academy of Management Journal*, an invitation which I accepted. A previous invitation had been declined because the University was unwilling to provide the institutional support required. One might question someone from IR becoming editor of *AMJ*. Interestingly, two colleagues from other universities reacted to the appointment in contradictory ways. One reacted "You might have known it, *AMJ* is still under the control of the OB crowd" and the other reacted "But you're not qualified--you're not OB!" *AMJ* was perceived at that time to be an outlet dominated by empirical investigation of what has come to be termed micro-OB. Linkages and distinctions between IR and OB were still in doubt.

What is termed OB (Organizational Behavior) evolved from the introduction of the behavioral sciences into management education starting in the 1960s. During that time IR began shifting towards the Human Resource Management focus, de-emphasizing labor-market analysis. George Strauss (1993) traces OB to its roots in IR and that certainly describes the Berkeley experience, where IR had never separated from the business school and never attempted to establish itself as an independent academic discipline. It was different at Minnesota. Whereas much of what is taught in OB was included in the IR program of study, the obverse was not the case. IR was still viewed as oriented towards the full range of IR topics, including professional HRM, whereas OB was oriented towards the application of behavioral sciences in the managing of subordinate organizations.

AMJ began to occupy much of my time. Because it was an association publication, I felt constrained as an editor to view the journal as the vehicle for furthering the association and not as subject to my personal interests and whims. Thus I strove to improve the quality of published research and to broaden the journal as an outlet for quality research from all divisions of the Academy regardless of subject and methodology. Field investigations and case studies utilizing interview methods, and research into strategy and organization-level analyses were introduced, expanding the *AMJ* coverage from its more traditional micro-OB focus to encompass the many divisions of the Academy with their different issues and research methodologies . While the strains of reviewing, editing, and guiding the journal at that time were great, there were numerous gratifying experiences of assisting authors to re-orient and revise submissions to qualify them for publication. On the whole, it was a rewarding, although trying, experience; I ended my term with the feeling that I had contributed to the development of a journal of quality empirical research worthy of the Academy, and a journal that reflected the full range of the Academy membership. That experience certainly heightened and broadened my knowledge of management scholarship through reading all of the many submissions of manuscripts reflecting the scholarship of the full range of professional divisions within the Academy. I also benefitted from the professional contacts with authors and reviewers and came to respect many with whom I had not had prior contact.

MY MOVE TO OWEN AT VANDERBILT

Industrial relations at Minnesota entered a rocky period during the late 1970s and early 1980s with continuing conflict over definition of the field and priorities for development. Despite Yoder and Heneman's insistence that IR was a distinct academic discipline, the faculty members at Minnesota were still recruited from the traditional disciplines of labor economics and industrial psychology and taught their respective concentrations in the IR curriculum from a disciplinary focus. The desired integration of related disciplines that characterized the focus of the 1950s was giving way to specialization in the different concentrations or sub-areas of IR. Meanwhile, the professional field was moving from traditional industrial relations to human resource management, from labor markets to work organizations. The "labor problems" focus of the 1940s was giving way to the problems of utilization and development of human resources in employment. The internal conflicts over priorities in staffing, student admissions, research priorities, and the like led to considerable tension and turmoil. George Milkovich, Bill Weitzel, Bill England, and Hoyt Wheeler had all migrated from Minnesota to situations they viewed as more interesting and I found myself increasingly isolated. In consequence, I explored various career alternatives which appeared. One of these was with the Owen School at Vanderbilt University.

The Owen School was only about ten years old and was building under the leadership of Samuel Richmond, recruited as dean from Columbia University. It offered only the MBA at that time, although a PhD was to be initiated within a year. The faculty was small, and the faculty in OB was relatively young and weak. At the same time, there were outstanding faculty in Finance and Marketing. The Owen School offered the opportunity to design and develop a program of "IR" within a business school and MBA program such as I had proposed at Minnesota in 1961. I was excited by the opportunity.

In addition to giving up many ties with the IRC and the University of Minnesota, the move to Vanderbilt also meant giving up Minnesota winters which I had come to look forward to and enjoy. Early on at Minnesota I had taken up skiing which I enjoyed. With the birth of sons, Charles and John, I switched to cross-country skiing and even rigged up a sled to pull my younger son John on a rope behind me. Minnesota and Wisconsin offer numerous opportunities for cross-country skiing and the county park system near Minneapolis made it possible for skiing day trips every weekend of the winter. Although Ursula never thrilled to skiing, she graciously tolerated the enthusiasm of the boys, Charles and John, and I and accompanied us. Minnesota winters, particularly those with lots of snow, had become a major attraction for me and one that was forsaken with the move to south to Vanderbilt. Charles also was leaving to study at Williams College with John to leave later to study at Amherst College. Minneapolis had been their home through boyhood, and this was an appropriate time to move. Ursula began the long venture to build a home in the south with which the family could now identify, Charles now teaching English at the University of Connecticut and John pursuing a career as a fine artist in New York.

At the Owen School, we introduced into the MBA curriculum two concentrations, a concentration in Human Resource Management intended for career entry into the HRM profession, and a concentration in Organization Management intended as a supplement to some other functional concentration, but not providing career entry. These concentrations were combined in an academic area titled Organization Studies and encompassed what I had learned as IR, with the exception of labor market analysis. This introduction of HRM into the MBA program was somewhat unique in MBA programs of study at that time. The evolution of OB in MBA programs since about 1960 cast OB as part of the common core of management studies rather than as a separate concentration, and the study of OB was as close as MBA students came to human resource management. Students opting for the practice of HR management were channeled to separate schools of IR (e.g. Cornell) or academic programs separate from the MBA (e.g., Minnesota). The cleavage between IR, now HRM, and business management study stemming from the 1950s continued at most institutions. The curriculum at Owen acknowledged that HRM can be a specialization of management just as are finance, marketing and operations, and that OB (termed Organization Management at Owen) is part of the common core of management studies.

It was hoped that faculty recruited to the area of Organization Studies would have specialized interests in one or the other concentration (OM and HRM), but that all would be qualified to teach in both concentrations. Later recruits who joined our efforts included John Deckop, who had worked with me on his Ph.D. at Minnesota, and Richard Daft, to balance the span of Organization Studies, Mahoney at the HRM end and Daft at the organization management end. With my retirement from the active faculty, I have since been succeeded by Barry Gerhart as the anchor for the HRM end of Organization Studies. The HRM concentration has become popular with MBA students at the Owen School, attracting many of the more intellectually capable. And it has proven successful in the marketplace for graduating student employment, many of the major employers interviewing at Owen for HR graduates only, despite the relatively small number of them compared with more traditional schools of IR.

Doctoral studies at Owen are offered in the Organization Studies area. The program is small and has only recently graduated students. One, Carol Graham, worked with Dick Daft on a study of "corporate crime", the violation of environmental laws and regulations. A second, Arlen Honts, worked with me on a study of the impact of negotiation setting upon behavior and outcomes. A third, Mary Watson, is working with me on completion of an analysis of the effects of corporate downsizing upon various measures of corporate performance. Others in the pipeline will be conducting research into ethical orientations in organizations, into corporate communication images, and into temporary and volunteer work.

Although now titled Organization Studies at Owen and an increasing number of other schools, I view this focus as a modern version of what I once knew as Industrial Relations. Certainly the focus is still upon the "world of work and employment" in one way or another; the combination of sub-disciplines provides the opportunity to elicit disciplinary confrontation in analysis and understanding, the approach I have found personally most rewarding and stimulating.

Whether because of career stage, the move to Vanderbilt, or some other factor, I have personally discovered more interests in the application of HRM and have, in recent years, consulted with boards of non-profit organizations and served as an expert witness consultant in employment discrimination litigation. The litigation experience reminds me that, while the issues and problems of HRM have changed since I first entered the field, issues and problems still remain. And they still benefit from the application of various traditional disciplines. The field of IR, now increasingly defined as HRM, would likely hold the same attraction and appeal to me as it did 40 years ago were I again starting off on a career.

POSTSCRIPT

An autobiographical analysis provides the opportunity to review the evolution of one's field of study as well as one's own career evolution. My field of study has carried a number of different labels over the years and has undergone differentiation as well as growth. What began as "labor problems" in the 1940s evolved into an inter-disciplinary field of study known as Industrial Relations in the 1950s. In general, it was viewed as a set of issues and problems relating to people as human resources at work, and calling for empirical study by related disciplines. While there were various relevant theories (e.g. negotiation, governance, motivation), there was no single over-riding and unifying theory. So called Human Relations, predominantly empirical observations lacking a theory, evolved during the 1940s and 1950s and was associated with IR, although it later provided the impetus for evolution of what is now termed Organizational Behavior. Interest in labor market analysis declined after about 1960 and was re-established in the discipline of labor economics, and IR interests shifted more towards issues of managing human resources within organizations. Part of this interest in organizations merged with sociology and social psychology and evolved into what is known today as Organization Theory. And the interest in managing human resources at work is now concentrated in what is termed Human Resource Management. A small portion of the original Industrial Relations continues today in much the same model as in 1960. The major growth of that original field of study, however, has been in the related specializations which it spawned over the years. I like to think of Organization Studies as an overarching umbrella linking these different specializations. Organization Studies is a field of study which benefits from the combined contributions of related disciplines and specializations. In this sense, it is not unlike the Industrial Relations model of the 1950s.

It appears to me that my personal evolution and that of at least one branch of IR moved in tandem. What first attracted me to IR was the focus upon the issues of human resource utilization in employment—the unemployment and hardship observed during the 1930s, the waste of abilities observed in the military and the auto industry where I worked, the frustrations of employees locked into a subservient authority relationship and a machine technology, and the frustrations of employers seeking increased cooperation and productivity. Industrial relations was cast as an applied field challenging the efforts of labor economists, industrial and motivational psychologists, sociologists, and labor lawyers. All had something to contribute to analysis of the issues and to fashioning improved methods. The challenges would change over time from massive unemployment, to reducing labor strife, improving skill training, motivating performance, employment discrimination, and design of work methods and organizations for improved performance. The contributions of what often appeared to be competing and conflicting academic disciplines fascinated me. Working with these competing disciplines provided insights not obtainable from any one of them. I continue to enjoy this challenge and have attempted in my teaching to excite students to the same challenge.

The effort to cast Industrial Relations as a separate and academic discipline was, in my opinion, a mistake. To cast it as a single discipline would have involved, somehow, a merger of different disciplines eliminating the conflict and contradictions I find fascinating and productive. Education in Industrial Relations today still maintains the model of related yet distinct disciplines. Professional education at the master's level parallels that of other models of professional education (e.g. MBA) with course work in fields of practice taught by faculties from different disciplinary backgrounds. Education at the PhD level involves concentration in one field with related study in other fields. The various definitions of different fields vary from school to school, but are dominated by the underlying and supporting disciplines regardless of label.

Looking backwards I realize that my career has been that of a student always seeking to learn and always challenged by unanswered questions. Learning was sought in research and in working with students as a teacher to find answers. Most recently I observed while waiting to donate blood at a Red Cross center a number of plaques honoring donors of 15 gallons of blood each. Some 80 individuals were honored, and casual observation indicated that 76 (95%) of them were male. The immediate challenge was to answer why the predominance of males in those donating 15 gallons of blood requiring a minimum of at least 20 years of donations. Alternative explanations might involve motivation (public spirit, qualify for time-off from work, or to earn a badge), proximity and ease (blood mobiles at work and males more likely to be employed), association of female roles with nursing and drawing (not giving) blood, and countless others. I may yet undertake study of the issue as a final challenge in my learning.

PUBLICATIONS

1952

Factors in union meeting attendance. *Labor and Nation, 8,* 41-45.

1953

With T. Lindbom. Practices of Minneapolis firms in the utilization of older employees. *Journal of Gerontology, 8,* 202-206.
What's happening to the older employee in industry? *Labor Law Journal, 4,* 329-333.
A suggested supervisory training program. *Collegiate News and Views, 7,* 15-17.

1954

How management communicates with employees. *Personnel, 31,*109-115.
With H. Fox, S. Walton, & W. Kirchner. *Leadership and executive development: A bibliography* (Bulletin 14). Industrial Relations Center, University of Minnesota.
With W. Uphoff. *Problems of union administration* (Research and Technical Report 15). Industrial Relations Center, University of Minnesota.

1955

With D. Perry. In-plant communications and employee morale. *Personnel Psychology, 8,* 339-346.

What do managers do? *Organization for management teamwork* (Research and Technical Report 17, pp. 10-18). Industrial Relations Center, University of Minnesota.

1956

With R. Nelson. Strengthening the management team. *Business News Notes,* School of Business Administration, University of Minnesota.

With M. Dunnette, & D. Perry. *Criteria of executive effectiveness* (Research Report). Air Force Personnel and Training Research Center, Lackland Air Force Base.

1957

With W. Doman, & T. Jerdee. Applying yardsticks to management. *Personnel,* May, 556-562.

With T. Jerdee. New way to look at managers' jobs. *Factory Management and Maintenance, 115*(12), 110-128.

[Review of: Blumen, Kogan, & McCarthy, *The industrial mobility of labor as a probability process.*] *Econometrics, 25,* 291-293.

1958

Weighted application blank analysis of contingency items. *Journal of Applied Psychology, 42,* 60-62.

The identification of management potential. *Proceedings of Annual Meeting,* Industrial Relations Research Association.

1961

Building the executive team: A guide to management development. New York: Prentice-Hall. [Dutch translation: *Vorming van een Leidinggevend Team.* Antwerp: Marka-Boeken, 1966.]

With T. Jerdee, & A. Nash. *The identification of management potential—A research approach to management development.* Dubuque, IA: William C. Brown Co.

Factors determining the labor-force participation of married women. *Industrial and Labor Relations Review, 14*, 563-577.

Influences of labor-force participation of married women. In N. Foote (Ed.), *Household decision-making* (pp. 11-24). New York: New York University Press.

With R. Woods. Developing an appraisal program through action research. *Personnel, 38*, 25-31.

1963

With W. Sorenson, T. Jerdee, & A. Nash. Identification and prediction of managerial effectiveness. *Personnel Administration, 26*(4), 12-22.

With T. Jerdee, & S. Carroll. *Development of managerial performance—A research approach.* Cincinnati, OH: Southwestern Publishing.

1964

Compensation preferences of managers. *Industrial Relations, 3*, 135-144.

1965

With T. Jerdee, & S. Carroll. The job(s) of management. *Industrial Relations, 4*(2), 97-110.

With G. England. Efficiency and accuracy of employee selection decision rules. *Personnel Psychology, 18*, 361-378.

1967

The real cost of a wage increase. *Personnel, 44*(3), 22-32.

Managerial perceptions of organizational effectiveness. *Management Science, 14*, B76-B91.

Criteria of organizational effectiveness. *Proceedings of Annual Conference*, Midwest Academy of Management.

1968

With W. Weitzel. Standards of effectiveness for credit unions. *The Credit Union Executive, 7*, 13-18.

1969

Managing time--A functional analysis of the manager's job. *The Credit Union Executive, 8,* 23-27.
With W. Weitzel. Managerial models of organizational effectiveness. *Administrative Science Quarterly, 14,* 357-365. [Reprinted in: E. Vrochla (Ed.), *Economics and social sciences: Theory of organizational design.* University of Koln, 1978.]

1971

With G. Milkovich. The internal labor market as a stochastic process. In D. Bartholomew & A. Smith (Eds.), *Manpower and management science* (pp. 75-91). New York: D.C. Heath.
With W. Weitzel, & N. Crandall. A supervisory view of unit effectiveness. *California Management Review, 13,* 37-42.
[Review of: W. Bowen & T. Finegan (Eds.), *The economics of labor force participation.*] *Industrial and Labor Relations Review, 24,* 291-293.

1972

With P. Frost, N. Crandall, & W. Weitzel. The conditioning influence of organizational size upon managerial practice. *Organizational Behavior and Human Performance, 8,* 230-241.
With G. Milkovich, & A. Annoni. The use of delphi procedures in manpower forecasting. *Management Science, 19,* 381-388. [Reprinted in: Sullivan & Clayborne (Eds.), *Fundamentals of forecasting,* 1977.]

1974

With P. Frost. The role of technology in models of organizational effectiveness. *Organizational Behavior and Human Performance, 11,* 122-138.

1975

With J. Newman, & P. Frost. Workers' perceptions of the four-day work week. *California Management Review, 18*(1), 31-35.

Justice and equity: A recurring theme in compensation. *Personnel, 52*(5), 60-66.

With G. Milkovich. Computer simulation: A training tool for manpower managers. *Personnel Journal, 54,* 609-612.

With G. Milkovich. The use of computer simulation in manpower management education. *Academy of Management Annual Meeting Proceedings.*

[Review of: R. Aronson, *The localization of federal manpower planning.*] *Industrial and Labor Relations Review, 28,* 157-158.

1976

With P. Frost. Goal setting and the task process. *Organizational Behavior and Human Performance, 17,* 328-350.

Organizational strategies for protection against back contamination. National Aeronautics and Space Administration, NGL 24-005-160.

1977

With L. Krefting. Determining the size of a meaningful pay increase. *Industrial Relations, 16,* 83-93.

With G. Milkovich, & N. Weiner. A stock and flow model for improved human resources measurement. *Personnel, 54*(3) , 57-66.

1978

The rearranged workweek: Evaluations of different work schedules. *California Management Review, 20*(4), 31-39. [Reprinted in: F. Schuster (Ed.), *Contemporary issues in human resource management,* Reston Publishing, 1980; and in *Administracion de Empresas,* Buenos Aires, Argentina.]

With W. Weitzel. Secrecy and managerial compensation. *Industrial Relations, 17,* 245-251.

With F. Hills. University budgets and organizational decision making. *Administrative Science Quarterly, 23,* 454-465. [Reprinted in: R. Birnbaum (Ed.), *Ashe reader in organization and governance in higher education,* Ginn Press, 1983.]

With G. Milkovich. Human resource planning models: A perspective. *Human Resource Planning, 1*, 19-30. [Reprinted in: L. Moore (Ed.), *Manpower planning for Canadians*, 1979; and Biles and Holmberg (eds.) *Strategic human resource planning*, 1980.]

1979

Compensation and reward perspectives. Homewood, IL: Richard D. Irwin.

Organizational hierarchy and position worth. *Academy of Management Journal, 22*, 726-737.

With G. Milkovich. Human resources planning and PAIR policy. In *Planning and auditing PAIR, IV* (pp. 2-1-2-30. Washington, DC: Bureau of National Affairs. [Reprinted in: J. Walker (Ed.), The *challenge of human resource planning*, Human Resource Planning Society, 1979; and in R. Beatty & C. Schneier (Eds.), *Personnel administration today.* Boston: Addison Wesley, 1978.

1980

Examples of middle range theory. In L. Moore & C. Pinder (Eds.) *Middle range theory of organizational behavior* (pp. 326-333). Boston: Martinus Nijhoff.

1981

An integrative model of job satisfaction and performance. In G.W. England, A.R. Neghandi, & B. Wilpert (Eds.) *The functioning of complex organizations* (pp. 51-74). Cambridge, MA: Oelgeschlager, Gunn & Hain.

With N. Weiner. A model of corporate performance as a function of environmental, organizational, and leadership influences. *Academy of Management Journal, 24*, 453-470.

With K. Wheeler. The expectancy model in the analysis of occupational preference and occupational choice. *Journal of Vocational Behavior, 19*, 113-122.

1982

Comparable worth and market wages. *Industrial and Labor Relations Report, 19*(2), Cornell University. [Reprinted in: R. Rowan (Ed.),

Readings in labor economics and labor relations, Homewood, IL: Richard D. Irwin, 1985.]

Compensating for work. In K.M. Rowland & G.R. Ferris (Eds.) *Personnel management* (pp. 227-262). Boston: Addison-Wesley.

With D. Pierson. Labor market and employer ability to pay as wage contour influences. *Southern Business Review, 8*(2), 9-31.

1983

With S. Rynes, & B. Rosen. Compensation, jobs, and gender. *Harvard Business Review, 83*(4), 170-178.

With G. Milkovich, & L. Dyer. The state of practice and research in human resources planning. In S. Carroll & R. Schuler (Eds.), *Human resources management in the 1980s* (pp. 2-1-2-29). Washington, DC: Bureau of National Affairs.

Conceptual approaches to the definition of comparable worth. *Academy of Management Review, 8*, 14-22. [Reprinted in: *Journal of Library Administration, 4*(2), 87-100; in S. Youngblood (Ed.), *Readings in personnel and human resource management,* 1983; and in D. Organ (ed.), *The applied psychology of work behavior,* 1986.

Perspectives of organizational approaches to planning. In G. Copa & J. Moss (Eds.) *Planning and vocational education* (pp. 81-101). New York: McGraw-Hill.

1984

With B. Rosen, & S. Rynes. Where do compensation specialists stand on comparable worth? *Compensation Review, 16,* 27-40.

Growth accounting and productivity. In A. Brief (Ed.), *Productivity research in the behavioral and social sciences* (pp. 56-70). New York: Praeger.

1985

Journal publishing and the organization sciences: An analysis of exchanges. In L. Cummings & P. Frost (Eds.), *Publishing in the organizational sciences* (pp. 14-34). Homewood, IL: Richard D. Irwin.

With S. Rynes, & B. Rosen. Three perspectives on comparable worth. *Business Horizons, 28*(1), 82-86.

[Review of: S. Biesheuvel, *Work motivation and compensation,* Vol. I & II.] *South African Journal of Psychology, 15*(3), 97-99.

1986

With J. Deckop. Evolution of concept and practice in personnel/human resource management. *Journal of Management, 12,* 223-241.

1987

Understanding comparable worth: A societal and political perspective. In L. Cummings & B. Staw (Eds.), *Research in organizational behavior* (Vol. 9, pp. 169-206). Greenwich, CT: JAI Press. [Reprinted in B. Staw & L. Cummings (Eds.), *Evaluation and employment in organizations,* Greenwich, CT: JAI Press, 1990.]

With R. Blake. Judgments of appropriate occupational pay as influenced by occupational characteristics and sex characteristics. *Applied Psychology: An International Review, 36,* 25-38.

1988

Productivity defined: The relativity of efficiency, effectiveness, and change. In J. Campbell & R. Campbell (Eds.), *Frontiers in industrial/organizational psychology: Productivity in organizations* (pp. 13-39). San Francisco: Jossey-Bass.

1989

Employment compensation planning and strategy. In L. Gomez-Mejia (Ed.), *Handbook of human resource management: Compensation and benefits* (pp. 3-1-3-28). Washington, DC: Bureau of National Affairs.

Multiple pay contingencies: Strategic design of compensation. *Human Resource Management, 28,* 337-348. [Reprinted in: G. Salaman (Ed.), *Human resource strategies.* Sage Publications, 1991.]

1990

With J. Deckop. Expert systems in human resource management. In R. Blanning (Ed.), *Foundations of expert systems in management* (pp. 269-300). Koln, Germany: Verlag.

Managerial expectations, style and productivity. *Proceedings of U. S. Competitiveness in the World Markets Conference* (pp. 8-14).

With J. Deckop. Workforce 2000: Compensation implications. *Proceedings of Annual Meeting, Industrial Relations Research Association* (pp. 507-517).

1991

Job evaluation: Anachronism or endangered species? *Human Resource Management Review, 1,* 155-162.

The symbolic meaning of pay contingencies. *Human Resource Management Review, 1,* 179-192.

1993

With J. Deckop. Y'gotta believe: Lessons from American- v. Japanese-management of U.S. plants. *Organizational Dynamics, 21*(4), 27-38.

With M. Watson. Evolving modes of work-force governance: An evaluation. In B. Kaufman & M. Kleiner (Eds.), *Employee representation: Alternatives and future directions* (pp. 135-168). Industrial Relations Research Association.

1996

Scholarship as a career of learning through research and teaching. In R. Andre & P. Frost (Eds.), *Researchers hooked on teaching* (pp. 112-124). Sage Publications.

1997

[Review of: S.E. Hills, *Employment relations and the social sciences.*] *Academy of Management Review, 22,* 295-298.

Reflections upon a stage in the maturation of AMJ and AOM. *Academy of Management Journal, 40,* 1432-1435.

ACKNOWLEDGMENT

Thanks to Peter Frost, Barry Gerhart and Donald Schwab for comments and reactions.

REFERENCES

Adams, J.S. (1965). Inequity in social exchange. In L. Berkowitz (Ed.), *Advances in experimental social psychology* (Vol. 2). New York: Academic Press.

Andre, R., & Frost, P.J. (Eds.). (1996). *Researchers hooked on teaching.* Thousand Oaks, CA: Sage.

Gordon, R., & Howell, J. (1959). *Higher education for business.* New York: Columbia University Press.

Hills, F.S. (1987). *Compensation decision making.* Hillsdale, IL: Dryden Press.

Industrial relations research: Ten tears of progress. (1955). Minneapolis: University of Minnesota Press.

The industrial relations center: University of Minnesota. (1956). Minneapolis: University of Minnesota Press.

Jaques, E. (1961). *Equitable payment.* New York: John Wiley & Sons.

March, J.G., & Simon, H.A. (1958). *Organizations.* New York: John Wiley & Sons.

Milkovich, G.T., & Newman, J.M. (1984). *Compensation.* Homewood, IL: R.D. Irwin.

Nash, A., & Carroll, S. (1975). *The management of compensation.* Monterrey, CA: Brooks/Cole.

Nelson, R. (1955). *The ten-year story of IRC.* Minneapolis: University of Minnesota Press.

Pierson, F. (1959). *The education of American businessmen: A study of university-college programs in business administration.* New York: McGraw-Hill.

Strauss, G. (1993). Present at the beginning: Some personal notes on OB's early days and later. In A. Bedeian (Ed.), *Management laureates* (Vol.3). Greenwich, CT: JAI Press.

Wallace, M.J., Jr. & Fay, C.H. (1983). *Compensation theory and practice.* Boston: PWS-Kent.

Whyte, W.F., Dalton, M. et. al. (1955). *Money and motivation.* New York: Harper.

Yoder, D., Paterson, D.G. et. al. (1948). *Local labor market research.* Minneapolis: University of Minnesota Press.

Andrew M. Pettigrew

CATCHING REALITY IN FLIGHT

ANDREW M. PETTIGREW

The good life requires sacrifice and commitment but also embodies contrasts and choices. As I sit here in a remote part of Herefordshire in England drafting this essay, I wonder both why I am doing it (beyond the automatic response to a generous invitation) and why I am doing it at this stage in my life. My nearest neighbor, a farmer John Powell, has just appeared and we have been joking that does someone know more about my life than I, for it appears strange to be writing an autobiographical essay having just turned 53 years of age. Intellectually I am just moving into another stage of my work where I am taking on a scale and complexity of theoretical and empirical inquiry that I have not attempted before. The new challenges involve combining comparative case study work with the surveying of organizational transformations in organizations in the UK, Europe, Japan, and the United States. This work also involves leading an international team of scholars based in universities in the UK, France, Japan, the Netherlands, Spain, Sweden, Switzerland, and the United States. Alongside this work is another large empirical project on boards and directors in the UK that I have waited 25 years to do.

Management Laureates, Volume 5, pages 171-206.
ISBN: 0-7623-0178-3

As an amateur historian I am also mindful of some of the weaknesses of the historical method and of the limitations of self-reflections of the past. Baroness Thatcher, or Mrs. Thatcher as she was then, knows these limitations well. As Prime Minister she visited the University of Warwick in 1987 to show approval for its history of educational innovation and achievement. She was invited to spend a couple of hours with a group of about 30 professors, some of whom had been asked to talk about their subject. As expected, Mrs. Thatcher used the occasion to display her aggressive intellect, and after 45 minutes and four departmental presentations, the score was Mrs. Thatcher 4, University of Warwick nil. Then the historians made their bid for fame. Mrs. Thatcher's opening salvo to the historians was "well the problem with reading history is that you learn more about the values of the historian than you do about the period under examination." This was quickly followed by "and how could some historian 30 years from now sit down and read the papers crossing my desk today really understand the circumstances of the time and how I judged and reacted to them." The historians responded to these methodological jibes as best they could, but then took the wise step of sitting back and listening. The more Mrs. Thatcher talked the more apparent it became that what she was really worried about was not the niceties of the historical method, but what historians would be saying about her in thirty-years time when her private state papers were made public.

The greatest sin a biographer can commit is to view the past from the narrow perspectives of his own time, to ignore the historical context and make assumptions about character and motive that are based on contemporary values and trends. All these fallibilities of the historical method (and more) apply to those who attempt an autobiographical essay. Autobiographies are occasions for self-congratulation and rationalization. They can also be opportunities for over-indulgent self-criticism, doubt and practiced concealment. They may also be settings for public appreciation of family, friends and professional mentors. Scientific autobiographies have an additional possibility—to reveal aspects of the practice of science that are nearly always excluded from scholarly publications and yet can be valuable messages about the conduct of inquiry for future generations.

A predisposition I recognize in myself is to look backwards and forwards and in so doing to tilt my gaze away from the present. I believe this preference is as much an emotional as it is an intellectual one and it has sometimes been fateful to my awareness of people and situations. Looking backwards is I think a deeply European and not just a British trait. I have always felt that European (and Asian) cultures have a deep texture that is not shared in North America and that has had an enormous impact on scholarship in those societies. Reading much (but thankfully not all) U.S. management literature there is an unwitting preference for the present and the future. The past is reserved for historians. The world starts from today. I have a deep curiosity and nostalgia for the past which extends way beyond my academic interests. My fascination with time, which is embodied in the title of this essay, is also reflected in a long-standing interest in antiquarian horology. This Herefordshire country cottage in which I am sitting dates from the 17th century and is full of treen and other practical implements of 18th and 19th century everyday agricultural life. But history is not just about artifacts, deep texture and events, it is also alive in the present and shaping the emerging future.

The preference I have for the future is indicative of the restless energy in my character. If I underplay the present it is because I am anxious to complete the task I currently have and move on. There is so much to do and so little time to do it. This trait, which has its downside, has been highly functional in an academic career. It has insured projects are completed, written up and disseminated. This restlessness has driven me to join a succession of new institutions, to cross intellectual boundaries, to help create a number of new academic and social institutions, and to assist the development of a number of fields of inquiry in organizational analysis and strategic management.

The overriding intellectual purpose of my work has been to catch reality in flight. My interest is in the dynamic quality of human conduct in organizational settings. Thus I have been preoccupied with how decisions are made, how power is won and lost, how organizational cultures are created and maintained and the relationship between continuity and change in organizations. The process studies associated with my name have all treated time seriously. I have tried to make time for time not only to reveal the temporal character of human conduct but to expose the relationship between human behavior and the changing contexts in which it is embedded. With this emphasis on the dynamic quality of human behavior, there is also a quest for embeddedness in social analysis. This is achieved partly by locating present behavior in its historical antecedents, but also by analyzing individual, group and organizational behavior in their sectoral, economic and political contexts.

Mindful of the analytical principle that human action should always be studied in context, I will follow this principle in structuring this essay. Autobiographical accounts have a natural historical flow and I will resist the temptation to present my scholarly life through themes rather than a chronology of people, institutions and ideas. I hope in this way not only to explore the what, why and how of any intellectual achievements associated with my work, but to link that description to the people and settings who have triggered, enabled and supported any such achievements.

FAMILY, CHILDHOOD, AND SCHOOL

I was born on 11 June 1944 in Corby, England. Corby is known for three things in the UK. It is a new town, it is a steel town and it is little Scotland located in rural Northamptonshire.

My father and mother and two older sisters and brother migrated from Airdrie in Scotland in 1934. My father (and his father) had worked for Stewarts and Lloyds, a Scottish Steel Company. A combination of the Depression and the opening of a new integrated Steel Works in Corby in 1934 drove my parents out of Scotland. They were the only siblings of their extended families to leave Scotland at that time. For them it was a big decision with many uncertainties. I have always admired them for taking this the biggest decision of their lives, which had a fateful impact on their children's future. I grew up in a loving and stable family atmosphere--something that I greatly value and my wife Ethna and I have tried to recreate in our own family.

I have been fortunate in having more than one founding experience in life. Going to Corby Grammar School in 1955 was the first, Yale University in 1969 was the second.

In most European societies there are two routes to social mobility, education or entrepreneurialism. I chose education or education chose me. I was lucky in my timing, but I took every advantage of the opportunity that opened up before me. Up until 1955 Corby did not have its own Grammar School, the nearest Grammar School being in Kettering some eight miles away. In this situation, there was a quota system for Corby children and only a group of 20 or so could go to Kettering. But in 1955, just as I reached the point of selection and passed the 11+ state examination, the first Grammar School opened in Corby and took into its first year a cohort of 100 or so children. Considering I was the first of my extended family to go to a Grammar School (and then University) my parents took this very calmly. To this day I can recall my father's warm hearted but ironic jibes about "life at the glamour school."

Although I did not fully appreciate it at the time, Corby was no ordinary Grammar School. Its founding headmaster was John Kempe, later to become headmaster of Gordonstoun, where most of the male members of the British Royal Family had their schooling. John Kempe was an unlikely person to become the leader of a new grammar school in a largely working-class town. He had been educated at a well-known British public school and Cambridge. He had been a decorated spitfire pilot in World War II, a member of the pathfinder expedition for the successful British led assault on Mount Everest in 1953 and the headmaster of an Indian boarding school before arrival in Corby in 1955. His educational philosophy was shaped by the ideas of the German educationalist Kurt Hahn who had founded Gordonstoun in 1933. The combination of John Kempe's idealism and style and the recruitment of a young, energetic and talented group of staff (Colin Dexter, the novelist was head of classics at Corby for a time) all contributed to the sense of excitement and achievement in the school.

On top of the conventional British diet of academic study and sport was added the Hahnian emphasis on mountaineering, outward bound schools and community service. Just before I left Corby Grammar School, my mountaineering and outward bound activities led to an invitation to join the Brathay Exploration Group expedition to Uganda. This expedition, financed by the British Broadcasting Corporation and Royal Geographical Society, took a group of 12 boys from various social and educational backgrounds into East Africa to work with local archaeologists and social anthropologists. Although by this stage I knew I was shortly to begin a Sociology degree at Liverpool University, the Uganda trip represented many firsts. First trip outside Europe, first experience of flying and first exposure to the practical realities of social science fieldwork.

Oddly enough, this first exposure to the social sciences in action involved a time series study of cultural change. On the Northern slopes of Mount Elgon, between 9,000 feet and 11,000 feet, the Musopisiek people of the Sibei kept cattle and sheep in clearings in the forest. They lived in long, low rectangular flat-roofed houses, which did not occur elsewhere in Uganda. In the late 1950s, round conical-roofed houses, characteristic of many other parts of East Africa, had been built in addition to the flat houses, and my task was to survey the distribution of the flat houses and their contents. The idea was then to conduct a later survey to measure the spread of the round houses as an indicator of the break-up of the old Musopisiek culture. Supported by Royal Air Force aerial photographs and a local guide I set off to complete this task. The results were later published by the expedition leader Ioan Thomas in the *Uganda Journal* (27(1), 1963, pp. 115-122). As is customary, the research assistance was acknowledged in a footnote to a footnote!

LIVERPOOL SOCIOLOGY 1962-1966

Although in my thoughts and deeds I am much more inclined to see people as potentates than pawns, I am always open to the possibility that the direction one takes in life is as much a result of chance and opportunities as it is rational intent. By the time I was 17, in 1961, I had just assumed I would go to university, although there was no tradition of university education in my family. Because I was studying history, geography, and economics at General Certificate of Education Advanced level, I had assumed history would be the obvious choice for university study. Then we moved house in Corby and I found myself living next door to Ray Jobling, who had been at Corby Grammar School and was now studying a subject I had never even heard of called sociology, at Liverpool. Ray made sociology sound intellectually challenging and socially relevant and I decided to follow him there. At that time, the two best Sociology Departments in the UK were at the London School of Economics and Liverpool. For me Liverpool had the edge, because of the Ray Jobling connection and because at that time it was the major (perhaps only) center of industrial sociology research in the UK university system. At that time most of the big names of British industrial sociology—Joe and Olive Banks, Tom Lupton, Enid Mumford, Bill Scott, and Joan Woodward, were working at Liverpool or had recently left.

Liverpudlians are a garrulous, witty crowd and I much enjoyed the period 1962-1966 spent in Merseyside. When things are going well Liverpudlians are a cocky, confident people and with the arrival of the Beatles in 1962/63 their humor was fuelled by a world-wide attention for all things associated with the Merseyside sound. I enjoyed this as much as anyone else in Liverpool, but I have to admit I spent more time playing rugby and watching the Liverpool football team than I did attending pop concerts.

The sociology boom in Britain was in its infancy in 1962 and the field was still trying to find its identity and status. There were some very able and committed sociologists at Liverpool and I had a good theoretical training and a sound introduction to industrial sociology. What I remember most about the department (housed appropriately enough in the former Bishop's Palace in Abercrombie Square) was the open rancor between the faculty. Ostensibly this was about whether sociology should be scientific and value free or interventionist and value laden, but the intellectual debates were sometimes carried out in a vicious and personal manner. I remember one day standing in a tutor's room (one of the leaders of the scientific faction) with a group of fellow students and watching our professor, Lord Simey, striding across Abercrombie Square with one of his supporters. Our tutor commented: "Look, here comes Don Quixote and Sancho Panza!" This is an aspect of academic life that still wrankles—the private and public belittling of colleagues' work, often without the care or courtesy of having read the work.

But the quality of the industrial sociologists at Liverpool deepened my interest in the subject. Their tradition was akin to what I had observed of the social anthropologists in Uganda. Out in the field observing, describing, and analyzing people in their social settings, interpreting any observed patterns in theoretical terms and then presenting the findings in scholarly monographs. Key examples of this theoretically informed British empiricism, that made the Liverpool tradition, are now rarely cited, but for the record include: *The Dock Worker* (Simey et al., 1954), *Technical Change and Industrial Relations* (Scott, Banks, Halsey, & Lupton, 1956), *Management in Britain* (McGivering, Matthews, & Scott, 1960), *Coal and Conflict* (Scott, Mumford, McGivering, & Kirby, 1963), and *The Computer and the Clerk* (Mumford & Banks, 1961). All these books, apart from the last, were published by Liverpool University Press.

The fourth year spent at Liverpool was to complete a strangely named Diploma in Industrial Administration. This was a postgraduate qualification in industrial sociology that provided a basic research training and a requirement to complete a three-month research project. Enid Mumford supervised the project—an interview based study of role conflict and strain among operational researchers. From this empirical study (and after enormous support by Enid Mumford and Joe Banks) I managed to publish my first refereed journal article in the *Journal of Management Studies*, May, 1968. I did not realize it at the time, but a year later this article was to provide an intellectual springboard for an appointment at Yale University.

MANCHESTER BUSINESS SCHOOL 1966-1969

In the summer of 1966 as I was nearing the end of the postgraduate diploma at Liverpool, Enid Mumford decided to leave the sociology department and take up a lectureship in industrial sociology at the newly opened Manchester Business School in Manchester University. Enid was at this point in her career beginning to develop a strong reputation for her work on the human problems of installing computer systems. She acquired a research grant for a new project and asked me to join her at Manchester to work as the full-time research fellow on the project. Tom Lupton left a professorship at Leeds University around the same time to become the first professor of industrial sociology at Manchester Business School. In 1970, following the lead taken by Derek Pugh at London Business School, Tom changed the title of his chair to Organizational Behavior.

Manchester Business School in 1966 was a lively and innovative place. The school had tentatively opened in 1965 in a city center office block until a new building could be constructed on the main university campus. From my position as a junior minnow in a pond rapidly filling up with every conceivable fish, Manchester was lively but also a confusing and often threatening place. Here was a new institution, with London Business School, supposed to be or become, the Oxford and Cambridge of university-based management education, trying to discover its identity, build a range of new teaching programs, recruit staff from a wide range of university disciplines and industrial backgrounds and also conduct research. For 95% of the academic staff this was the first time they had left their disciplinary departments to walk through the door of a business school. Identity crises were legion, uncertainties regular, conflicts inevitable, but the school quickly got on its feet and attempted (perhaps unwisely in retrospect) to innovate too much, too soon.

My prime responsibilities were research but we were all encouraged to learn how to teach MBA students and I did my share of tutorials and course development. Considering I was then just 22 years of age and with no industrial experience or teaching record, real risks were being taken. But even bigger risks were being taken with course design. I remember sitting in bewilderment in a mixed group of economists, sociologists, psychologists, anthropologists and former managers to design a course on "analysis of the environment." London Business school went for the conventional functional and disciplinary course offerings. Manchester from the start attempted interdisciplinary teaching around big themes such as analysis of the environment. We thus had young academics still trying to discover and get on top of their discipline, and managers trying to make the transition into academia, also confronted with the complexities of designing and successfully implementing interdisciplinary teaching. This was an early lesson about the need to control levels of complexity in creative settings.

Thankfully I was still insulated from many of the pressures of educational innovation. Enid Mumford had secured the funding for my research post, designed the project outline and negotiated access for the study. My task was to use a combination of participant observation, interviewing and documentary analysis to study the implementation of a large new computer system in Littlewoods, a major UK retailer headquartered in Liverpool. This project was an early lesson on how and why the rational intentions of research design can be overturned by circumstances, leaving the researcher with the choice of withdrawing from the study or taking advantage of the new situation to rethink and recreate a new study. What happened in Littlewoods was that the decision to purchase the computer equipment was so protracted and full of conflict that I was unable to study the implementation of the computer system in my research contract. The project therefore was reconceived while in process as a decision-making rather than an implementation study.

From this decision-making study evolved first my Ph.D. (1970), and my first book, *The Politics of Organizational Decision Making* (1973). Enid Mumford and I later co-operated on another book, *Implementing Strategic Decisions* (1975), which also drew partly on the Ph.D. data set. The Ph.D. also produced two refereed journal articles, one in *Sociology* (1972) and the other in *The Sociological Review* (1973). These were to be my last articles in mainstream sociology journals—thus far!

However, the Ph.D. was not just a source of publications, it also represented a crucial step in the development of my scholarly identity and point of view. These early building blocks included an interest in time, social process and social structure, the crucial role of longitudinal research designs and historical analysis in revealing social processes, and the tremendous potential in interdisciplinary theorizing. There is also a need to take over-theorized and difficult concepts such as power and politics into the field, to underpin concepts with data and make some empirical claims about how and why decision outcomes are shaped by power and conflict in organizational life. I get considerable satisfaction from the fact that *The Politics of Organizational Decision Making* is still cited in the literature on power, politics, and decision making some twenty-five years after it was published and twenty years after it went out of print.

Enid Mumford played a crucial role as supervisor of my Ph.D. She opened the door for the research access, funded the research, supported me emotionally in some very difficult fieldwork situations and provided the standards for me to aim for. She was and still is an inveterate optimist. Her attitude was, everything is possible until proven otherwise. Of course, not everything is possible but if you assume it is, most of the time it may indeed be (nearly) possible. I have followed this maxim throughout my research career and I believe it to be one of the reasons why I have been successful at negotiating access to research sites that other scholars may have assumed were unattainable. I do believe creative pursuits have more than their share of stresses, why add to them by forever looking on the dark side?

But I must retreat in this chronology to recognize the most important thing that has happened to me in my personal life—marriage to Ethna Moores in July 1967. Our time in Liverpool had overlapped by three years, but we did not meet until she returned to the Manchester area to begin her teaching career and I to begin my appointment at the Manchester Business School. It has been my good fortune to marry the finest person I have met.

YALE—ADMINISTRATIVE SCIENCES 1969-1971

Out of the blue on Saturday, April 12, 1969, I received an overseas telegram from Chris Argyris, then departmental chairman of Administrative Sciences at Yale University. I have kept the telegram, it said "Can offer teaching position for $10,500 for nine months. Letter follows. Professor Chris Argyris, Yale University."

I don't think I even checked up what 10,500 US$ was in pounds sterling. The offer was instantly accepted and Ethna and I began planning our move to New Haven, Connecticut.

Behind the sudden telegram was the professional hand of Chris Argyris. His interest in me had been triggered by a number of factors. The 1968 *Journal of Management Studies* article he had liked. At that time the Administrative Science (Ad.Sci) department at Yale was an unlikely mixture of psychologists and operations research (OR) people. Chris wanted to broaden the base of the behavioral side of the department by recruiting a couple of sociologists (Bliss Cartwright was recruited at the same time). He also saw in my interest in OR people at work a possible bridge between the behavioral and OR groups in Ad.Sci. I later discovered he had checked me out with Tom Lupton. In any case, it was a low risk option for Yale—I was only being offered a nine month appointment.

Although I had developed very quickly as a field researcher at Manchester Business School and subsequently benefited enormously from a five-year stay at London Business School, I still consider the two years spent at Yale to be the most significant in my career and life. As Ethna and I often say, Yale changed our lives. For this we shall be forever indebted to Chris Argyris.

As Ethna and I arrived in New Haven in August 1969, I was just 25 years old, still 9 months away from completing my Ph.D. and had not yet taught a complete course on my own. There was everything to learn in a society then in turmoil and in an elite educational institution in an academic culture of which I was a complete innocent.

By the time we arrived in New Haven, Chris Argyris had had to step down as Chairman of Ad.Sci because of a brief period of ill-health. Bob Fetter, the new chairman met us and he and his wife Audrey graciously let us stay with them for a few days until we found somewhere to live. Eric Denardo, another of the OR professors, helped us to find an apartment and we quickly settled into life at Yale.

I was astounded by the quality of people and professionalism of academic life at Yale in general and the Ad.Sci department in particular. As I arrived in my office, the previous year's academic report landed on my desk. I noticed that several of the behaviorists in the Ad.Sci department had published 6 to 8 articles in top journals in the previous 12 months and they also had a string of articles forthcoming. My first reaction was one of admiration and disbelief. The second was "I cannot compete with this!" The Yale group was young, ambitious and talented. In addition to Wight Bakke and Chris Argyris, it included Ed Lawler, Dick Hackman, Tim Hall, Ben Schneider, Clay Alderfer, Roy Lewicki, and Gerrit Wolfe. Notable doctoral students were Bob Duncan, John Wanous, Dave Brown, Bob Kaplan and Larry Zahn. Although the British academic groups I had then been exposed to had talented individuals, none had this critical mass of quality people and they certainly were not producing academic output at this rate. Of course, what I was also seeing at Yale was a different academic culture, different style of research and different reward system. In Britain the quality research monograph and scholarly review of a field were still prized over journal articles. The Yale research was also more tightly circumscribed and more quantitative than the sociological work I had been used to in England and this meant publishing lead times were shorter though competition to enter the best journals still much tougher than in Europe.

Exposure to the psychologists at Yale reinforced my belief in interdisciplinary thinking. This was helped by the openness of people such as Chris Argyris, Tim Hall, and Ben Schneider to approaches they would not necessarily have used themselves. Tim Hall and Ben Schneider were particularly supportive of my attempts to finish my Ph.D. and the methodological part of my thesis was greatly influenced by their extensive knowledge of data analysis in the behavioral sciences.

There were some interesting divisions between the Yale psychologists. The joke at the time was that the group were divided into the IPIs (the interpersonally incompetent) and the IPCs (the interpersonally competent). The former were industrial/organizational psychologists (Division 14 of the American Psychological Association) who represented the hard edge of scientific rigor and neutrality. The interpersonally competent subgroup were using sensitivity training, and increasingly other behavioral techniques, to research and intervene in social systems. The two new sociology recruits were automatically allocated to the interpersonally incompetent! The tensions between these two subgroups were real, but were more often displayed in father-figure tensions with Chris and in joking relationships than in deep personal tensions across the overall groups. Indeed, the Yale setting is still the most intellectually vigorous, productive and yet genuinely supportive academic environment I have worked in.

But the Yale Ad.Sci department's days were numbered. In my second year at Yale, Chris Argyris announced he was leaving to go to Harvard.

Ed Lawler, Tim Hall, and Ben Schneider had either decided to leave or were contemplating it. Having successfully completed my Ph.D. in the academic year 1969/70, I was invited to stay a further year and then offered a regular tenured position. But the atmosphere in the department was changing and I had by this stage been encouraged by Derek Pugh to take a lectureship back in England at the London Business School. Reluctantly, Ethna and I returned home, quite different people from what we had been two years earlier. Academically, I had grown enormously and I now had an academic network (and respect for U.S. scholarship) that will carry me through my life. Our first child Martha was born in New Haven in February 1970, and I acquired a life-time companion in diabetes. This was a lot to achieve in two years.

The Ad.Sci department at Yale and London Business School could not have been more different. Here was another opportunity to learn and develop as an academic. Ad.Sci was a small, very high quality group of scholars (with little institutionalized contact with the business world), set in an established, elite institution. London Business School (LBS) was at that time an aspiring elite institution filling up with mostly UK scholars who had been trained either in British social science departments or US business schools. LBS was already programmatically quite complex with a two year M.Sc (later re-named MBA program), a plethora of executive programs, a Ph.D. program and a developing set of research groupings of which the Organizational Behavior Research Group (OBRG; led by Derek Pugh) was closest to my research interests.

As I arrived at LBS in September, 1971 (as a Lecturer in Organizational Behavior) a change of institutional leadership was imminent. Arthur Earle, a Canadian businessman, was just about to retire as Principal and was to be succeeded by Jim Ball, one of the founding Professors of Economics. This move was fateful to the LBS's development. It assured the political supremacy of Economics and Finance, assisted the development of a mixed scholarly and policy oriented culture in the school, and hastened LBS's acceptance as a member of the economic, political and educational elite within, first of all, the capital and, then, the country of England.

In Ad.Sci., Organizational Behavior (OB) had been center stage on a very small stage. At LBS, Derek Pugh's international research reputation and Charles Handy's teaching and political skills insured OB was on stage, but not in a starring role. Derek Pugh located himself with his research group in an externally pleasing but internally grubby building adjoining the recently redeveloped main LBS building. Derek attracted a talented group of young scholars of whom John Child, Roger Mansfield, Roy Payne, and Lex Donaldson have turned out to be the most notable. I was located in the main LBS building along with nearly all the full-time teaching staff. The OBRG at LBS did not seem to gel as the Aston team had done in the 1960s and, although individual scholars were productive, no clear team-oriented work emerged. The periodic OBRG seminars were lively and often acerbic. I remember commenting at the time that the absence of any apparent Hypocratic oath among the OB fraternity at LBS had not prevented the emergence of a hypercritical oath. This was mostly the product of the energy and ambition of quality creative people, however, and there were no permanent casualties (as far as I am aware) from the intellectual combat.

My teaching experience at Yale had been relatively low pressure contact with small groups of able undergraduate and post-graduates. This was to change at LBS where all teaching was to largish groups of MBAs or executives and where there was already a strong culture of performance assessment of teaching efforts. I looked around and quickly decided early that public failure was non-contemplatable and yet I needed some space to learn how to teach MBAs and executives. Fortunately for me Charles Handy was available as a mentor and coach and I watched him in action and tried to learn as much as I could. I remember going to him for advice as I was preparing my first 10 week OB course for the London MBAs. I presented a logically unimpeachable ordering of the material and waited to see what would happen. "Well Andrew" was his reply, "there's a rational way of doing this and a psychological way of doing it. You've done the rational bit, what about the psychological bit?" He then went on to explain that in this high pressure culture first impressions count with students and, therefore, you should start with the material you are most confident in presenting, not what seems intellectually the right place to start. Once you've won the psychological and reputational battle in the first and second classes, you can then return to your appropriate logical ordering of the material. Twenty-five years later and after innumerable MBA classes, I am still following Charles's sound advice.

The Yale experience had taught me that academics needed to publish and I needed no encouragement from LBS to do so. The main priority at that time was to publish from my 1970 Ph.D. thesis. My strategy was to produce two refereed articles (which eventually appeared in *Sociol-*

ogy, 1972, and *The Sociological Review,* 1973) and a book (1973). With no experience of dealing with publishers, I approached one of the top London literary agents for advice. They made contact with Tavistock publications and I was offered a contract in a new series *Organizations, People, Society,* edited by Professor Albert B. Cherns. I shall always be very grateful to the Tavistock copyeditor who spent hours on her own and many hours with me turning my Ph.D. thesis into a readable manuscript. Given the commercial pressures on publishers today, that kind of coaching is regrettably no longer available for novice authors.

The Politics of Organizational Decision Making (1973) turned out to be an important moment in defining my intellectual identity and reputation. In many ways it was a counter-cultural book. By the early 1970s the appearance of the computer and the availability of statistical packages had given a tremendous boost to quantitative social science.

Case studies were perceived by many academics to be regressive. That's what Gouldner, Selznick, Lipset, and Trow did in the 1950s and 1960s. The political analysis in the 1973 book and the attempt to empirically study power relations in organizational settings were also somewhat out of character with the rational tones of contingency theory then beginning to firmly take hold in management research. My own personal excitement about my first book contrasted sharply with the slow sales and apparent lack of external interest. But it appears many more copies were read than sold and, as I began to go to European conferences, I became aware that scholars in Scandinavia and the Netherlands were beginning to use it.

In the late 1960s and the 1970s business schools in Europe looked more to the United States than to Europe for role models and reference points. The UK certainly took this view and many young scholars were encouraged to spend time studying, teaching, and researching in the best U.S. universities. In 1973, however, Ford Foundation money was instrumental in founding the European Institute for Advanced Studies in Management in Brussels. This small research institute was quickly picked up by a number of European governments and became a key staging point in many European junior academics' careers and development. London Business School was drawn into the net and, in the academic year 1973-1974, Alan Dale, Stuart Timperley and I were each invited to spend four months there supporting doctoral students from various European countries and helping to plan and run a variety of international academic seminars. This experience was massively educational for all three of us. From my perspective, it was another crucial academic turning point. I was now able to build a European academic network to complement the one that was being built in North America.

As my Ph.D. publications were being prepared, I began to think of my next empirical research projects. Two lines of inquiry presented themselves. One was to build on the research I had done in my Diploma and Ph.D. on specialist experts in organizations, the other was to look for another study of decision making and change in organizations. While at Yale I had noticed in the UK national press that a rather famous private boarding school in Scotland, Gordonstoun School, was changing from single sex to co-education. I knew the headmaster, John Kempe, from his time as headmaster of Corby Grammar School and I wrote to him asking if I could study this process of change. Once back in England the correspondence continued and, after a number of visits to the school, the idea was approved by the Governing Body. Thus began a fascinating study that has never been properly written up. I received a small travel grant from the OBRG fund (Derek Pugh was very open-minded) and Will McQuillan and I did some interviewing there. I followed this up with much more extensive interviewing of staff, pupils and governors right back until the School's foundation in 1934. Kurt Hahn, the German founder of the School, had fled to England in 1933. His behavior as a classic educational entrepreneur fascinated me and I began to read widely on the birth processes and early development of educational, religious, and other organizations. The Gordonstoun data and the theoretical reading on the creation of organizational cultures led to a 1976 conference paper and a 1977 European Institute Working Paper (77-11), which were eventually re-worked for a paper in the *Administrative Science Quarterly* "On Studying Organizational Cultures." The interview and archival data I have on Gordonstoun are certainly unique and now with the passage of time and mortality probably irreplaceable. I have all these data and remain determined eventually to prepare a book on the social and organizational history of Gordonstoun.

The Gordonstoun study is of note because it was the first exposure I had as a social scientist with elites in British society. Elites in most societies are adept at shielding themselves from the unwelcome gaze of social analysts and my route to this group reaffirms the old maxim that to get to elites you have to go through other elite members. Eventually I was able to interview Prince Philip and Prince Charles (both Gordonstoun old boys). My link to them was via Lord Brabourne, a son-in-law of Earl Mountbatten. Lord Brabourne, in 1974, was a Governor of Atlantic College, a sister school of Gordonstoun in the "round square circle." At the end of our interview he said to me, "Well, you know, Philip would be interested to talk to you about Gordonstoun." My response was the innocent, "How do I arrange that?!" Well, said Lord Brabourne, "I'm seeing him this weekend, I'll ask him." Within a week I had a letter from Lord Brabourne indicating Prince Philip had agreed to an interview and would I now write formally to his principle private secretary. I wrote immediately, explaining who I was and what had transpired, and received a very polite but cool response asking for more details. Further correspondence ensued and then a letter asking me to write back in about 4-6 months. I assume that gap was to make security checks, for when I wrote again, I had an appointment within a month.

The interview with Prince Philip was fascinating but terrifying. It took place in 1975 when the British Royal Family had an even more distant, but as yet untarnished place in the British social consciousness. I was asked to appear at Buckingham Palace. The interview was to take place in his study. I was allocated one hour. Philip's private secretary met me at the Palace door and escorted me to the study and told me where to stand so I would be directly facing Philip as he entered the room. Philip and I were introduced and we left unaccompanied to his study. Then the problems began.

I had done my homework on Philip and was careful to introduce myself as having nothing to do with the press and media. I explained the study aims, guaranteed him anonymity and then asked if I might tape record the interview. A silence ensued and Philip snapped back, "Where's your notebook?" I repeated parts of my introductory statement again and there was another even longer silence. The apprehension I felt before entering the Palace was now escalating into anxiety. I thought I was going to be thrown out before I could begin the interview. I broke the silence by making an offer. "After the interview I will provide you with a typed transcript of the interview so you know exactly what was said." A shorter silence ensued. "No," said Philip, "I'll give you a typed transcript of the interview." When the interview finished, Philip rang for the butler, asked for the tape, and said have this typed up and sent to Dr. Pettigrew. I got the typed transcript unedited. The tape was returned, but wiped clean of his voice. Notwithstanding the tense beginning, the interview was successful. I obtained the information I needed and at the end of the conversation Philip inquired if I would like to talk to Charles about the School. I met Prince Charles within a few months. This encounter was more relaxed and informal and I still have the tape recording of the interview, but this time it was transcribed outside the Palace by myself. As far as I am aware, these two interviews are the only social science encounters with members of the British Royal Family,

In 1975 a chance encounter with Mike Browning, then a Divisional Personnel Manager in Imperial Chemical Industries' (ICI) Agricultural Division, led me into another study of change that was to have a much bigger impact on my thinking and reputation than the Gordonstoun study. Mike Browning was a delegate on a one-week executive course at LBS and heard me talking around a model of the evolution of specialist activities in organizations written up in a 1975 *Personnel Review* article. Afterwards he drew me aside and said you have just described and analyzed the development of the organization development group in Agricultural Division, would you consider doing a small scale study of us and then feedback the results in a team workshop. After a few days reflection, I phoned Mike and said I would be much more interested if the study could be comparative, if we compared and contrasted the birth and development of the organization development (OD) groups in different parts of ICI. Within a few months I had negotiated access to the corporate headquarters of ICI and three of its four largest UK divisions—Agricultural, Petrochemicals, and Plastics. Mond Division joined the study in 1978. ICI provided a two-year research contract and Dennis Bumstead joined me at LBS to help carry out the research.

The story of the ICI research is a long one. The project lasted from 1975 to 1985, when *The Awakening Giant* was published. I will pick up the chronology during the next phase of my career at the University of Warwick.

By late 1975 I saw no future at LBS. Most of my contemporaries (John Child, Roger Mansfield, Malcolm Warner, Roy Payne, Ray Loveridge) had left for chairs elsewhere. I was approached by Roger Fawthrop, then Chairman of the School of Industrial and Business Studies at the University of Warwick and asked if I would apply for a new Chair in Organizational Behavior at Warwick. At first I said no because Martha, our oldest child, had just gone out of remission with leukaemia. She went back into remission, however, and appeared to be stabilizing again, and Ethna and I decided I should put in a late application. I was offered the job in May 1976, when I was still just 31, and took up the post in October, 1976.

I arrived at Warwick laden with concern. Martha had gone out of remission again and was not going to live. I stopped travelling to Warwick in late November and Ethna and I cared for Martha at home until she died on December, 27, 1976. You never completely recover from your own child's death. Time is never an adequate healer. Matthew, who was now four, had been born just a few weeks before Martha's diagnosis with leukaemia. Edward had been born just 10 months before Martha's death. William our youngest son was born two-years later in 1978. Our sons have had a stable and happy upbringing and are all making much of their lives.

WARWICK 1976—PRESENT

Although I was very excited about my appointment at Warwick, by the time I took it up my heart was not in it. I travelled back and forward from the London area where my family still was, but would rather not have bothered. The small OB group I inherited were not strongly committed to research in a business-school setting and my task was either to develop or disperse them. In the end the latter was the only option and without exception they have either retired, left academia, or have moved on to other educational posts.

The School of Industrial and Business Studies at Warwick has long since changed its title to Warwick Business School. For the past ten years, it can justifiably claim to be one of the premier research-led schools of business in the UK. This was not the case in 1976. The School was very small, isolated from much of academia and business and was very parochial. With the notable exception of industrial relations (which had an outstanding Industrial Relations Research Unit; IRRU) the School did not have a strong research culture or achievements. Hugh Clegg, the founding Professor of Industrial Relations and George Bain, the second director of the IRRU, were key academic figures in, and in George's case, loosely linked to the School.

What saved me emotionally and intellectually at this early stage at Warwick was the support of Ethna and the academic excitement of the ICI study.

By 1977 Dennis Bumstead and I had prepared a report on the initial work on the OD groups in ICI, but I could see the potential in developing the study from this analysis of the uses and limitations of specialist change resources, to examining the wider processes of strategic change in the company. ICI has always been a very networked company and I found the key to widening the study was moving through the various company networks and hierarchical levels. In turn, I was accepted first in the OD network, then the divisional personnel managers' network, then the works managers' network, then the divisional board level, until finally I had access at the very top to the Main Board. This process took several years and was finally capped in 1982 when John Harvey-Jones, a supporter of OD and my research, became Chairman and Chief Executive of the company.

ICI is an elite institution in Britain and would have remained impenetrable without that kind of long-term relationship building. But there are always levels of understanding and depths of appreciation in case-study work and this was my personal learning about these issues. But with this closeness also has to come a certain distance to remain impartial and to try and develop a suitable analytical framework to locate all this marvelous detail of reality in flight.

In 1981 the award of a personal research grant from the Social Science Research Council allowed me to collect more interview data on the ICI responses to the early 1980s recession. I also spent a nine-month period as a visiting scholar at Harvard Business School. This provided me with more space to analyze the interviews and begin the process of drafting *The Awakening Giant*. At Harvard, Robert H. Miles, Paul Lawrence, Mike Beer, Dick Walton, and Alfred Chandler all helped me to test and refine my ideas.

Meanwhile the School of Industrial and Business Studies at Warwick was beginning to awaken. In 1982/83 George Bain was appointed, first of all, to a teaching post in the School and, then, was elected to be School Chairman. George spent the next seven years driving the School forward through an unrelenting growth pathway. New colleagues arrived, others retired and still others built upon the atmosphere of psychological success to do their own institution building. Out of this atmosphere and process I decided to build on the impact of the 1985 publication of *The Awakening Giant* and create the Centre for Corporate Strategy and Change.

WARWICK—CENTRE FOR CORPORATE
STRATEGY AND CHANGE 1985-1995

Why create a university-based research center? In Britain in 1985 the dominating policy issue in all aspects of organizational life was change. In Mrs. Margaret Thatcher we had a right-wing Conservative leader with a revolutionary agenda who looked as if she was going to maintain power for long enough to drive through that program of transformation in both the public and private sectors. The experience of researching and writing *The Awakening Giant* left me with a mission that theoretically sound and practically useful research on change should involve the continuous interplay between ideas about the context of change, the process of change and the content of change. That study also provided me with an analytical approach to management research that combined multiple levels of analysis (firm, sector, political and economic context), with the collation and analysis of time-series data collected through historical and real-time analysis. Central to the methodological approach was the use of the longitudinal comparative case study.

The theme of change, supported by the above analytical and methodological requirements, provided the mobilizing intellectual idea and purpose for the Centre for Corporate Strategy and Change (CCSC). Linked to this mission was a strongly held view that the understanding of processes of change in their contexts needed to be as firmly embedded in social science knowledge as it was in the world of policy and practice. The Centre for Corporate Strategy and Change thus needed an active and diverse dissemination strategy to complement its philosophy of combining theory and practice, intellectual rigor and relevance. Eventually (see Pettigrew, 1997) this ambition to meet the double hurdles of scholarly quality and relevance was crystallized around a view of partnerships in knowledge production. The aim was not just to disseminate ideas through multiple networks of scholars and practitioners, but to build partnerships for the co-funding, co-production and co-dissemination of research. This remains an unfulfilled ambition and a rallying cry for social science, in general, and management research, in particular, for the twenty-first century.

The Centre for Corporate Strategy and Change started therefore with a real and ambitious intellectual purpose, but yet was grounded in a solid experience of empirical inquiry. But big ideas needed to be operationalized into sub-themes and projects and those projects needed financial and human resources to make them happen. From the outset I could see that a single stream of research in the Centre for Corporate Strategy and Change would be vulnerable to changes in the intellectual and financial market for knowledge and, therefore, I talked metaphorically of the need for at least a two-legged stool. In fact, for the whole of the period of my directorship of the Centre we always had a three-legged stool. Between 1985 and 1995 the Centre has pursued five research themes, always maintaining at least three at any point in time. These are:

i.   Strategic change and competitiveness 1985-1992;

ii. Human resource change 1985-1995;

iii. Public sector change 1986-;

iv. Strategic change and the internationalizing firm 1993-

v.   Boards, directors and corporate governance 1993-.

Over this 10-year period Centre staff generated approaching £5 million of research grants, contracts and other sponsorship. We built a consortium of private and public sector sponsors, who although they contributed only 20% of our total resource base, allowed us to maintain key research staff in position beyond existing contracts and experiment with new research areas independent of external funding processes. This financial record is quite exceptional within the UK context and is a reflection of the entrepreneurial spirit and culture of collective self reliance built in the Centre.

The minimum critical mass for a research center such as the Center for Corporate Strategy and Change is four to six full time research staff plus a director. The Center began in October 1985 with a director, four senior research fellows and a secretary. With the appointment in autumn, 1986, of two further senior research staff and the beginnings of our public sector research, the Center was in critical mass.

Since 1986 the Center has been able to sustain an interdisciplinary group of scholars beyond the critical mass size. The team has included individuals trained in organization theory, strategic management, economics, sociology, psychology, history and social policy.

The Center has developed a number of high quality young scholars. Five of them have been promoted to Professor and others are likely to achieve that form of recognition. Looking back it is clear that the first generation of staff, Richard Whipp, Chris Hendry, Ewan Ferlie, Lorna McKee and Paul Sparrow were the more talented and had the biggest impact on developing the Center's character and their various fields of research. Some of the present younger generation, however, may yet leap-frog them in terms of academic distinction.

The major lesson for me in funding and directing the Center for ten years is how little an individual can achieve and how much more is possible when a talented group of scholars can work together in a sustained way around a common intellectual theme, using a similar methodology. The academic contributions of the Center may be claimed by Center staff, but such claims are empty without the support of our peers in the academic world. There are justifiable claims however, that Center staff have contributed to empirical work on competitiveness and change, to the links between business strategy change and human resource management, to the strategies and structure of international firms, the impact of professionals on innovation processes, the development of the new public management and of quasi markets in the UK public sector and the study of boards and directors. Theoretical and conceptual developments are also claimable on change processes in organizational settings, thinking about the pace and receptivity of change, the development of learning organizations and quasi markets and power and influence processes at the top of firms. We have also reflected analytically about the theory and practice of conducting longitudinal research in organizational settings. Such claims are underpinned by a vast corpus of published writing. In its first ten years, staff of the Center for Corporate Strategy and Change presented several hundred conference papers, published 24 research monographs, 120 journal articles and 75 chapters and contributions to books.

Twenty years on from the 1965 foundation of the London and Manchester Business Schools, the face of British management education and research was quite different. Most university and many polytechnic institutions now had departments of business and/or management studies and a proliferation of MBA programs of varying quality had emerged. This growth had, of course, meant a considerable expansion of academic positions in business schools and a rise in interest and activity in management research. A number of specialist academic associations were by this time in place, ranging from marketing to industrial relations and information systems, but there was no serious management association with a focus on research equivalent to the Academy of Management in the United States.

My experience and network in U.S. academia led me to regularly attend the annual conference of the (US) Academy of Management. In 1985 at the San Diego Conference Cary Cooper, of the University of Manchester School of Management, and I concluded why did we not go back to the UK and set up a British Academy of Management. Within months a committee had been formed and Cary and I emerged as first President and Chairman of the Executive Committee of the British Academy of Management (BAM). The inaugural conference was held at Warwick University September 13-15, 1987, and shortly, thereafter, the scholarly journal—the *British Journal of Management* was launched. BAM now has a firm place in the professional life of many UK management scholars and is helping to support the development of the management research community in the tough research performance culture in universities at the end of the twentieth century.

In 1995 I decided to retire as director of the Center for Corporate Strategy and Change, although all my research is still located within the Center's portfolio of work. My research is now concentrated in two areas. These are the study of the conduct and power relationships in the boards of the top 250 public limited companies, and studies of the strategy, structure, systems, processes and transformation of international firms. In this latter area, the Center's work has stimulated partnership arrangements with universities in the United States, Japan, Korea, France, Germany, the Netherlands, Sweden, Switzerland, and Spain. International comparative work, using surveys, data bases, and comparative case studies, is examining the role and performance consequences of network forms of organizing and the transformation of large enterprises in the United States, UK, Japan, and Continental Western Europe. The Center may yet become known in its next stage of development for combining international mapping studies with longitudinal comparative case studies.

This essay may well have exposed all my earlier fears of the limitations of self reflections of the past. I have tried to reveal some of the untidiness and surprises of an academic career but also I hope the need to create order and intellectual identity in the life of a scholar. Research is the most personal of activities although it is often carried out in project teams and centers and is, of course, deeply embedded in a community of academicians. One of the pieces of advice I always offer to younger researchers is to recognize the personal qualities of the research process and their own strengths and weaknesses. Find out what you are capable of doing well and do it. Don't be led by older generations who have probably been equally personally driven but are now offering over-determined choices for the next generation. I have tried to follow this maxim myself and sometimes it has worked and other times it hasn't. But I remain convinced of the crucial social and political aspects of the research process. Research is a craft process and not just a technical act and in that craft process personal considerations and qualities are vital.

PUBLICATIONS

1967

The outsiders. *Personnel and Training Management*, (November), 30-33.

1968

Inter-group conflict and role strain. *Journal of Management Studies*, 5(2), 205-218.

1972

Information control as a power resource. *Sociology*, 6(2), 197-204.
Managing under stress. *Management Today*, (April), 42-46.

1973

The politics of organizational decision making. London: Tavistock.
Occupational specialization as an emergent process. *The Sociological Review*, 21(2), 255-278.

1975

With E. Mumford. *Implementing strategic decisions*. London: Longman.

Occupational specialization as an emergent process. In G. Esland et al. (Eds.), *People and work* (pp.258-274). Edinburgh: Holmes McDougal.

Strategic aspects of the management of specialist activity. *Personnel Review, 4,* 5-13.

Towards a political theory of organizational intervention. *Human Relations, 28*(3), 191-208.

The industrial purchasing decision as a political process. *European Journal of Marketing, 9*(1), 4-20.

1977

Strategy formulation as a political process. *International Studies of Management and Organization, 7*(2), 78-87.

1979

On studying organizational cultures. *Administrative Science Quarterly, 24*(4), 570-581.

1980

The politics of organizational change. In N.B. Anderson (Ed.), *The human side of information processing.* Amsterdam: North Holland.

1982

Strategy formulation as a political process. In B. Taylor & D. Hussy (Eds.), *The realities of planning* (pp. 94-99). Oxford: Pergamon.

Towards a political theory of organizational intervention. In M.D. Hakel, M. Sorcher, M. Beer, & J.L. Moses, *Making it happen: Designing research with implementation in mind* (pp. 41-60). Beverly Hills, CA: Sage Publications.

1983

Patterns of managerial response as organizations move from rich to poor environments. *Educational Management Administration, 2,* 104-114.

1985

The awakening giant: Continuity and change in imperial chemical industries. Oxford: Basil Blackwell.

With A. Thompson, & N. Rubashow. British management and strategic change. *European Management Journal, 3*(3), 165-173.

Contextualistic research: A natural way to link theory and practice. In E.E. Lawler (Ed.), *Doing research that is useful for theory and practice* (pp. 222-248). San Francisco: Jossey Bass.

Examining change in the long-term context of culture and politics. In J.H. Pennings (Ed.), *Organizational strategy and change* (pp. 269-318). San Francisco: Jossey Bass.

Contextualist research and the study of organizational change processes. In E. Mumford (Ed.), *Research methods in information systems* (pp. 53-75). Amsterdam: Elsevier.

With C. Hardy. The use of power in managerial strategies for change. In R. Rosenbloom (Ed.), *Research on technological innovation, management and policy* (pp. 11-45). Greenwich, CT: JAI Press.

1986

With C. Hendry. The practice of strategic human resource management. *Personnel Review, 15*(5), 3-8.

Some limits of executive power in creating strategic change. In S. Srivastva (Ed.), *The functioning of executive power* (pp. 132-154). San Francisco: Jossey Bass.

Cultura organizzativa: una famiglia di concetti. In P. Gagliardi (Ed.), *Le Imprese come culture* (pp. 51-66). Torino: ISEDI.

The management of strategic change. In G. Parston (Ed.), *Managers as strategists: Health service managers reflecting on change* (pp. 106-127). London: King Edward's Hospital Fund.

1987

[Editor]. *The management of strategic change.*, Oxford: Basil Blackwell.

Researching strategic change. In A.M. Pettigrew (Ed.), *The management of strategic change* (pp. 1-13). Oxford: Basil Blackwell.

With P.R. Sparrow. Britain's training problem: The search for a strategic human resource management approach. *Human Resource Management, 26*(1), 109-27.

Context and action in the transformation of the firm. *Journal of Management Studies, 24*(6), 649-670.

Theoretical, methodological and empirical issues in studying change. *Journal of Management Studies, 24*(4), 420-426.

With R. Whipp, & R. Rosenfeld. Understanding strategic change processes: Some preliminary British findings. In A.M. Pettigrew (Ed.), *The management of strategic change* (pp. 14-55). Oxford: Basil Blackwell.

With C. Hendry. Banking on HRM to respond to change. *Personnel Management*, (November), 29-32.

1988

[Editor]. *Competitiveness and the management process.* Oxford: Basil Blackwell.

With L. McKee, & E. Ferlie. Understanding change in the NHS. *Public Administration, 66*(3), 297-317.

Introduction. In A.M. Pettigrew (Ed.), *Competitiveness and the management process* (pp. 1-8). Oxford: Basil Blackwell.

With P. Sparrow. Contrasting HRM responses to the changing world of computing. *Personnel Management*, (February), 40-45.

With C. Hendry. Multi-skilling in the round. *Personnel Management*, (April), 36-43.

With P. Sparrow. How Halfords put its HRM into top gear. *Personnel Management*, (June), 30-34.

With C. Hendry and P.R. Sparrow. Changing patterns of human resource management. *Personnel Management*, (November), 37-41.

With L. McKee, & E. Ferlie. Wind of change blows through the NHS. *Health Service Journal*, (November 3), 1926-1998.

With L. McKee. Managing major change. *Health Service Journal*, (November 17), 1358-1360.

With E. Ferlie. AIDS: Responding to rapid change. *Health Service Journal*, (December 1), 1422-1424.

With P.R. Sparrow. Strategic human resource management in the UK computer supplier industry. *Journal of Occupational Psychology, 61*(1), 25-42.

With P. Sparrow, & C. Hendry. The forces that trigger training. *Personnel Management*, (December), 28-32.

1989

With C. Hendry, & P.R. Sparrow. *Training in Britain: Employer's perspectives on human resources.* London: Her Majesty's Stationery Office.
With M.B. Arthur, & C. Hendry. *Training and human resource management in small to medium sized enterprises: A critical review of the literature and a model for future research,* Sheffield: The Department of Employment, Training Agency.
With L. McKee, & E. Ferlie. Managing strategic change in the NHS. *Health Services Management Research, 2*(1), 20-31.
With R. Rosenfeld, & R. Whipp. Processes of internationalisation: Regeneration and competitiveness. *Economia Aziendale, 7*(1), 21-47.
With R. Whipp, & P.R. Sparrow. New technology, competition and the firm: A framework for research. *International Journal of Vehicle Design, 10*(4), 453-469.
With R. Whipp, & R. Rosenfeld. Culture and competitiveness: Evidence from mature UK industries. *Journal of Management Studies, 26*(6), 561-585.
With R. Whipp and R. Rosenfeld. Il management del Cambiamento strategico e operativo. *Review Kybernetes, 24,* 36-46.
Longitudinal methods to study change: Theory and practice. In R.M. Mansfield (Ed.), *New frontiers of management* (pp. 21-49). London: Routledge.
With R. Whipp, & R. Rosenfeld. Competitiveness and the management of strategic change processes: A research agenda. In P. Tharaken, & A. Francis (Eds.), *The competitiveness of European industry: Country policies and company strategies* (pp. 110-136). London: Croom Helm.
With C. Hendry, & P.R. Sparrow. Linking strategic change, competitive performance and human resource management: Results of a UK empirical study. In R. Mansfield (Ed.), *New frontiers of management* (pp. 195-220). London: Routledge.
Issues of time and site selection in longitudinal research on change. In J. Cash, & P. Lawrence (Eds.), *The information systems research*

challenge: Qualitative research methods (pp. 13-19). Boston: Harvard Business School Press.

With R. Whipp, & R. Rosenfeld. Managing strategic change in a mature business. *Long Range Planning, 22*(6), 92-99.

With E. Ferlie. The politics of progress. *Health Service Journal, 12*(1), 44-46.

With L. McKee. Hospitals do not hurry. *Health Service Journal, 26*(1), 102-104.

With L. McKee, & E. Ferlie. Hints on how to ring the changes. *Health Service Journal, 16*(2), 200-202.

1990

With C. Hendry, & P.R. Sparrow. *Corporate strategy change and human resource management.* Sheffield: The Department of Employment, Training Agency.

With E. Ferlie. Coping with change in the NHS: A frontline district's response to AIDS. *Journal of Social Policy, 19*(2), 191-220.

With C. Hendry. Human resource management: An agenda for the 1990's. *International Journal of Human Resource Management, 1*(1), 17-43.

Studying strategic choice and strategic change. *Organization Studies, 11*(1), 6-11.

Longitudinal field research on change: Theory and practice. *Organization Science, 1*(3), 267-292.

With C. Bennett, & E. Ferlie. *Developing services for HIV/AIDS: Organisational learning in district health authorities* (pp. 20-22). London: Department of Health Yearbook of Research and Development.

1991

With R. Whipp. *Managing change for competitive success.* Oxford: Basil Blackwell.

With C. Hendry, A.M. Jones, & M.B. Arthur. *Human resource development in the small-to-medium enterprise* (Research Paper Series No. 88). Sheffield: Employment.

With E. Ferlie, L. FitzGerald, & R. Wensley. The leadership role of the new health authorities: An agenda for research and development. *Public Money and Management,* (Spring), 1-5.

With C. Hendry. Getting training and development into the organisational blood stream. In M. Silver (Ed.), *Competent to manage: Approaches to management training and development* (pp. 193-201). London: Routledge.

Organizational climate and culture: Two constructs in search of a role. In B. Schneider (Ed.), *Organizational climate and culture* (pp. 413-433). San Francisco: Jossey Bass.

With S. MacDonald, P. Gustavsson, & L. Melin. The learning process behind the European activities of large UK and Swedish firms. In H. Vestergaard (Ed.), *An enlarged Europe in the global economy* (pp. 1-30). Copenhagen: European International Business Association.

With C. Hendry. Human resource change and the changing skills of the human resource. *Professional, Vocational Training,* No. 1, CEDEFOP, Berlin.

With E. Ferlie, L. Fitzgerald, & R. Wensley. The leadership role of the new health authorities: An agenda for research and development. *Research for Action,* Paper 1, February.

With L. Fitzgerald. Boards in action: Some implications for health authorities. *Research for Action,* Paper 2, February.

With L. Cairncross, & L. Ashburner. Membership and learning needs. *Research for Action,* Paper 4, November.

1992

With E. Ferlie, & L. McKee. Shaping strategic change: Making change in large organisations, the case of the NHS., London, Sage.

With C. Hendry. *The processes of internationalisation and the implications for human resource management: A literature review.* Sheffield: Department of Employment.

With R. Whipp. Managing change for competitive success: Bridging the strategic and the operational. *Industrial and Corporate Change, 1*(1), 205-233.

With E. Ferlie, & L. McKee. Shaping strategic change: The case of the NHS. *Public Money and Management, 12*(3), 27-33.

With C. Hendry. Patterns of strategic change in the development of human resource management. *British Journal of Management, 3*(3), 137-156.

On studying managerial elites. *Strategic Management Journal, 13*(Special Issue), 163-182.

The character and significance of strategy process research. *Strategic Management Journal, 13*(Special Issue), 5-16.

With R. Whipp. Managing change and corporate performance. In K. Cool (Ed.), *European industrial restructuring in the 1990's* (pp. 227-265). London: Macmillan.

1993

[Editor]. With L. Zan, & S. Zambon. *Perspectives on strategic change.* Amsterdam: Kluwer.

With R. Whipp. Managing the twin processes of competition and change: The role of intangible assets. In P. Lorange et al. (Eds.), *Implementing strategic processes* (pp. 3-42). Oxford: Blackwells.

With E. Ferlie, & E. Cairncross. Introducing market like mechanisms in public sector: The case of the NHS. In L. Zan, S. Zambon, & A.M. Pettigrew (Eds.), *Perspectives on strategic change* (pp. 235-250). Amsterdam: Kluwer.

With R. Whipp. Leading change and the management of competition. In J. Hendry, G. Johnson, & J. Newton (Eds.), *Strategic thinking: Leadership and the management of change* (pp. 199-228). Chichester: John Wiley.

With L. Zan, & S. Zambon. Introduction. In L. Zan, S. Zambon, & A.M. Pettigrew (Eds.), *Perspectives on strategic change* (pp. ix-xxi). Amsterdam: Kluwer.

With E. Ferlie, & L. Cairncross. Understanding internal markets in the NHS. In I. Tilley (Ed.), *Managing the internal market* (pp. 69-81). London: Paul Chapman Publishing.

1994

With I. Lapsley. Meeting the challenge: Accounting for change. *Financial Accountability and Management, 10*(2), 79-92.

1995

With T. McNulty. Power and influence in and around the boardroom. *Human Relations, 48*(8), 1-29.

Longitudinal field research on change. In G.P. Huber & A. Van de Ven (Eds.), *Longitudinal field research methods* (pp. 91-125). San Francisco: Sage.

On studying managerial elites. In H. Thomas, D. O'Neal, & J. Kelly, *Strategic renaissance and business transformation* (pp.437-472). Chichester: J. Wiley.

Information control as a power resource. In D.J. Hickson (Ed.), *Managerial decision making* (pp. 302-318). Aldershot: Dartmouth Publishing.

Blijvend veranderen voorwaarde voor duuzare verbeliering. *Kwaliteit In Bedrijf*, (8 December), 6-9.

1996

With E. Ferlie. Managing through networks: Some issues and implications for the NHS. *British Journal of Management, 7*(Special Issue, March), 81-99.

With T. McNulty. The contribution, power and influence of part time board members. *Corporate Governance An International Review, 4*(3), 160-179.

With E. Ferlie. The nature and transformation of corporate headquarters: A review of recent literature and a research agenda. *Journal of Management Studies, 33*(4), 495-523.

With E. Ferlie, L. Ashburner, & L. Fitzgerald. *The new public management in action*. Oxford: Oxford University Press.

1997

Slagen en falen bij transformatie van organisatievormen. *Nijenrode Management Review*, (March-April), 49-60.

The double hurdles for management research. In T. Clarke (Ed.), *Advancement in organisational behaviour* (pp. 277-296). Aldershot: Ashgate.

1998

With T. McNulty. Control and creativity in the boardroom. In D. Hambrick, D. Nadler, & M. Tushman (Eds.), *Navigating change: How CEOs, top teams and boards steer transformation* (pp. 226-255). Boston: Harvard Business School Press.

With T. McNulty. Sources and uses of power in the boardroom. *European Journal of Work and Organizational Psychology, 7*(2), 197-214.

Success and failure in corporate transformation initiatives. In R. Galliers, & W. Baets (Eds.), *Information technology and organisational transformation* (pp. 271-289). Chichester: Wiley.

What is a processual analysis? *Scandinavian Journal of Management, 13*(4), 337-348. [Special Issue on Conducting Processual Research]

Forthcoming

With T. McNulty. Strategists on the board. *Organisational Studies.*

Karlene H Roberts

HAVING THE BUBBLE

KARLENE H. ROBERTS

One of my earliest memories is of being taken by my parents (in my hat and white gloves) to San Francisco's Chinatown. There we saw old women hobbling around and my parents told me of the Chinese custom of binding female children's feet. Small feet were considered beautiful, and having bound feet meant women were unable to perform taxing physical tasks, and could not run off (Levy, 1992). The process of getting small feet was lengthy and extremely painful. The practice probably began in the twelfth century in the courts of China, where women did not have to do burdensome work. Ultimately, it spread through the classes to women required to do heavy work. Once ingrained, like other customs, it was difficult to dislodge. It is a strong reminder that we are all bound by the norms and customs of our societies and our times, which place us in boxes.[1] Just as Chinese mothers placed their daughters in boxes by binding their feet, I wonder what boxes we place our children in.

In this series there is the box in which William Foote Whyte found himself bound by polio, Vic Vroom's brush with death box, etc. The evidence suggests, though, that women traditionally have been placed in smaller boxes then men. Sometimes, too, it is easier for men to hide the

Management Laureates, Volume 5, pages 207-242.
Copyright © 1998 by JAI Press Inc.
All rights of reproduction in any form reserved.
ISBN: 0-7623-0178-3

limitations their boxes place on them. It is difficult to hide one's gender, though the gifted pianist and saxophonist, Billy Tipton, managed to do so for an entire career. Her biographer, Diane Middlebrook, claims this was pure acting and a realistic response to the male dominated world of jazz in the 1930s (Lehrman, 1997). Only at the time of Tipton's death in 1989 did her three sons realize their father was in reality a woman, a secret thought to have contributed to her death. Some women of my generation have struggled, often at great sacrifice to escape some of their "boxes." This is the story of my boxes.

LAUNCH! LAUNCH!

I was born in San Francisco into a good sized, midwestern, middle-class, family. My mother (Doris Hosman) was one of eight children. My father (Carl Hahn) was one of three sons. I am an only child. Three of my grandparents were college educated. My paternal grandfather was a banker in Twin Falls, Idaho, and my maternal grandfather was a Methodist minister, who sequentially served ministries all over Nebraska. My mother and father met at the University of Nebraska where they were both active in drama and their Greek Societies. My maternal grandfather, on a Methodist minister's salary, put all eight of his children through college. When I asked my mother why he bothered with the daughters, she said that when the first child was old enough to go to college (a son) my grandmother put her foot down and said that if grandfather was going to do it for one, he was going to do it for all eight. My father's brothers were college educated. The cultural diversity represented in my family runs all the way from Pennsylvania Dutch to German, with a little English and Scandinavian thrown in.

After college (and in the midst of the depression) my mother was hired as a drama teacher at Central High School in Omaha, and my father landed one of the few jobs open to his business school graduating class in Great Falls, Montana, at Carpenter Paper Company. My mother had to request permission from her employer to marry. Early in their marriage they moved from Montana and settled more permanently in northern California.

When I was four my parents bought their first home in Millbrae, California, where I was raised except for an interlude during World War II. My father enlisted (along with his close friends) as a naval officer after the bombing of Pearl Harbor. We spent most of the war years in southern

California where my father worked with naval aviation at Lockheed. Except for my mother's sometimes precarious health (she lost a baby and had other difficulties), those were fun years for me. We were plunked right into the middle of the movie industry. We lived across the street from a major movie studio and after school my friends and I would sit on the studio fence watching Roy Rogers, Dale Evans, Trigger, and all the rest making movies. We used to eat often at a little restaurant that was a favorite of Lucille Ball and Desi Arnaz, and Rex Harrison picked me up in front of Grauman's Chinese Theater and kissed me (which drove my mother wild because all of Hollywood was to her view "wicked"). Later one of my college classmates and I would see John Wayne at the, then famous, Brown Derby Restaurant. After World War II we returned to Northern California and lived for almost a year in San Francisco's Marina District. I love San Francisco, even its fog approaching like "little cat's feet."[2] My parents bought their second house in Millbrae. Millbrae was a community that sociologically and physically grew up the hill just to the west of the San Francisco International Airport. And we grew with the community, owning sequentially three homes on the hill. My mother took care of our house and ran the grammar school lunch program for a few years and my father worked as a middle manager in San Francisco.

My parents were active in community theater. When I was in the fifth grade I managed to get one of the better "kid" roles in a local production of "I Remember Mamma." Because of her involvement, the community theater director knew my mother could coach me. This was the one thing I did as a kid that was more in partnership with a parent rather than in a parent-child relationship. The production went on for several weeks. I had to have special permission to be late to school each day because shows ran late on weeknights.

I completed grammar and high school in Millbrae. From my bedroom I had a view of the San Francisco airport. One could see small planes wafting in from the skies. Recently I went back to that house. I was struck by the crowd of behemoth 747s and DC-10s and their only somewhat smaller sisters, lumbering over every inch of airport property.

FAIR WINDS AND A FOLLOWING SEA

In the early throes of high school I met a girl who was to become my lifelong good friend. Diane Bailiff and I come out of similar boxes and since high school and until recently, have done life VERY differently. Diane has done life much like Gayle Sheehy (1995) says, women our age do life. Sheehy says about the Silent Generation:

> As teens they showed the lowest rates in the twentieth century for almost every social pathology of youth...By the time they reached the age of 24, over *one half* of Silent Generation males and *70 percent* of the females were married.... the women who graduated from college by age 20 to 24 (5.4 percent...) went comparison shopping in their senior years for the best husband products... There weren't a lot of expectations that female Silents would turn out to run for Congress or state legislature or mayor or governor.... [there was] a surge in divorces and displaced mothers.... I found a remarkable surge in efforts by Silent Generation women to expand their knowledge *after* the age of 40. In 1991 nearly a million women over 40 were enrolled in college nationwide. (1995, pp. 29-33)

Diane was very popular and had the attention of the "right" boys, from the football players to the class president. She was president of the Girl's Association, Secretary of the Student Body, and a host of other things. I got good grades and was editor of the yearbook. We hung out a lot at both of our homes, mine the relatively Germanic home in which hugging was a rarity and hers the physically warmer home in which people hugged a lot. Diane's father was an executive with Sears Roebuck. We both worked at Sears during holidays, which paid very well. We also did some synchronized swimming together. Recently we were reminiscing about our teen-age years. We recall going into San Francisco (with our hats and white gloves), and our mothers reminding us to "remember your breeding." I'm sure Diane never had to be told this because she more quickly understood the rules than I did, but my mother constantly told me the boys wouldn't like me if I acted too smart (a box). For comparative purposes I will return to Diane in this essay.

Our group spent as much time as we could at the local (and first) Mel's Drive-In, like the one featured later in *American Graffiti*. We drove our parents crazy because a bunch of us "fraternized" with football players from another local high school. John Madden was in that group of boys and my father spent much of his time kicking those kids out of our house, which was incongruous because my father, until his death, was a staunch football fan (and a financial supporter of University of Nebraska football) and loved John Madden. For the most part, I grew up in Ozzie-and-Harriet land.

Those students from my high school who went to college went to the University of California at Berkeley or San Jose State.[3] Four of us went to Stanford (two men and two women) and this was the first time I felt marginalized, but not for gender reasons. Because of my grades, I was not admitted to Stanford on a regular basis but told that if I attended summer session 1955 and did well, I could return in winter session 1956 (when some number of fall admits had failed). My parents and I long deliberated whether I should instead go to Cal or to one of the Seven Sisters. The Ivy League was still all male and I was not much interested in going to a girl's school. Thus, five days after high school graduation I entered Stanford. Diane entered San Jose State the following fall (1955), and those of the rest of my classmates who went to college entered college in the fall.

My mother reports that she took me to Stanford, turned away, and realized I was gone forever. She was right. Although I was scared stiff that first quarter (and got the best grades I've ever gotten) I have never enjoyed anything more than I enjoyed Stanford. In many ways the classical education at Stanford was wasted on women because, in our own minds, we were there to "get a man" (a box). And, the "gentlemen's C" was still very much in vogue for both males and females (another box). The classical education was superb, featuring a year long course in western civilization (much like Columbia's western civ, and Chicago's and St. John's great books courses). It is a shame classical education no longer exists. Maybe it could be resurrected in conjunction with a broader vision. Western Civ combined with courses in the history of art and the history of religion did far more for me than courses in my major, psychology, because they gave me a broader world view. In fact, I chose the major because, at the time, it had fewer requirements than did many other majors. The psychology department faculty was superb.

Stanford enrolled its first class of 559 students in October, 1891. One fourth of the class was female. By 1899 Jane Stanford was alarmed because women students were approaching 40% and she was concerned that Stanford might turn into a women's college and, thus, be inappropriate as an institution founded in memory of her son. She amended the university's charter to limit enrollment of women to 500 at any one time. This limitation remained in effect until 1933 when the Board of Trustees voted to maintain the same proportion of men and women that had existed in 1899. This limit on the number of women at Stanford continued until 1972 (Fetter, 1995). I don't recall seeing a single student of color at Stanford while I was there. One woman had a child. She was not permitted to live in the dorms with the rest of us, even though her child was living with its grandparents.

By my sophomore year I had almost forgotten who Diane was (or anyone else from my high school except those at Stanford). A fellow student (a year ahead of me), Jim Guthrie, had a very attractive roommate (all roommates then were same sex). Jim and I introduced Diane to his roommate. Ultimately Diane married the roommate and Diane's, Jim's, and my lives, have had interesting intersections since then. I think our comparisons are interesting because it places my life against the backdrop of another woman who lived her early life in a more traditional way, and against the backdrop of a more traditional male who did many of the same things I did. Jim came from a very different set of boxes than did Diane or I.[4] Jim and I would later enjoy long academic careers at the University of California.

Although I tried to take advantage of the opportunities Stanford provided, I missed out on some. For example, I was offered a chance to participate in the first Stanford in Europe program. My father (despite growing business problems) urged me to do so. I announced that I would surely get to Europe within a year or two after graduating from Stanford so no need to go now. Summers provided interesting breaks from school. I worked as a lifeguard and swimming instructor at my high school, worked a summer in Yosemite,[5] and as a summer intern in Washington, DC (where the great fun was to try to glimpse Senator John F. Kennedy in the Senate subway).

Graduation was then upon us. Diane had married and dropped out of San Jose State to work to help her husband finish college. She and her husband had a baby and prepared to move on so he could work on a Ph.D. in philosophy at Penn State. Jim was finishing a master's degree in education and about to take a high school teaching job even further north in California, and I had yet to find a HUSBAND. My closest female friend in college was at Stanford Med School and most of my female classmates were preparing for WEDDINGS, or beginning to work as teachers or secretaries. I looked at the activities of both my parents and the males and females in my graduating class and concluded that the men were having all the fun. In my parent's age group, the men were also in a broader world than the women were. I could see they also carried the vast majority of the burdens. My father was caught in what we call today "re-engineering" and having to think about starting his own small business at age 52 (all this while he was still paying my huge

Stanford tuition; the sole provider box). My mother worried about what the "Jones's thought" about everything (a box for her).

A LOOSE CANNON

I felt my choices were limited.[6] Several things were *acceptable*. I could try to go into nursing, social work, or K-12 teaching until I was MAR-RIED (a box). Stanford launched a huge capital campaign and offered me a clerical job UNTIL I WAS MARRIED. Diane's box was also getting smaller. She was working to help her husband through school (and mother their first child) when she became pregnant—with twins. Diane saw her profession as wife and mother. Accepting surplus food as a graduate student's wife was embarrassing to her, but she accepted as her personal challenge learning to use homemaker skills; such as cooking, sewing, mothering, and wifing. I chose social work and headed to Columbia University's MSW program.

In the early 1960s New York was a great place for two kinds of people—students and the very rich. Students got discounts to all kinds of things. I didn't find the School of Social Work either practically or intellectually stimulating and didn't do well. But New York City glistened and was much fun. I loved Fifth Avenue shops, the museums, Broadway, the whole thing. I hated school.

At Columbia I met a fellow student who would occupy my life for a number of years. Don Roberts was completing his undergraduate years and enjoying the process. This was despite the fact that Don was putting himself through Columbia with a combination of loans and work. He was the son of a construction worker and was raised in a non-Mormon family in Salt Lake City. Don was very aware of being an outsider in the Mormon community. He longed to get out of it and did. He majored in English at Columbia.

I returned to California where I began working for Pacific Gas and Electric Company (PGandE) as a clerical worker, the only kind of job then open to women at PGandE (a box). I also talked to the Department of Psychology at Berkeley about entering its Ph.D. program. I hadn't had some of the more rigorous psychology courses at Stanford one needed in Berkeley's Ph.D. program. If your goal should be getting a husband doesn't it make perfect sense to avoid the hard courses? I took those courses at Berkeley, did well, and entered Berkeley's Ph.D. program in 1961. The next summer I visited my parents (who had moved to southern California) with my roommate, a Ph.D. student in anthropology. In a long diatribe my mother explained her embarrassment that I wasn't yet out of school.

One day in 1961 I saw Don Roberts walking across the Berkeley campus. He was working on a master's degree in English in order to become the Great American Writer. In 1962 I took a leave of absence from the Psychology Department and worked for a year on a research program in educational psychology at Berkeley. I traveled all over the midwest and east collecting data on recent high-school graduates.

Because Don was the answer to my mother's prayers, and some of mine, I extended the leave until fall 1964. We were married at the Stanford chapel in 1963 and went to Hawaii where he had an offer to teach undergraduate English at the University of Hawaii.[7] We decided that I'd make do and find a job doing whatever I could find a job doing. I worked on a project in educational psychology and we saved some money. John Kennedy was killed just after we arrived in Hawaii, which probably made us a little more serious about considering our futures.[8] Rock fever (or island claustrophobia) also contributed. Looking back, I think that year may have been the only truly happy year of the marriage, at least it was the only year that had any carefree quality about it.

SWABBING THE DECKS

We returned to northern California in 1964, and I resumed school. Don took a job with the *Wall Street Journal* in its Educational Services Department. At the time it was reputed that Educational Services only hired men over six feet tall. Some men and all women were in a pretty limiting box if they wanted to work for the *WSJ*.

My mentors at Berkeley were an extraordinary group of men. I started out in clinical psychology (a woman could always go into clinical practice and follow a husband), but soon switched to industrial psychology because I liked the subject matter better (and because Lyman Porter, my advisor, was pretty convincing about its merits). I also reasoned that doing so would broaden my job possibilities because, except for clinical and industrial psychology, the only job opportunities for Ph.D.s in psychology were in academe. The problem is that Berkeley socializes its Ph.D. students to believe the *only* "correct" job is in *academe* (another box). I was successfully socialized. It never occurred to me that there might not be any jobs available for me.

I planned to take my orals in late 1966, but my faculty (Lyman Porter, Ed Ghiselli, and John Campbell, with Ray Miles as the outside examiner) were all disappearing come summer, 1966. This was a full six months before I planned to take my oral exams. By this time Don was in the Ph.D. program in communication research at Stanford and was commuting from Berkeley. We were both exhausted. Mason Haire and Lyman Porter suggested we try to go to Europe for the summer. They had just been there doing the famous Haire, Ghiselli, and Porter (1966) international management study. They worked it out so I could spend time with Elliot Jaques' program at the Tavistock Institute. The spring floods came to Yuba City where Don's parents lived. I felt they expected me to take them into our little Berkeley apartment (less than 400-square feet with little heat) and take care of them (a box), and I said I just couldn't do that, take orals within three weeks and then head to Europe. I was certainly willing to give up the Europe part, but I didn't think one easily and flippantly said to mentors who had arranged my orals in the face of their own needs to leave Berkeley that things had changed. I don't know the extent to which Don argued my case with his parents. I do know my position caused a lot of friction in our family. I think that year was possibly the beginning of the juggling act that has characterized my life ever since.

I took my orals, the faculty dispersed, and we headed to Europe on five-dollars a day (eight years after my Stanford opportunity). I worked at "the Tavi" and Don floated the streets of London, loving the fact that around every corner was one more historically important thing about English literature. We then headed across Europe and back to the United States on a three-month whirlwind. We had saved enough money on our five-dollar a day budget to stop at Columbia on the way home and pay off Don's college loans.

Back again at Berkeley I became the head teaching assistant, which was a major honor, and finished my Ph.D. under Ed Ghiselli's direction in 1967. It is an irony because Ghiselli, one of the leading psychometricians of the time, directed a thesis without a single number in it. My thesis was about leadership transition in organizations and drew from data Ray Miles had left over following a study he had done at Berkeley. I completed my Ph.D. at Berkeley without ever running a rat and with a thesis that didn't have a single number in it—two things no other Berkeley Ph.D. in memory had done. Somehow I had avoided those boxes. I never did another piece of research that didn't include numbers until

1985, a reflection of the fact that until very recently organizational science has been dominated by quantitative research. In 1967 I took a job as a research associate at Stanford's Graduate School of Business, and we lived near Stanford.

DON'T GIVE UP THE SHIP!

Don completed his Ph.D. the following year and had every good job offer in his field (our grades and performance were equally good). I had none and didn't go into the job market in which male faculty members called their male friends in other universities to recommend their male students. Job listings weren't posted (Theodore, 1986, p. 30). My mentors told me they would be in touch with community colleges in whatever geographical area Don took a job. While I think Don would have engaged me in the decision about what we were to do, there was no decision for me to engage—society had seen to that (a box). Don remained at Stanford on soft money which later turned into hard money. One reason he decided to stay at Stanford was that I had "pick up" jobs in the area and no job anywhere else.

Stanford's business school had a tenure track job opening in my field and they hired Larry Pinfield. *Simultaneously,* I maintained my research associate job at the School of Business, did a research project at Stanford Research Institute (now SRI International), and took a lecturer position in psychology at Berkeley; so my resume would show both research and teaching similar to the typical male's resume. A job at a community college was not going to allow me to do that. The only other couple getting Ph.D.s at Berkeley at the same time were Jack and Carol Vale (in psychometrics and experimental psychology). They decided on another strategy, to take two jobs at a less prestigious university. Their marriage failed before Don's and mine, and they both left psychology.

I've often thought my best work at the time was my review of crossnational research on organizations. It was inspired by the classic Haire, Ghiselli, and Porter study, encouragement given me by Ed Ghiselli during my oral to do cross-national work, and the availability at Stanford of Hal Leavitt who hired me as a research associate, and Claude Faucheux who helped me frame the piece. For many years it was cited as a classic in cross-national management.

One day in 1969 I was walking down the hall in Tolman Hall (home of Berkeley's Psychology Department and School of Education), when

I ran into Jim Guthrie who had returned to Palo Alto to teach. He was now married and had three children. He entered the Ph.D. program in education at Stanford,[9] then went to Washington with John Gardner (Secretary of Health, Education and Welfare in the Johnson Administration) in 1966, and finished his Ph.D. in 1967. He came to Berkeley in 1967 as an assistant professor. He had interviewed at Harvard, Berkeley, and Northwestern. I was not to have an assistant professorship until 1970.

Writing in 1973, Berkeley sociologist Arlie Hochschild said:

> ...the classic profile of the academic career is cut to the image of the traditional man with his traditional wife. To ask why more women aren't full professors, or "full" anything else in the upper reaches of the economy, we have to ask first what it means to be a male full professor—socially, morally, and humanly—and what kind of system makes them into what they become.
>
> The academic career is founded on some peculiar assumptions about the relation between doing work and competing with others and getting credit for work, getting credit and building a reputation, building a reputation, building a reputation and doing it while you're young, doing it while you're young and hoarding scarce time, hoarding scarce time and minimizing family life, minimizing family life and leaving it to your wife—the chain of experiences that seems to anchor the traditional academic career. Even if the meritocracy worked perfectly, even if women did not cool themselves out, I suspect there would remain, in a system that defines career this way, only a handful of women at the top (Hochschild, 1994, pp. 126-127).

During the period from 1968 to 1970, John Campbell (at Minnesota) and Chuck Hulin (at Illinois) tried to get me considered for jobs in their psychology departments. I went both places for interviews. Had I been offered a position in a psychology department my research would not look at all like it does today. I like to take a much broader brush to a problem than is characteristic of most research done in psychology departments. For that I am grateful to my business school setting. John later told Don and me that Minnesota didn't want to offer its job to a woman. I was very unhappy and becoming depressed. I recall thinking my unhappiness was all my fault for wanting to do something other than scrub kitchen floors, the traditional female role (a box). Jim often noted how much attention my mother gave to this task. I suggested to Don that it was my problem and we considered putting me into Agnew State Hospital until I could get the thing straightened out.[10] He probably thought that was a little extreme but I was unhappy enough to seek psychological counseling, which didn't work either because the therapist (as well as our parents) couldn't understand why I was unhappy *only* playing house.[11]

DAMN THE TORPEDOES—FULL SPEED AHEAD

The Business School at Berkeley had a job opening and was looking seriously at Bill Ouchi. Bill wasn't very far along with his thesis. In 1970, however, I got the position and was informed that I would come up for tenure six years after my degree (having spent three of those years in positions unconducive to research). Thus, I would be up for tenure in 1973. In 1970, 3.2% of the tenured faculty at Berkeley was female. In Psychology and Sociology no woman had been recruited to tenured positions since 1923. In 1970 the Berkeley Academic Senate (all ladder faculty) included 2% women full professors, 6% women associate professors, and 4% women assistant professors. Sixty percent of the publishing female scholars at Berkeley had lecturer and research titles. In 1972 it is estimated that nationally the social science labor pool had in it 17.9% full-professor, 14% associate professor, and 16% assistant-professor women.[12] There were fourteen assistant professors in the School of Business. I was the only woman. Of those fourteen only two of us remain today. My students were predominantly male. The business school program had 693 undergraduate students, 117 were women; and 565 graduate students, 51 were women.

To give another idea of what Berkeley was like in those days my colleague, Denise Rousseau, a Berkeley Ph.D. (1977), discovered a position paper written by Robert Tryon in the 1960s about the advisability of admitting women to the program. He cited statistics from Berkeley and other universities on the likelihood of women graduates becoming professors and concluded that few did because they married and left the field. Denise wondered why Tryon didn't say anything about the impossibility of women getting jobs in the field (a box). In 1971, 2.8% of the Ph.D.s awarded nationally in business and 24% of the Ph.D.s. awarded in psychology went to women (Spencer & Bradford, 1982, p. 8).

I was grateful for a tenure-track job at a very good university, and like so many women of the time (Theodore, 1986). I looked at the crumbs thrown other women and felt lucky. I was beginning to meet a number of women hired to permanent lectureships or not hired at all. Simeone points out that women in male dominated jobs should compare themselves to similar men, rather than to women excluded from these positions (Simeone, 1987). I feel that had I not been married (a condition that might have led to the perception that I was somewhat "safe") I would not have gotten my job, though the data show that at the time women were not hired *because* they were *single* and were not hired *because* they were *married* (Theodore, 1986). They were just not hired.

My new status gave me an opportunity to apply for research grants, which I could not previously do (making one box larger). In my early years on our faculty, Ray Miles often picked up huge teaching loads to protect me against a heavy teaching load. I have always been grateful to him for this. Ray is one of the nicest colleagues anyone could have (anywhere).

Don and I bought a home near Berkeley. We were urged to move by the School of Business when I was appointed to the faculty (hence Don did the long commute). We had a very traditional marriage. At that time university faculty entertained each other (something I would find hard to believe they do as much of today since both partners in many marriages work). Our social life included both faculties, but primarily the Berkeley faculty. In addition, Stanford underwrote faculty to entertain advisees annually (my recollection is that it was at $3 per head). That sent powerful messages to their faculty about social expectations (and put them into a box). We couldn't reasonably entertain Stanford students so far away so I packed picnics for Don to take to Stanford for his students. The traditional nature of our marriage was reflected in lots of ways. One that I've thought about over the years is that whenever our parents visited (during many holidays) they talked with Don about his work, but NEVER with me about my work. I once asked my mother why this was so. She said Don did such interesting work (his area is the effect of television on children's behavior) that it was fun to talk with him about it and they simply couldn't understand what I did. When our parents visited I was expected to provide traditional entertaining, including expansive meals, etc. My mother thought it was wonderful that Don would help me clean up.

In 1970 Charles O'Reilly walked into my life and over the next few years we had a remarkable publication record together. At the same time Lyman Porter asked me to collaborate with him on a chapter on organizational communication for the first *Handbook of Industrial and Organizational Psychology*. These events (plus federally supported research programs) allowed me to do in depth work in the area of organizational communication. Charles was an absolute delight to have around. He liked to write the middle sections of *Journal of Applied Psychology* pieces and I liked to write the beginnings and ends.

In 1972 Don and I adopted a child. Brett came to us in early December, when he was five weeks old. My tenure case went forward to central campus near the day Brett was born. Some years later a former dean of the Business School told me he was certain that had I looked pregnant (a box) I would not have gotten tenure. Berkeley didn't have maternity leave for faculty members so I began teaching three weeks after Brett came. And our parents finally had something to talk with me about.

Being a mother was fairly frightening. Although one would never know it today, Brett seemed so vulnerable and I was panicked that I'd not be able to juggle all the roles. I didn't want to let my grad students down and neither did I want to do things that would jeopardize Brett. Diane was living in Stevens Point, Wisconsin, where her husband was on the faculty of the University of Wisconsin campus there. She recalls a conversation with her husband at the time Brett came in which they both agreed that I couldn't possibly be a mother and have a career.

As is true of any other academician, part of my job included travel and Don was very good about caring for Brett when I was gone. One year when Brett was small, I nearly equally split my time between Washington, DC and Berkeley. I would arrive home on Friday night and spend the weekend shopping, doing laundry, and cooking and freezing meals for Don and Brett so I could head out again the following Monday (the box was my expectation that the career was acceptable as long as I did the other traditional things married women did). It was a nightmare. Fortunately, Brett was an easy going and wonderful baby.

SMOOTHER SAILING

I received tenure in 1973. Jim received tenure in 1974. In 1973 Diane and her husband and their three children escorted thirty Stevens Point students to Munich and in 1974 she served on the Stevens Point Library Board and was President of Children's Arts.

The Roberts and O'Reilly research took off into a long study of the first F-14 fighter squadrons the Navy introduced into the fleet. We were looking for a way to study groups that had to work together to accomplish some task. I applied for research money from the Office of Naval Research which, at the time, supported considerable organizational research. The commanding officer of the first F-14 squadron was looking for someone to study groups in his squadron. The match was made in heaven. Much of the work was done in San Diego. We often took flights to San Diego that stopped in Orange County where I would hand Brett through the gate to my parents. The reverse occurred for the pick up. A number of people told me that Charles was initially concerned that if or when Brett came my research productivity would fall. The University of California has compared my productivity to that of my colleagues enough times since then to support the notion that Brett didn't interfere with my productivity.

In fall, 1974 Chuck Hulin and I went with our families on sabbatical to the University of Washington in Fred Fiedler's lab. We wanted to complete a book on research methodology and actually made good headway on it while there. It was wonderful to have the time to think about various approaches to understanding organizational behavior and Chuck's and my skills were complementary. Unfortunately, we had to return to our universities before the book was complete. The book languished and in 1976 we asked Denise Rousseau to breathe fresh life into it and help us finish it. Without Denise that book might still be sitting on our desks. Denise has always been a good sounding board, friend, and colleague. The book is one of the first attempts in our field to help researchers deal with the problem of linking constructs across levels of analysis.

Within a nano-second after returning from Seattle, in early 1975, the phone rang and it was Karl Weick (then at Cornell) with "an offer I hope is too good for you to refuse." Karl chaired a research advisory panel for the National Institute for Education which funded research on schools as organizations. His panel represented all forms of social science. For four years we gave away money which is always fun to do. From the mid-1970s until the end of the 1980s, I served on many journal editorial boards and enjoyed thinking about crafting research. It was a complementary task to the Roberts, Hulin, and Rousseau book. Thinking about research to support was also complementary to these activities. The panel offered me many opportunities to meet scholars from other fields and from my own, including Janice Beyer and Bill Starbuck.

Charles completed his Ph.D. in 1976 and went to UCLA. I was promoted to full professor in 1978, right on time. In 1979 Diane received her bachelor's degree in Theater from the University of Wisconsin at Stevens Point. Jim was promoted to full professor in 1980.[13] Up to this point his and my progress are relatively similar. A short time later Berkeley hired Charles and we were admonished not to do any more research together so we might demonstrate our independence from one another. Our interests had diverged by this time anyway, but I've missed his friendship in the ensuing years. To compensate, however, Bill Glick came to Berkeley as a Ph.D. student and was front and center for the next event in my life.

OBE[14]

In 1980 Don left our marriage and moved to Palo Alto where he continued his career at Stanford. I had an eight year old son to raise, and a career to foster. Bill was my student, which, no doubt, put him in a very stressful situation. To his credit he has more than overcome these early frustrations and we wrote some very interesting papers together, including our review of the job characteristics approach to task design which John Campbell (then editor of *Journal of Applied Psychology*) goaded us into writing. Don and his new partner insisted that they were better suited than I was to parent Brett and her two children, and that Brett should live with them. I recall during the break up of the marriage Don asking me what I wanted. My answer was something about how I didn't know what I wanted having spent all my life marching to what I felt was someone else's drumbeat. Yet, if one looks at my life compared to most women my age, it doesn't look that way at all.

Our family home was unsuited to my single parent role because it was on three levels, nestled into a steep hill, which kids really couldn't get around easily, and I couldn't wash the windows or sweep the roof. In 1982 I sold that home and moved to a flat area in a quiet suburban community where Brett could get from place to place on his bike. Like most other middle-class parents, we lived in a community in which it was expected that parents would donate time to their children's school, athletic events and activities (a box). Until Brett graduated from high school I was in his schools on a weekly basis in the absence of his father, and although I didn't coach any of his teams, I went to all the soccer, baseball, football, etc., games. Male coaches were generally rude to me. I was never included in the social network of the school system.

At some point, early in the single parent years I took stock of where I was and what I could offer myself and Brett. One of my conclusions was that whereas academics don't make a lot of money they have opportunities for travel, so Brett has been to Canada, Europe, and Asia and across a good part of the United States. When Nakiye Boyacigiller was a Ph.D. student at Berkeley she introduced Brett (age 9) to "overseas travels with mom" by going to England with us. I thought watching us would be perfect birth control for Nakiye who would certainly not want to have children after being the subject of some of Brett's antics. It didn't work. She has two lovely children and a full blown career in our field. It has been wonderful to watch her bloom into a mature, competent, professional. I have enjoyed many funny and frustrating moments travelling with Brett. He summed up our crazy situation during a trip to Hong Kong and China when he was twelve. He ordered me to "quit wandering off." He thought the kid was supposed to do the wandering, not the mom.

In 1984 my life changed dramatically. In the spring of that year I happened to be at a university lunch with my political science colleague, Todd La Porte. We exchanged a few words about our common interest in organizations in which errors could have catastrophic consequences, but which usually don't commit the errors (high reliability organizations). We had both worked in such organizations (The FAAs air traffic control operations, and Pacific Gas and Electric Company's nuclear power plant at Diablo Canyon). Another such organization came to our attention. After its first overseas deployment the Navy's new nuclear powered aircraft carrier, the USS Carl Vinson, was home ported in Alameda, California (just a hop skip and jump from UC Berkeley).[15] Its second captain knew about my earlier work with F-14s. I met him and we talked about the possibility of doing some research on his ship on the way organizations learn to mitigate risk. In these kinds of organizations "two 'atta boys' don't equal one 'ah shit'."

Todd, other colleagues including Karl Weick, students, and I brought together ship officers and managers from the FAA air traffic control system in the Bay Area, and PGandE's nuclear power plant at Diablo Canyon. The ship sponsored a one day workshop in which managers from these units could talk about their common challenges. As Karl comments in volume 3 of this series, ours is an enduring friendship, which I think is made better through the work we began then and continue today. We make no attempt to publish more than a small amount of it together. Over the years we've worked out the collegiality and it seems to work best this way.

At the end of the workshop there was some mumbling about letting a research team onto the ship during some part of a deployment. My heart went to my feet because by Act of Congress in those years no woman was assigned to sea duty (a box). I was about to hand this goody over to my male colleagues when a Navy officer suggested I persist. I did and spent some part of the next four years at sea with the Navy.

During the first two years of doing the research in the three organizations, we sponsored intermittent workshops in which we discussed our findings with the organizational participants. Too often researchers misinterpret the meaning of their data and we wanted to avoid this problem. This research process continues in the work we're doing today.

The problem with me going to sea during the first year of the work was as one naval officer said to me, "sending you to graduate school before letting you go to kindergarten." I boarded the Carl Vinson when she was at high readiness and about to deploy into the Indian Ocean from Japan. It is better to try to learn about this kind of organization early in her 18 month readiness cycle when there are just a few people aboard, the pace of work is manageable, and everyone is learning. As a result of my naivete some very funny things happened to me at sea.

I wanted Brett to join me in the Orient after my first "at sea period." Christmas, 1984, drew near. My parents had stayed with Brett until his school was out, then his father picked him up for Christmas. Don put him on a plane for Hong Kong the day after Christmas. My mother was concerned that, at age 12, he was too young to be trusted on an airplane to Hong Kong. Don suggested to her that it's tough to get lost on a 747. But the family didn't know that I was stranded in Manilla. Through a series of miracles I managed to arrive in Hong Kong two hours before Brett did. During his growing up we had a lot of near misses. I recall one evening calling Brett at 5 p.m. from Washington, DC, just as my plane was taking off for San Francisco. He was older then and I told him to do his homework and I would be home in time for "Cagney and Lacey," a TV program we both enjoyed, which came on at 10 p.m. I scurried through the door just in time to watch it with him.

The Berkeley research group decided that the first team aboard the carrier would determine the major research areas to be tackled initially. For a novice, an aircraft carrier, particularly one launching and recovering aircraft every 48 to 60 seconds day and night, is a very intense and bewildering environment. It didn't take long to recognize that probably the biggest research payoffs would be in the study of decision making, culture, structure, and adaptation to technology. I addressed part of each of these issues and have published papers on all of them.

How these issues play themselves out in fast paced, technologically sophisticated environments is interesting. For example, the structure of Navy aviation operations is enormously rigid when nothing very interesting is going on. As the practice for battle heats up (simulating the battle), flexibility takes over, people have to be trusted to do their jobs in the way they were trained to do them, and the job of the commanding officer is to have the big picture (or bubble). Micro managing is not only unsatisfactory in such situations, it can be disastrous.

As soon as I returned from my first "at sea period" in January, 1985, I became associate dean of the undergraduate school of business at Berkeley. I had no idea how I was going to do that job, teach, raise a child, go to sea, do research in the other organizations I was studying, and write proposals for research funding. In 1986 I became the third woman Fellow in the Academy of Management. I understand the first woman Fellow was John Slocum's (volume 4) aunt. Jim served as Dean of the School of Education from 1980 to 1983, and as chair of the faculty from 1985 to 1988. Diane divorced in 1983 and was Director of the Higher Education Location Program (providing toll free access to all information about the University of Wisconsin system) at the University of Wisconsin and working on a Ph.D. in educational administration at Madison.

I've ridden four of the Navy's nuke carriers, and was aboard both the USS Enterprise and the USS Carl Vinson during the filming of "Top Gun." Fortunately by that time I knew a whole lot more about what to do aboard an aircraft carrier than did a Hollywood film crew. Getting on and off aircraft carriers is an interesting experience if the carrier is not tied to a pier (it truly is a postage stamp out there), as is doing deck work at night. Our work has received very good press and had good extramural funding. I've been personally fortunate to have the sponsorship of the second of Vinson's captains (Tom Mercer), who retired as a two star admiral, and the friendship of Tom and his wife, Becky.

In 1987 the then provost of the professional schools at Berkeley made a tongue-in-cheek appointment. He put me on the chancellor's oversight committee for the ROTC at Berkeley (which has an interesting history going back to the 1960s). I've served on many campus faculty committees and done all the jobs one should do in the business school, but this was definitely the strangest. That committee was composed of only white male faculty members with some sort of experience or history with the military, and the way one retires from it is to leave the university or die.

That same year Denise Rousseau and her husband, Robert Cooke, separated. Our Berkeley research project had three co-principal investigators, two Berkeley colleagues and myself, and was supported by ONR and NSF. The project purchased, at a research discount rate, a large number of copies of the culture instrument Rob and Denise developed from Rob's consulting firm. Rob filed a law suit against *me* for copyright infringement even though the project was lead by three co-principal investigators. The single publication (at that time) using his instrument was co-authored by Todd La Porte, Denise, and myself. The suit lasted until 1996. Rob also requested the American Psychological Association and the American Sociological Association to censure Denise and me. It was terribly costly in time and stress and was ultimately thrown out by two courts of law and considered frivolous by the APA and ASA. Another box to deal with.

AT THE EDGE OF THE ENVELOPE

In 1991 I was asked to serve on one of the committees of the Marine Board of the National Academy of Science.[16] Through this work I met Bob Bea on our Civil Engineering faculty, who was a member of the Marine Board and also of the National Academy of Engineering. Bob graciously introduced me to the civilian maritime industry in which there was growing concern with risk because of the 1989 Exxon Valdez accident. About the accident, our doctoral student Bill Moore and I wrote that it was caused by the failure of a whole system of organizations.[17]

Bob and I designed some research together in the safety area and were able to attract sufficient money to Berkeley to support a number of business and engineering graduate students. We have some interesting difficulties working together because of our different disciplinary paradigms. I am completely inductive and he completely deductive. We speak very different languages and see as important different aspects of the work. One adds to this the different paradigms in engineering and business education and the situation becomes prickly. We've spent a number of years trying to work across these paradigm induced boxes.

Within the last few years I've also had the good fortune of becoming acquainted with managers in other arenas who, for one reason or another, have had to be more concerned with reliable operations. Three things seem to drive increased sensitivity to reliability: (a) the fear being subjected to television news coverage, (b) the environmental movement, and (c) the cost of litigation. We've worked with some of the major regulatory agencies (the U.S. Coast Guard, the U.S. Navy, the Federal Aviation Administration, the Mineral Management Service of the Department of Interior, California State Lands Commission, etc.) on safety policy, and on working to minimize the limitations of their accident data bases. Today we can learn little or nothing from existing data bases about the precursors to accidents because they fail to include organizational data at all, and when they do include operator data they do so in a form that is not useful to people trying to understand how accidents occur (e.g. it's a training problem—what training problem?).

In 1996 the Navy established a Quality Management Board to assess aviation safety in response to losing three F-14D Tomcats and one Marine Harrier. I serve on that board, have just joined the Human Factors Standing Committee of the National Academy of Science (with Ben Schneider, Dan Ilgen, Terry Connolly, and others), and am on the Board of Advisors for the newly established National Patient Safety Foundation of the American Medical Association. We're designing and conducting research on reliable operations with oil companies, commercial airlines, firefighters, pediatric intensive care units, and police negotiators, surely activities that could go well into the next century.

Brett has been in college and on his own since 1991. My father died in 1988. Since 1991 my mother's health has deteriorated. She requires almost constant care, some of which I provide. It is heavy, depressing, and stressful work. Recently one of my colleagues literally screamed that I shouldn't devote time to my mother because it was interfering with our work. If one colleague says this, others think it, just as they did when Brett was born. The data show that in the United States elder care is handled primarily by women relatives; wives, sisters, and daughters (a box).[18] I would feel very guilty if I didn't do this. Many men my age seem to expect that wives and sisters are responsible for caring for aging parents.

Other discontinuities also exist between men and women in academe. I am the lowest paid full professor in the OB area at Berkeley, and by quite a substantial amount. As Simeone states:

> Current research shows that the salary gap still exists, and that it continues to widen as one moves up the ladder.... the longer women have been employed, the

> smaller their salary is likely to be in relation to men. A 1977 study of science doc-
> torates showed that in the social sciences there was a 2.8 percent difference
> between male and female assistant professors, but a 13.1 percent difference at the
> full professor level.... These data demonstrate the cumulative effects of discrim-
> ination, as discrimination against women early in their careers is perpetuated and
> magnified as their careers progress. (Simeone, 1987, pp. 31-31)

I make eighty-one cents for every dollar the man who was promoted to the same rank at the same time I was makes. And this is before consulting, summer monies, endowed chairs, etc., which have all advantaged the men in our department, and others across the country. In 1994 Jim converted his Berkeley earnings into retirement and took a much higher paying job at Vanderbilt University. Had he stayed at Berkeley, for every dollar he made I would have made sixty-five cents. In 1997 Diane became Dean of Student Affairs in her university. Her salary is comparable to that of her male and female counterparts across her state's higher education system.

I have never been denied a merit increase at Berkeley and always came up for them "on time," but was never accelerated. One way faculty members at Berkeley accelerate their salaries is to demonstrate their "market worth." I could not do this when Brett was younger because I was afraid that a trip to the marketplace might also result in a trip to child custody court (a box). I didn't want to put Brett in the position of having to choose where to live or who to live with. I didn't want to risk losing him. Although I'm willing to and love doing research on risk I'm not willing to engage in it, at least not in those proportions.

UNODIR[19]

What would I have done differently? Been born later. Eliminate some of the nagging fears and anxieties I have about being accepted by my colleagues. But, *un*less *o*therwise *dir*ected I plan to continue with the research that intrigues me. I don't think anyone in the organizational sciences has had the opportunity to go into as many interesting and different organizations as I have. I enjoy working on the policy issues that seem to be just coming to focus in a world far more environmentally sensitive than it has been in the past.

As one can see my career is different from that of most women, even college educated women, my age. It is also clear that while Jim and I began at Berkeley relatively similarly (probably because somehow I made up the first three years of it when he had a "real" job and I didn't), today we are anything but similar with me doing exactly what Simeone states, dropping further and further behind.

I'm not the first woman on the faculty in the School of Business. The 1970-71 catalog lists an *emeritus* female *assistant* professor of accounting. The other emeritus faculty member listed in that catalog was a male *full* professor. Indicative of organizational structural impediments to women belonging to the faculty is the existence on campus today of *The* Faculty Club and The Women's Faculty Club. Denied the privileges of The Faculty Club the first academic women joined together with librarians, administrative assistants, faculty wives and women graduate students to form a women's faculty club. The image of the middle class American woman's role in society in place after World War II has not been altogether dispelled, at least among an older population. As Doris Goodrich presents it:

> ...housewives were "homemakers," houses were "homes" and "togetherness" described the most rewarding marital relationship. The family unit was centered on super-mom, a model of skillful housekeeping, motherly sensitivity, and selfless devotion to others. This ideal American family lived in Suburbia, a new kind of community composed of people of the same age group, sharing similar racial characteristics and socioeconomic backgrounds. In this community, conformity was the ruling ethic; children were taught to subordinate their individuality to the welfare of the group. (Goodrich, 1994, p. 22)

Talk about boxes! In response to this, Jim said, "it works." It did work for most traditional males and their traditional homes, but it didn't work for me. As Karl Weick pointed out to me not long ago, I've been at the starting line of three major areas of organizational research; cross-national, communication, and high reliability organizations. I've also contributed to the research methodology literature. Today we're embarking on a new journey into risk mitigating organizations as systems. Risk mitigating organizations are often severely regulated. Even if they're not they usually have interesting interdependencies with other organizations, all working together to mitigate risk. A growing example of this is in the health industry. I was also at the starting line of the field's inclusion of women. It is hard to be at the starting line. But my experience might be a lesson to others that boxes can be used in some interesting ways. They can and do confine. They can also be stacked and used as building blocks to accomplishments people seek. It has not been and never will be easy for men and women to figure out how to stack boxes and use them as stepping stones, rather than to let them weigh them down.

PUBLICATIONS

1964

With D. Fitzgerald. Semantic profiles and psychosexual interests as indicators of identification. *Personnel and Guidance Journal,44*(8), 802-806. [Also in *Proceedings* of the American Psychological Association, Los Angeles, California]

1968

With R.E. Miles, & L.V. Blankenship. Organizational leadership, satisfaction and productivity: A comparative analysis. *Academy of Management Journal, 11*, 401-414.

1969

With E.J. Webb. Unconventional uses of content analysis in social science. In G. Gerbner, O.R. Holsti, K. Krippendorff, W.J. Paisley, & P.J. Stone (Eds.), *The analysis of communication content: Developments in scientific theories and computer techniques* (pp. 319-339). New York: Wiley.

1970

On looking at an elephant: An evaluation of cross-cultural research related to organizations. *Psychological Bulletin, 74*, 327-350.

1971

Leadership sift in organizations. In H.C. Kindgren, D. Byrne, & F. Lindgren (Eds.), *Current research in psychology: A book of readings* (pp. 431-435). New York: John Wiley. [Also in *Proceedings* of the American Psychological Association, (1970) *5*, Miami, FL]
With G.A. Walter, & R.E. Miles. A factor analytic study of a job satisfaction items designed to measure Maslow need categories. *Per-

sonnel Psychology, 24, 205-220. [Also in *Proceedings* of the American Psychological Association, (1970) *5,* Miami, FL]

1972

With W.K. Graham (Eds.), *Comparative studies in organizational behavior.* New York: Holt, Rinehart and Winston.

1973

With D.H. Rost. GrundEragen empirish-pedagogischer forschungs hinweise zum vrstandnis und zur Kritik Erfahrungs-wissenschaftlicher untersuchungen in der erziehungswissenschaft, GFPF Materielen, *5,* Frankfurt A.M. [Criteria of empirical educational research: Aspects of understanding and criticism.]

With F. Savage. Twenty questions: A management strategy for utilizing various measures of job satisfaction. *California Management Review, 15,* 82-89.

With N. Logan, & C.A. O'Reilly. Job satisfaction among part-time and full-time workers. *Journal of Vocational Behavior, 3,* 33-42.

With C.A. O'Reilly. Job satisfaction among whites and non-whites: A cross-cultural approach. *Journal of Applied Psychology, 57,* 295-299.

A symposium: Cross-national organizational research. In K.H. Roberts, & C.C. Snow (Eds.), *Industrial Relations, 12* (whole number).

1974

A thousand ways: A flexible design for behavioral research in multinational organizations. R. Holton & S.P. Sethi (Eds.), *Management of the multinationals* (pp. 368-376). New York: Free Press.

With C.A. O'Reilly. Information filtration in organizations: Three experiments. *Organizational Behavior and Human Performance, 11,* 253-265.

With C.A. O'Reilly. Failures in upward communication in organizations: Three possible culprits. *Academy of Management Journal, 17,* 205-215.

With C.A. O'Reilly. Measuring organizational communication. *Journal of Applied Psychology, 59,* 321-326.

With C.A. O'Reilly, & G.E. Bretton. Professional employees' preference for upward mobility: An extension. *Journal of Vocational
Behavior, 5*, 139-146.

With D.H. Rost. *Analyse and bewertung empirischer untersuchungen.*
Weinham, West Germany: Beltz.

With C.A. O'Reilly, G.E. Bretton, & L.W. Porter. Organizational communication and organizational theory: A communication failure?
Human Relations, 27, 501-524.

1975

With C.A. O'Reilly. Individual differences in personality, position in the
organization, and job satisfaction. *Organizational Behavior and
Human Performance, 14*, 144-150.

1976

With L.W. Porter. Organizational communication. In M.D. Dunnette
(Ed.), *Handbook of industrial and organizational psychology* (pp.
1553-1589). Chicago: Rand-McNally.

With C.A. O'Reilly. Relationships among components of credibility
and communication in work units. *Journal of Applied Psychology,
61*, 99-102.

With N. Cerruti & C.A. O'Reilly. The effect of training designed to
increase organizational communication in work units. *Nursing
Research, 25*, 197-200.

With F.J. Smith, & C.L. Hulin. Ten year job satisfaction trends in a stable organization. *Academy of Management Journal, 19*, 462-468.

1977

With L.W. Porter (Eds.). *Communication in organizations.* Middlesex,
England: Penguin.

Communications in organizations. In B. Wolman (Ed.), *International
encyclopedia of neurology psychiatry psychoanalysis and psychology.* New York: Van Nostrand Reinhold.

With C. Folkins, C.A. O'Reilly, & S. Miller. Physical environment
and job satisfaction. *Community Mental Health Journal, 13*,
24-30.

With C.A. O'Reilly. Task group structure, communication, and effectiveness in three organizations. *Journal of Applied Psychology, 62,* 674-681.

1978

With C.L. Hulin, & D.M. Rousseau. *Toward an interdisciplinary science of organizations.* San Francisco: Jossey-Bass.
With S. Miller, S., C.A. O'Reilly, & C. Folkins. Factor structure and scale reliabilities of the adjective check list across time. *Journal of Consulting and Clinical Psychology, 46,* 189-191.
With C.A. O'Reilly. Organizations as communication structures: An empirical approach. *Human Communication Research, 4,* 283-293.
With C.A. O'Reilly. Supervisor influence and subordinate mobility aspirations as moderators of consideration and initiating structure. *Journal of Applied Psychology, 63,* 96-102.

1979

With C.A. O'Reilly. Some correlates of communication roles in organizations. *Academy of Management Journal, 22,* 42-57.

1980

With L. Burstein (Eds.). *New directions in methodology: Aggregation issues in organizational science.* San Francisco: Jossey-Bass.
With S.B. Stafford. Exporting: U.S. influence. *The Exporter, 7*(11), 17.

1981

With W.H. Glick. The job characteristics approach to job redesign: A review and critique. *Journal of Applied Psychology, 66,* 193-217.

1982

With W.H. Glick, & N.L. Rotchford. A frame of reference approach to investigating part- and full-time workers. *International Review of Applied Psychology, 32,* 327-344.

With N.L. Rotchford. Part time workers as missing persons in organizational research. *Academy of Management Review, 7*, 228-234.

1983

With N. Boyacigiller. Survey of cross national organizational researchers: Their views and opinions. *Organizational Studies, 4*(4), 375-386.

With A. Beckenstein, & L. Gabel. A manager's guide to antitrust compliance. *Harvard Business Review, 60*(5), 94-102.

1984

With N. Boyacigiller. Cross national organizational research: The grasp of the blind men. In B.M. Staw & L.L. Cummings (Eds.), *Research in organizational behavior* (pp. 423-475). Greenwich, CT: JAI Press.

Organizational communication. In F. Kast & J. Rosenzweig (Eds.), *Modules in management*. Chicago: SRA Associates.

With W.H. Glick. Hypothesized interdependence, assumed independence. *Academy of Management Review, 9*, 722-735.

1985

With R. Blair, & P. McKechnie. Vertical and network communication in organizations: The present and the future. In R. McPhee & P. Thompkins (Eds.), *Organizational communication: traditional themes and new directions* (pp. 55-78). Beverly Hills, CA: Sage.

With W. Boeker, R. Blair, & M.F. Van Loo. Analysis of the effectiveness of organizational initiatives designed to facilitate the advancement of women in management. *California Management Review, 27*, 147-157.

1987

With F. Jablin, L. Putnam, & L.W. Porter (Eds.), *Handbook of organizational communication*. Beverly Hills, CA: Sage.

With N. Euske. Evolving perspectives in organizational theory: Implications for communication research. In F. Jablin, L. Putnam, K.H. Roberts, & L.W. Porter (Eds.), *Handbook of organizational communication* (pp. 41-69). Beverly Hills, CA: Sage.

With G.I. Rochlin & T.R. La Porte. The self-designing high-reliability organization: Aircraft carrier flight operations at sea. *Naval War College Review, 40*, 76-90.

1988

With S.B. Sloane. An aggregation problem and organizational effectiveness. In B. Schneider & D. Schoorman (Eds.), *Facilitating organizational effectiveness* (pp. 125-144). Lexington, MA: Lexington Press.

1989

With G. Gargano. Managing interdependencies in high reliability organizations. In M.A. Von Glinow & S. Morman (Eds.), *Managing complexity in high technology organizations* (pp. 147-159). New York: Oxford University Press.

With D.M. Rousseau. Research in nearly failure free high reliability organizations: Having the bubble. *IEEE Transactions on Engineering Management, 36,* 132-139.

New challenges to organizational research: High reliability organizations. *Industrial Crisis Quarterly, 3*, 111-125.

With W. Glick, P. Weissenberg, D. Whetton, J. L. Pearce, A. Bedeian, H. Miller, & R. Klimoski. Reflections on the field of organizational behavior. *Journal of Management Systems, 2*, 25-39.

1990

Some characteristics of one type of high reliability organization. *Organization Science, 1*, 160-176.

Managing high reliability organizations. *California Management Review, 32*, 101-113.

1991

With D. Hunt. *Organizational behavior*. Boston: PWS Kent.

1992

Structuring to facilitate migrating decisions in reliability enhancing organizations. In L. Gomez-Mejia & M.W. Lawless (Eds.), *Advances in global high technology Management: Top manage-*

ment and executive leadership in high technology (Vol. 2, pp. 171-
192). Greenwich, CT: JAI Press.

1993

New challenges to understanding organizations. New York: Macmillan.
Some aspects of organizational culture and strategies to manage them in
   reliability enhancing organizations. *Journal of Managerial Issues,
   5,* 165-181.
With W.E.D. Creed, & S.K. Stout. Organizational effectiveness as a theoretical foundation for research on reliability enhancing organizations. In K. H. Roberts (Ed.), *New challenges to understanding
   organizations* (pp. 40-53). New York: Macmillan.
With W.H. Moore. Bligh reef dead ahead: The grounding of the Exxon
   Valdez. In K.H. Roberts (Ed.), *New Challenges to understanding
   organizations* (pp. 157-167). New York: Macmillan.
With W.E.D. Creed. Epilogue: In K.H. Roberts (Ed.), *New challenges to
   understanding organizations* (pp. 168-172). New York: Macmillan.
With C. Libuser. From Bhopal to banking, organizational design can
   mitigate risk. *Organizational Dynamics, 21,* 15-26.
With K.E. Weick. Collective mind and organizational reliability: The
   case of flight operations on an aircraft carrier deck. *Administrative
   Science Quarterly, 38,* 357-381.

1994

Organizational behavior. In V.S. Ramachandran (Ed.), *Encyclopedia of
   human behavior* (Vol. 3, pp. 367-376). San Diego, CA: Academic
   Press.
Functional and dysfunctional organizational linkages. In C. Cooper &
   D.M. Rousseau (Eds.), *Trends in organizational behavior* (Vol. 1,
   pp. 1-11). Sussex, England: Wiley.
With S.K. Stout, & J.J. Halpern. Decision dynamics in two high reliabil-
   ity military organizations. *Management Science, 40,* 614-624.
With M. Grabowski. Human systems in the marine industry. In *National
   Academy of Science, Marine Navigation and Piloting: Minding
   the Helm.* Washington, D.C.: National Academy Press.

With D.M. Rousseau, & T.R. La Porte. The culture of high reliability: Quantitative and qualitative assessment aboard nuclear powered aircraft carriers. *Journal of High Technology Management Research, 5,* 141-161.

1995

With R.L. Klein, & G.A. Bigley. Organization culture in high reliability organizations: An extension. *Human Relations, 48,* 771-793.

1996

With M. Grabowski. Human and organizational errors in large systems. *IEEE Transactions on Systems. Mans and Cybernetics, 26,* 2-16.

With M. Grabowski. Organizations, technology, and structuring. In S.R. Clegg, C. Hardy, & W. Nord (Eds.), *Handbook of organization studies* (pp. 409-423). London: Sage.

A non-linear life. In D. Cyr & B. Horner-Reich (Eds.), *Scaling the ivory tower: Stories of women in business* (pp. 161-172). Chicago: Praeger.

With R.G. Bea. Human and organization factors in designs, construction and operation of offshore platforms. *Journal of Petroleum Technology.*

With T. Mannarelli, & R.G. Bea. Learning how organizations mitigate risk. *Journal of Contingencies and Crisis Management, 4,* 83-92.

With R. Bea. Crisis management and the near miss. *Surveyor* [Quarterly Publication of the American Bureau of Shipping], September, 20-23.

1997

In their own words. In R. Field, *Human behavior in organizations: A Canadian perspective* (2nd ed.). Toronto: Prentice Hall Canada.

With M. Grabowski, & J.R. Harrald. Decision support and organizational forms in a high velocity environment: Responses to catastrophic oil spills. In M. Grabowski & W.A. Wallace (Eds.), *Advances in expert systems for management: Evaluation and value in knowledge based systems.* Greenwich, CT: JAI Press.

With M. Grabowski. Risk mitigation in large scale systems: Lessons
from high reliability organizations. *California Management
Review, 39,* 152-162.
Lessons from other industries. In *Proceedings* of the 1996 International
Workshop on Human Factors in Offshore Operations. New York:
American Bureau of Shipping.

1998

With M. Grabowski (in press). Risk mitigation in virtual organizations.
Organization science.

ACKNOWLEDGMENTS

"Having the Bubble" is having the larger picture of an event, an organization,
or any other entity. My thanks to Diane Bailiff, Jim Guthrie, Kathy Johnson,
Joanne Martin, Donald Roberts, Christina Rosen, Denise Rousseau, George
Strauss, and Karl Weick for reading an earlier version of this. I didn't make all
the changes they suggested. Though I didn't ask him to comment on this I will
always be grateful to Brett for being there. I am indebted to the women who
preceded me in academe and dedicate this to those who follow.

NOTES

1. Define "boxes" however you like. That is the essence of sense making.
2. Probably a "Caenism." Herb Caen was San Francisco's most popular newspaper columnist until his death in 1996. When I was in high school I interviewed him for
a class project.
3. In the United States in 1959 5.9% of females over 25 had four years of college.
In 1956 two times as many men as women completed college (Bureau of the Census,
1960, p. 109).
4. He went to public school in Virginia and San Francisco and attended Pasadena
City College before entering Stanford. He reports he was not terribly happy at Stanford.
5. I worked as a maid, Jim worked there as a manager.
6. Jim did not feel his choices were limited. Diane had already made her choice
and the issue of choices didn't occur to her again until some years later.
7. One had to be pretty careful that whoever one married was acceptable to the
family. One of my cousins fell in love with a Jewish naval officer. Her family threatened
to disinherit her if she married him (a box). She never married.
8. Jim reports that the Kennedy assassination also had a huge impact on his career
choice. Diane was living with her family in Las Vegas. Shortly before the assassination,
Kennedy had been in Las Vegas and she and her husband took their children to see his

motorcade. She says, "the days that followed convinced me of the value of ceremony as a signal for the critical moments in our lives. I needed to know when closure had been reached."

9. In later years Jim commented that he felt the appropriate thing for him to do after graduation from college was to marry and have children.

10. Arleigh Hochschild (1994) calls something like this "autodiscrimination."

11. Carolyn Heilbrun discusses something similar: "My avoidance of therapy is, however, a generational one: in my young adult days had there been therapists sympathetic to feminism and with genuine, post Freudian understanding of the conflicts in women's lives, I could certainly have consulted one" (1997, pp. 121-122). A similar comment is made by Dorothy Smith (1994, p. 53).

12. By 1988 the average percent of female *full* professors in the Ivy League was 7.8 and in the Big Ten 8.6 (Academe, Bulletin of the American Association of University Professors, March-April 1989, Appendix 1, 22-65.)

13. In 1981 women's share of full professorship jobs nationally was 6.5% (American Association of University Professors, cited in Nine month faculty salaries for 1981-82. *Chronicle of Higher Education*, 7 July, 1982, p. 10). Berkeley first promoted a woman to full professor in 1918. She had been on the faculty since 1904 (Clifford, 1989, p. 12).

14. Overcome By Events.

15. The Nimitz class carriers displace 96,000 tons of water and have decks three football fields long. They carry over eighty aircraft, 6,000 men (then), and serve 18,150 meals a day. The technical manuals would form a pile as high as the Washington monument (555 feet). In this organization when a decision is made to turn right 6,000 people turn right.

16. Following the end of her short marriage to Larry Cummings, Diane completed her Ph.D. in 1991 and took a job as Associate Dean for Student Life at the University of Wisconsin at Whitewater.

17. Other pieces with Bob, his students, and mine have resulted from the collaboration.

18. Department of Transportation (1996), personal communication.

19. It is customary for Navy ship captains to radio their intentions to their commanding officers just before disappearing over the horizon, followed by UNODIR.

REFERENCES

Bureau of the Census. (1960). *Statistical Abstract United States*. Washington, DC: U.S. Department of Commerce.

Clifford, G. (1989). *Lone voyagers*. New York: City University of New York, Feminist Press.

Ervin-Tripp, S. (1995). Women activists in the seventies: Multiple routes to affirmative action.

Fetter, J.H. (1995). *Questions and admissions: Reflections on 100,000 admissions decisions at Stanford*. Stanford, CA: Stanford University Press.

Goodrich, D. (1994). Varieties of sociological experience. In K.P. Meadow & R.A. Wallace (Eds.), *Gender and the academic experience: Berkeley women sociologists*. Lincoln: University of Nebraska Press.

Haire, M., Ghiselli, E.E., & Porter, L.W. (1966). *Managerial thinking*. New York: Wiley.

Heilbrun, C. (1997). *The last gift of time*. New York: Dial Press.

Hochschild, A. (1994). Inside the clockwork of male careers. In K.P. Meadow & R.A. Wallace (Eds.), *Gender and the academic experience: Berkeley women sociologists*. Lincoln: University of Nebraska Press.

Lehrman, S. (1997). Billy Tipton: Self-made man. *Stanford Magazine*, (May/June), 50-51.

Levy, H.S. (1992). *The lotus lovers: The complete history of the curious erotic custom of footbinding in China*. Buffalo, NY: Prometheus Books.

Sheehy, G. (1995). *New passages: Mapping your life across time*. New York: Random House.

Simeone, A. (1987). *Academic women working towards equality*. South Hadley, MA: Bergin and Garvey.

Smith, D. (1994). A Berkeley education. In K.P. Orlans & R.A. Wallace (Eds.), *Gender and the academic experience: Berkeley women sociologists*. Lincoln: University of Nebraska Press.

Spencer, M.L., & Bradford, E. (1982). Status and needs of women scholars. In *Handbook for women scholars*. San Francisco: Americas Behavioral Research Corporation.

Theodore, A. (1986). *The campus troublemakers: Academic women in protest*. Houston, TX: Cap and Gown Press.

Wickham Skinner

GETTING TO SEE WHAT'S OUT THERE

WICKHAM SKINNER

PART 1

Life Before Becoming A Professor

With one older and one younger sister I grew up in Cincinnati. Both parents frequently reminded us that some of our ancestors had been illustrious. They included a general in the War of 1812, a congressman, a naval admiral, and an ambassador to Greece, Latvia, and Turkey. My father was a civil engineer and my mother was an artist. They were certainly independent-minded, and, Alice, my wife of 51 years says that I am independent-minded, too.

My father only worked for himself, as a consulting engineer, and never built any kind of an organization. He had a secretary, occasional "rod men" for his surveying, and an office downtown, but he seemed to count on his reputation to make the phone ring.

Clearly it rang often until the depression hit. He built a fine colonial house in the close-in suburbs, bought a new Packard touring car, took up golf and joined a modest country club. Business was good,

Management Laureates, Volume 5, pages 243-284.
Copyright © 1998 by JAI Press Inc.
All rights of reproduction in any form reserved.
ISBN: 0-7623-0178-3

but it was tied to construction and the depression had a terrible impact on his income.

When my father's business dropped off, my mother, an art teacher and supervisor before she married, went back to teaching, this time as a first grade teacher in a private school. She was good at it and liked it, but it was tiring and I think it was a discouraging turn of events. For she was a free spirit and the time pressures, steady demands on her and financial stringency certainly made life more of a struggle than she had expected.

There simply was no money. She was given $5.00 a day to buy the groceries and run the house. One winter I had no sweater, another no jacket, and several winters no gloves. Somehow they held onto the house, kept the cars running and we always had very merry Christmases. I wore hand-me down clothes, very good ones, from the son of a wealthy and kind friend of my mother's.

Now this may sound very grim, and I do remember needing that winter jacket, but in fact it was not grim for me at all. I know it was terribly hard for my parents to have my father's promising career cut back by hard times, but my childhood could not have been happier. Sure, I was always hoping things would go better for my parents, but for me growing up as I did was wonderful. Here's why:

First off, both parents were loving and supportive, always encouraging a somewhat hesitant son to be doing more daring and enterprising things. Secondly, my two sisters were fun to be with. The older one and I were closer, partly because we had gotten started together before the younger one came along, and partly because after the fifth grade we were always in the same class together in school. But we all three took bike rides and roller skated and played outside together and had great fun. For twelve or more years we all went to the Swedenborgian church for Sunday school. Year after year we all received prizes for perfect attendance.

What I remember from Sunday school (and from my grandmother) was the importance of being kind. I am not claiming that I am always kind; far from it, but that was the imprint from Sunday school. I was the peacemaker between the two girls and somehow seemed to have a role of trying to make everyone, including my parents, happier.

I had two great neighborhood friends, Sam Wilson and Jack Hollister, and we played touch football in the fall and baseball the rest of the year. We were in and out of each other's homes day and night, I visited them at their summer homes, especially loving Sam's seacoast place in

Maine. We never argued with each other. We invented imaginative games of all sorts, inside and out; I had my bicycle and when neither of my two friends were around I happily rode my bike for miles.

I did all the work around our house for five to twenty-five cents an hour. If I didn't cut the grass because I was away visiting my friends, it did not get cut. The family depended on me completely and I think I rather enjoyed coming through as needed.

As a teenager I was embarrassed that our house desperately needed painting and our cars were not only old but were of old-fashioned designs. But though that did bother my sisters, those things were fairly minor to me.

Another positive factor in my happy childhood was sports. I was taught baseball and football by two wonderful uncles and by kind classmates. The uncles were often unemployed because of the depression and they came over to our house and spent hours throwing and catching and punting with me. My father was interested in sports but had not been much of an athlete and was too busy at his work or waiting for clients to coach me. But those uncles did and, after a slow start, I became a fair athlete, making the grade school and high school teams in baseball, basketball, and football.

I was totally enthusiastic about sports but never a star. An end in football, I played five years in grade school, four years of high school, and several years in college and never scored a touchdown! But I always expected to and looked forward to every game as the day when I would do something heroic. The fact that I never did just did not bother me—our teams lost again and again but we all loved playing and always expected to win.

Besides my happy life at home and with my two boyhood friends and constant sports the school which I attended from K to 12 must have contributed enormously to my development. It was a small private school in Cincinnati. My mother arranged scholarships for all three of us somehow, and to the best of my knowledge year after year we were educated there without paying tuition. The teachers at University School were outstanding. It was a no-nonsense school in terms of standards and grades but they made it interesting and important.

I had remarkable classmates for those 12 years and would love to describe many of them. But two in particular, Bob Steiner and Joe Weiss were my intellectual leaders and kind, fun-loving friends. We are in close communication to this day. They have both gone onto outstanding careers of extraordinary importance, with impact on a national scale. More on this later. The spirit of the school was a combination of seriousness about education, get ready for college, cooperate together and be supportive of each other, and sports and drama and dances, learning to be courteous and kind to each other. A most remarkable place.

My high school teachers in Latin, English, History, Mathematics, and Chemistry are unforgettable. I was a good student but clearly well behind Joe and Bob and one other. I do believe I had to work harder to keep up, but I did that. Of those of us who took the College Boards all but one of us passed with at least three honors.

Before leaving this part of the story I want to tell about an amazing set of parallels in the careers of Bob Steiner, Joe Weiss and myself, three members of the twelve student University School Class of 1941. Steiner had great success in business. He led his toy company into daring new investments, including the very first advertising of particular toys on national television. The company grew, prospered, and he subsequently sold it. Financially secure, he became an adjunct professor in marketing and a writer in economics, his master's level degree. He was then invited to become an academic visitor on the staff of the Federal Trade Commission and went on to publish many articles in the most prestigious journals of economics, marketing, advertising, and law.

The significance of this, however, is not just his success but that he became a rebel against certain conventional, accepted rules and standard wisdom of economics. He has fought with increasing success to change the way economists analyze consumer goods industries and the premises concerning the importance of distributors and the relationships between manufacturers and distributors' margins. Recently he found a major set of errors in the census designations by the omission of those enterprises that are conventional manufacturers except that they manufacture offshore for their own brand names. This change will be included in the 1997 census of manufactures under "Own-Brand Marketers." Independent-minded? Yes, indeed!

Joe Weiss went to medical school and became a psychiatrist. After about fifteen years of practice he became gradually convinced that much of psychiatric theory and practice was just wrong and often did more harm than good. He began to develop his own theory and attracted around him a group of researchers and practitioners. Over the next ten years he tested and improved his ideas. This has resulted in three books, a series of articles, including a well known piece in *Scientific American*, speeches and papers all over the country and abroad. He has changed his field and is steadily influencing his profession to adopt radical changes in its ideas concerning how psychiatry works. To go up against conventional Freudian concepts and techniques and carry it off successfully is independence of mind of the first order.

I mention Weiss and Steiner in connection with myself because we all became rebels in our fields. We were each polite and collegial with our associates, quite amiable in fact, and worked closely within our fields and institutions. But we all three steadily and forcefully rejected many of the concepts and conventions which prescribed our work.

Our thinking processes were similar in that we all constantly tested the theories we were handed against practical experience. We all found, myself included as the reader will soon see, that the theories we were taught and that we were supposed to teach and apply simply did not fit reality. What was really going on was not explained by accepted theories: Weiss with people, Steiner with distribution margins and pricing behavior, and myself with the management of factories.

Many of our mutual friends have asked "Just what was going on at that school you attended? Was it certain teachers, or the educational processes, or did you just influence each other? What was it that made 25% of that class go off and become rebels and each try to overturn certain basics of their separate professions, and in fact actually carry it out?" I cannot answer those questions other than to speculate that our teachers encouraged our imagination, questions and dissent. The atmosphere was one of inquiry rather than dogma or authority.

We three worked entirely alone, for though close friends, we did not attempt to advise or influence each other, and in fact only learned of each other's accomplishments after they became fact. I am immodest to include myself with Joe and Bob for they have always been ahead of me but I take pleasure in claiming to share that independent-mindedness. We all demonstrate a near-reckless abandon which takes over when we are indignant with theories which are out of synch with reality.

Before concluding this ramble I will add to Alice's observation about independence of mind the sense that three other characteristics, one cognitive and the other two emotional, have also been at play: first, a compulsion to wrestle with causes and effects until they made sense; second, a drive to be well thought of, and, third, a happy disposition. Somehow I think these were important givens or acquisitions.

I am only too aware that these characteristics are not necessarily strengths nor do they regularly lead to success. For example, those of us who must somehow try to make sense of complex mixtures of facts and other data before moving ahead can get hung up, our heads in analytical glue, while more free minds dash ahead with verve, intuition, and freedom to ramble. And a happy disposition can sometimes be pretty complacent!

But University School and days spent with Weiss and Steiner had to end. I was admitted to M.I.T., Cornell, and Yale and went off to college in the fall of 1941, picking Yale as less technically narrow, and choosing chemical engineering as my major. Yale was a shock at first, mostly because everyone seemed so smart and sophisticated. I waited on table for my room and board and the rich preppies were often cruel and cliquey. After an only fair year as a freshman I did well scholastically and socially thereafter. But I remember those "bright college years" at Yale as ones of war-time when everything was downright serious, flat-out work, and going to college summers and all around the calendar.

I was a good engineering student but only fair in chemistry. The business side of the chemical industry was fascinating, though, and also on the plus side were truly exciting courses in English literature. The course that I took in industrial administration, to be described later, under an inspiring professor, Elliott Dunlap Smith, was the highlight of my college career. Though I did not realize it at the time, Professor Smith's fascination with "the executive" inspired me away from engineering forever.

Deferred from the military long enough to graduate, I was in and out of college with an engineering degree in two years and nine months. I tried to get a Navy commission but by that time in the war the Navy had plenty of officers. Very disappointed, I volunteered for immediate induction, and soon found myself a private in the army infantry. I learned to shoot the M-1 rifle, Browning Automatic Rifle, machine gun, throw grenades, and use the bayonet. But days before being shipped to the war in Europe I was suddenly transferred to the Engineer Corps for duty on the Manhattan Project, making the atomic bomb at Los Alamos, New Mexico.

At Los Alamos my first job was as an engineer on a team separating highly radioactive elements for testing implosion effects. Later I became an industrial engineer and did process analysis for a small plant machining RDX, the explosive surrounding the uranium to be imploded to set off the bomb. I learned some industrial engineering and I was overwhelmingly impressed by the fantastic, valuable insights to be gained from measuring and analyzing material and manpower flows. This led me, as I will shortly describe, to begin to be ready to act upon an ever latent powerful interest in managers. My compass turned to the Harvard Business School.

Now just a few more facts, the first being of utmost importance: My wife, Alice, is most remarkable and extraordinary. Beautiful, energetic, disciplined, cooperative, but best of all, very wise, quietly supportive, and an amazingly perceptive listener. With a disposition happy as mine. Sounds like a great combination? Right!

We have two children, now grown into responsible, energetic and most interesting people: Polly and Charles. We are close, I believe, as parents, children, and three grandchildren and we are most indebted to them all for steady love and understanding.

My life has included several other enduring loves. The first is sailing, boats, and the ocean. When I got my first job I bought my first boat within six weeks and I have had two to eight boats at all times ever since. We have cruised from the Chesapeake to Newfoundland in our forty foot cutter, CALLIOPE, and all along points in between. A parallel interest is in flying and I have a 181 horsepower four seater Piper Archer which I fly, mostly in Maine.

Competitive sports have been a passion: softball in an industrial league in Minneapolis (where I actually did hit some home runs and make some spectacular catches in center-field, a hero at last!), and squash during Harvard days and tennis thereafter. I try to play tennis two or three times a week and love trying to win and the feeling of being well exercised, win or lose.

Finally, those who know me would describe an ever-constant love for the state of Maine, its coast, lakes, mountains, and particular people found nowhere else.

Putting all this together, I should live on the coast, have a house on a harbor, lots of shoreline, a dock and acres of woods, a tennis court, be 22 minutes from the airport, and have several boats on several moorings in the harbor in front of our house. Fortunately, I am pleased and very thankful to report that what is described above is exactly that. Lucky me. It is gorgeous.

One confession: a better known article of mine is "The Focused Factory." My friends would report that Wickham's life runs to the contrary of his admonition to production managers: "keep operations focused!" But between writing, speaking, work as a trustee of the University of Maine System, president of the Farnsworth Museum in Rockland, four corporate boards, seven boats, one airplane, tennis, and 28 acres to take care of, they say that my life is not focused. They are wrong, of course, but that's another story for another time.

This essay now shifts to recount events and processes which led to the rebellion of a manufacturing professor and the subsequent development of some unconventional ideas.

PART 2

Developing New Concepts of Manufacturing Management

This story is about a professor and the impacts of some of the enduring traditions of academia on his process of working out some ideas. My all-consuming concern centered on industrial managers and why that profession, so important to the nation, was apparently failing us. But in pursuing this passion I was constantly ricocheted around by academic pressures and constraints.

I can see now that the academic surroundings in which I worked held back my progress and yet ultimately pushed the process along. For example, the process included a narrow escape from the sticky webs of academic research traditions, which almost ended the trip before it really began. But, happily, another aspect of academic life was instrumental in ultimately working out some new ideas: it was the stimulation of the teaching process that led me to finally perceive some useful concepts that had been waiting out there all along for me to get to see.

A FIRST PRESENTATION

It all began when the writer innocently took a stand against his superiors' wisdom and, like the minute-men at Lexington when they were finally driven to rebel, was thoroughly whipped in the first battle of what turned into a war. Like battered, beaten, and stomped on. It was bad, really bad.

What started the fight, it is clear now, was that when speaking at my first ever seminar to the "Production" Area of about 19 faculty members of the Harvard Business School, my unambiguous message was that what most of them were researching and teaching was irrelevant to the growing production problems of the day. What I said is on the record: "The U.S. production manager is attempting to fight big battles with small weapons," and the "small weapons" were those being provided by academics. Now, with good reason, one might wonder why I could have been so arrogant and untactful and, indeed, self-defeating, but, honestly, I really expected them to be excited and intrigued by my new ideas.

They were excited all right, excited like hornets whose nest has just been stepped on by a blundering hiker. They swarmed all over me until the hour grew late and, venom exhausted, the room emptied.

I drove home, shaken and severely discouraged. I had worked very hard on my presentation. Meeting me at the door, my wife, Alice, asked eagerly "how did it go?" I told her, "it was terrible." We lit a fire, sat down and had a martini, I recollect, and after hearing of my disaster, she said "Well, are you right or wrong?" I thought a moment and said "I'm right. I'm sure I'm right." She said then calmly, "Well, you'll be O.K. then."

Now, in retrospect, it is at first surprising that I was sure that I was right and neither humbled by my betters nor frightened away from my line of reasoning. I was no gutsy hero and never have been (and that disaster did scare this non-tenured lecturer in his fourth month on the faculty into sliding silently underground with those new ideas). But the fact was that I had come across early but undeniable signs of industrial deterioration and that it was management related made me indignant that my colleagues at a professional school of management were wasting their research efforts and teaching academic stuff that seemed really silly.

Thus bruised by my first compulsive brush with academic orthodoxy, I went to earth with my nascent ideas, overtly concentrated on teaching and course development, wrote a book on international manufacturing, and tried to be an all-around good citizen, not bothering my colleagues again with heresy of any sort for a full five years.

My instinct for silence was appropriate, actually, because these "ideas" of mine were mostly about what was wrong, both in industry and academic production teaching and research, but said nothing whatsoever about why it was all happening or what to do about it.

MOVING INTO ACADEMIA

I knew that something was wrong because I had been taught to be critical and to challenge both management and academic thinking as usually wrong or myopic: I benefitted from living with a grandfather who was fascinated with mechanics, an extremely analytical, engineering trained father, and an artist mother with an artist's eye for detail. Fortunately, as mentioned, I had highly demanding high school teachers and brighter-than-me yet supportive high-school colleagues. Subsequently, I studied and worked for the Yale professor, Elliott Dunlap Smith, who was in love with improving the practice of management. It was he who filled me with a near spiritual awareness of the enormous potential of managers for good and evil and, hence, the moral obligation of a mighty sense of responsibility.

College followed military service, but then my thinking life exploded with the experience of exciting, demanding, indeed thrilling analytical breakthroughs nearly three times a day in the Harvard Business School (HBS) MBA classrooms where I was a student in 1946 and 1947. Being "wrong" in my pre-class recommendations three times a day, five days a week, was humbling but in fact the power of in-depth analysis produced great confidence, confidence that hard-worked analyses yielded exciting, and usually contrarian insights. Contrarian! I liked that role.

A full decade with the Honeywell Corporation followed the MBA. Tough bosses and unambiguous jobs provided a dose of demanding, no-nonsense years, six in production, two in marketing and sales, and two as a divisional finance officer.

But Honeywell gave me one more gift and that was to train me in the process of leading management development classes. That process reminded me of my earlier, near-mystical admiration of my Harvard MBA instructors and their non-directive teaching styles, and a pledge I had made to myself ten years earlier to consider a teaching career after five years in industry. Figuring that I could always return to industry, but if I didn't try out teaching now I might never do it, I resigned to return to HBS and the doctoral program in late 1958.

After twelve months of case-writing which took me into fifteen companies in twelve industries while pursuing the standard menu of doctoral courses and exams, I wrote a thesis that concerned U.S. companies manufacturing abroad. But then to my great surprise and pleasure suddenly there came an invitation to join the HBS faculty. Four-months later there I was, giving that disastrous seminar, late one afternoon in December, 1960.

Everyone could give a seminar about their research and, though I was flat out 100% teaching that first fall, the signal was clear that I should be "doing some research" and report on it in a faculty seminar. I decided that because I had been away from academia for ten years I should catch up on what I'd been missing. Therefore what I should do would be to learn about the academics' new concepts and techniques and see their importance. This would serve to help me update myself with the field and my colleagues.

So that is what I was researching at odd moments, until late one evening after an area seminar in October, 1960, a doctoral student kindly asked me about my progress and then suggested an add-on: saying "Why don't you not only study these new concepts and techniques but at the same time from your present and recent casewriting in industry come up with a sense of what is happening in industry and then see whether the new stuff from academia is now or will be useful in solving current industrial problems?"

His name is Henry B. Eyring and that chance conversation changed everything and set me on a track I have never left. For what I discovered, and knew for sure after 16 months in the field and researching the new techniques, was that we had a complete mismatch between problems in industry and academic research and teaching and that, of course, is just what I arrogantly told the Area staff at the fateful seminar.

INDUSTRY AND PROFESSORS

The problems in industry were rife, and hard to miss when one got out into factories. They infected quality and productivity, equipment and process technology, labor morale, investment in facilities, the role of industrial managers in top management, the growing loss of industrial markets to foreign competitors, the emergence of sick industries...that was all starting to occur in the late 1950s while academics were still teaching time and motion study and being titillated by simulation, linear programming, "operations research" and heuristic algorithms.

The problem was that operations management professors were so absorbed in intellectually exciting new techniques that they did not perceive what was taking place in our factories. It is still astonishing that that could happen at a case-oriented, manager centered school of business. MIT or Chicago or Berkeley? Yes, easily, but at HBS?

I think it was an unusual and slippery time in HBS history, largely in the Operations field but also reflecting an uneasiness throughout the School due to the acceleration of changes incorporating more quantitative techniques in all subjects. In Operations the pressure for change was especially strong because many HBS professors in other fields were concerned that we in operations management might be falling behind intellectually. As a case in point we had been kicked out of executive programs because executive students found our content dull and low-level. Our colleagues in other areas considered us a "sick," weak area at the School. Therefore several very capable new hires had been made from distant doctoral programs devoted to simulation, game theory, and quantitative techniques and those newcomers were riding high.

For me to tell the Area that they were misdirecting their time must have seemed pretty insolent. New employee tells his seniors that they are nuts. Surprise! Seniors take great pleasure in a sixty minute thrashing of raw recruit.

After my pummeling at the seminar it was obvious that my ideas were politically incorrect. Socially I felt accepted and the HBS faculty attitudes toward me were friendly and supportive, especially around my teaching and course development. Nevertheless, within the Production Area it was clear that my lack of enthusiasm for getting into depth on the new quantitative concepts and techniques was giving me at age thirty six an image of being an old-fashioned representative of a dying species whose years were numbered. I did manage to get promoted to Associate Professor, a five-year appointment, probably simply because I was pretty hot in the classroom and a few other "old-fashioned" professors, of senior rank, backed me.

But I was driven by a compulsion to make sense of things and thereby be able to teach and write something important because it was useful. I became a rebel and slunk off underground to try to figure out by myself what was going on in industry and what should be done about it.

WORKING OUT SOME IDEAS

My problem, starting with the seminar but continuing after my promotion, was that I was long on criticism but short on remedies. U.S. industry was failing the country on all counts, but no one that I could find in academia or industry seemed to be able to analyze what was wrong other than the surprisingly rapid surge of new foreign industrial competence, quelled wholly, it appeared, by cheap overseas labor. How to compete with Japan and Germany, for example, seemed impossible when their costs were so much lower.

To show how smart I am, it took me eight years to figure out an answer! Let me turn now to describe that process; it's pretty self-centered of course, but the rationale for this series of essays is to explore the processes of intellectual development. My process was slow; perhaps I set a new record in that department.

The first three years, marked by the December, 1960 fiasco, were null and void in the "why" and "what to do" columns. I was teaching the first-year course and it was all uphill because the students found it so low-level and operational that they could not imagine themselves ever holding such positions. So 191% of my energy went into trying to make my sections in that course educationally exciting in spite of the drab content.

In that period the only real accomplishment toward my unspoken goal of learning what American industry needed was, beginning in 1962, taking my "seminar" ideas, gradually expanded, out to alumni and industrial groups beginning in 1962 in speeches. These speeches said, in effect, "we are slipping badly in our industrial prowess and we'd better watch out." Those speeches reflected my thinking at that time. I laid the blame on top management's lack of focus on the production function, failure to invest in modern equipment, and excluding top-production managers from top-management councils. I protested that great marketing and financial manipulation and sharp control systems could not make a company competitive. Audiences reacted well because I'd jolted them. Very few thinking people were thinking about manufacturing.

Back at the School no one paid any attention to what I was saying off campus, which was probably just as well because some sharp colleague would have criticized my shallow explanations and I would have been shot down again. I think I realized that my "answers" to our industrial problems were weak and vacuous so I was uneasy enough to keep my own counsel and avoid challenges. I knew I wasn't ready to tackle my colleagues again.

Fortunately my assignment in years 4, 5, and 6 brought me closer to being "ready." I was asked to teach "Advanced Production Problems," (APP) a course started in 1946 by John McClean that had been successful over 17 years but was suffering from out of date case material when I took it over in 1964. The conceptual basis of the course was a focus on the production function in one industry at a time.

The idea, a very effective one pedagogically. was to demonstrate that companies in one industry—with one marketplace and one technology and one set of economics and one external environment—usually differed substantially in their basic manufacturing policies, and their results differed accordingly. Three classes were devoted to understanding the technology of an industry. These sessions were devoted to grasping the fundamental physical processes, the equipment choices, and the key operating decisions affected by the equipment and process technologies. These also included lots of numbers: output per hour, operating costs, capital costs, setup and changeover times, product ranges and specs, and skill levels of operators.

The next three classes focused on the industry: competitors, market shares, financial results, norms for key costs of goods sold, and trends in the industry. Then we turned to cases. All in all this was a set of powerful notions, the industry focus invented by McLean and then developed and refined and taught with great effectiveness by Abe Zaleznik. Jim Bright, David Rodgers, and Stanley Miller.

In two fascinating hours in his office Miller taught me how to teach APP. What you do, he said, is to get the class to analyze the operating problem(s) in the case and then to back up and examine, first, their implicit manufacturing policies and, then, their competitive issues. This analytical process always demonstrated a conflict between the manufacturing policies and the company's competitive strategic situation, which conflict produced the operating problem. Pow! Wow! It was dynamite in the classroom. (Incidentally, these conflicts are as present today, typically in 95% of every company I enter or study, as they were in the 1960s. But that is getting ahead of the story. More later.)

In three years I updated all six industries and the course was always over-subscribed and got the highest possible student ratings. Each class ended in powerful, fresh insights that gave the students a mind-blowing sense of their own potentials. About a dozen students with whom I have kept up have told me that this course changed their professional lives, leading in some cases to their own businesses or top-management positions to which they say they climbed based on constant study of an industry's technology, economics, competitors, and manufacturing policy alternatives.

Curiously, none of my predecessors had ever written up for managers the wisdom offered in this course. I wrote it up as a personal statement for my tenure decision three years later but, like my predecessors, totally missed perceiving the implications for U.S. industry for another three years.

Now, 30 years later, this seems amazing. Something was still missing. I wasn't ready to write to managers about manufacturing policy. It was great in the classroom, but somehow I did not latch onto a sense that there was something in the basics of the course that might apply to restoring the rapidly declining fortunes of American industries.

In the cases I taught I saw the problems of manufacturing policies as internally non-congruent and externally non-supportive of corporate competitive strategies—and those cases were typical and not uncommon—but I did not relate that set of ideas to the U.S. manufacturing scene as a whole. Intellectually I was as aware as ever of our deteriorating industrial prowess but had made no progress in coming up with "why's" or "what to do's" of any genuine use.

I did, however, finally get over my fear of irritating my colleagues and despite being non-tenured decided to place my concerns about U.S. industrial decline into an article. Called "Production Under Pressure." It was accepted by the *Harvard Business Review* (HBR) and published in 1966. The article was important because it was a lone voice and the message surely needed broadcasting, The article said that we were in trouble externally from foreign competitors and internally from lack of top management attention and investment. The solution recommended was to restore management attention. I must admit that it was intellectually no starburst and it received scant notice from readers.

Except for one or two senior professors, my colleagues were totally silent. Why? I am sure that it was because I failed to probe and dig for fundamental causes and solutions. I cannot fault my colleagues for their indifferent yawns; years later they took notice after managers, consulting firms, and the business press took up my ideas.

But to get better ideas it took another three years, five more formative experiences, and one really new discovery to electrically integrate all these separate concepts and experiences into a single unified theory.

Two of these learning experiences were provided by demanding students who insisted on "why's" and "what to do's" and forced the teacher to sweat and strain for greater depth and clarity and integrity of ideas. The first students were second-year MBA's and the second, several years later, were AMP's (Advanced Management Program, i.e., senior executives).

The MBA course was called MOPO (Management of Production Operations). Its focus, started by Professor Arch R. Dooley a year earlier, was on the application and implementation of new industrial technologies, both hardware and software. The hardware, for example, consisted of new equipment such as automated, numerically controlled machine tools, and real-time on-line controls, computer-linked boxes at the workplace that fed production and inventory information back to a central office. The software were such developments as Materials Requirements Planning (MRP), job-shop scheduling systems, Monte Carlo gaming programs, work sampling, and even simple simulations and models for inventory control and reduction of lead-times. All neat stuff, offering managers substantial benefits.

The only problem, we discovered, was that no matter what it was, it never worked. The hardware or software was usually O.K. The problem was that the new gear was hobbled by or interfered with the existing equipment or systems or habits or skills of the workers and supervisors and staff. So each case was a disaster scene and usually the investment or change that looked so promising to the students, as well as to the company, turned out to be a fiasco. It was enough to make teacher and students and indeed managers cautious and gun-shy. "Nothing new ever works" could be the conclusion. "Always let another company go first," was heard around the classroom. This seemed like great wisdom but it was pretty shallow. It would certainly be of little use to managers who needed new technologies for turning around non-competitive factories.

Of course it was not enough for good students either, and I was forced to dig deeper. At just that moment I was asked to address the annual meeting of the Numerical Control Society (NCS) of America and I put those ideas from the MOPO course into a paper called "The Stubborn Infrastructure of the Factory." The notion was pretty simple but it helped me and it helped my students. And the enthusiasm of the conference audience was tremendous! I clearly was onto something useful and maybe its simplicity made it better.

The idea was simply that numerical controlled machinery was not catching on and fulfilling its obvious potential, because to work well it required changes in the production control system, supervision, maintenance, process specifications, job content, wage systems and/or etc., etc., etc. Any one element of the infrastructure of the factory could bring NC down and render it ineffective. No wonder it was catching on slowly and the NC Society members were frustrated and disappointed.

In the MOPO course this was the troubled outcome of every new hardware or software technology: it was shot down or crippled by some extraneous part of a factory's infrastructure. If the students and their instructor learned nothing else, they learned to recognize that infrastructure was as important as new technology and that it needed to be designed to fit and support whatever was new.

Though the NCS paper was a hit at the conference, somehow it never occurred to me to broaden it a bit and publish it in a management review or journal. This was in spite of the fact that many analysts of the U.S. manufacturing dilemma at the time were urging that the answer to cheap foreign labor was surely to be found in moving faster on installing new manufacturing technologies. But no one else seemed to realize that our disappointing progress in this direction was largely due to noncongruent infrastructures. In hindsight opportunity was staring at me once again. But I still wasn't ready, partly, at least, I think because the ideas seemed neither profound nor "complete."

One outcome of this line of thought was that I began to work on an article that broadened the "stubborn infrastructure" concept into a look at companies' experiences in installing new hardware and software technologies. What I observed was that new technology A surfaced another problem X that when solved by new technology B resulted in another problem, Y. Nothing was ever all right at once. I called this the "Anachronistic Factory"because one or more parts of the factory were always out of date. I suggested the obvious: do a more complete, integrated job of planning changes and in 1971 published an article with this title, but rightly, it made no great bang.

Although the issues were right in front of me, I did not pick them up and wrestle with the questions sitting there: Why the piecemeal planning everywhere? When careful "planning" was attempted the factory still did not work well for long. Why is something nearly always out of kilter? And, as I always asked my impetuous, always critical students eager to "fire that stupid manager!", why do smart people do dumb things? Why are our experienced, well trained industrial managers looking so badly? The deeper layers of analysis were right out there.

The AMP class finally furnished the catalytic spark. AMP's were tough to teach, partly because they were experienced and successful people and usually sure that they were right, especially when a high proportion came to the same conclusion. After being banished for many years, the Production Area had regained a place in their curriculum on a trial basis mostly because of the success of the manufacturing policy course in the MBA. I had given my confident promise to the course head that my eight classes would be a great success. The heat was on. I'd asked for it; the whole production area was watching. We could not afford to fail.

The first six classes went well. The AMP's wrestled heartily with cases in which manufacturing failures threatened to bring down whole companies. Dramatic, important, the cases were mostly Fortune articles, authentic and in the national view. The AMP's were fascinated with how such great companies with such previously successful manufacturing records could get into such trouble. I pushed them hard, wondering myself. But in the early morning before the seventh class, somewhat desperate to understand more myself and to have something useful for the class to chew on, suddenly it all began to come together.

I saw that the companies had gotten into trouble in manufacturing because experienced production executives had applied their hard-earned wisdom and the conventional premises of their profession to reach fundamental manufacturing policy decisions that were just plain wrong. They did not work. Disasters followed. Consternation. Disbelief.

How can manufacturing managers go wrong by applying the conventional premises of industrial management developed and tested and improved over a century? Can the "making of continuous improvements" be wrong? By maximizing productivity? By minimizing excess capacity? By keeping inventories low? By consolidating operations into one big, efficient facility? By minimizing indirect labor and overhead, by keeping "burden rates" low, by using time standards and tight labor controls? By mechanizing, automating and computerizing to the utmost? By investing in brand new, green field facilities?

In fact all the foregoing were "wrong" in the companies we studied and were being "wrong" in U.S. industry, for they were resulting in plants with structures and infrastructures that were internally non-congruent and, thereby, in dissonance. The equipment may have been chosen for high-volume production, the plant capacity set for low capital investment, the make/buy balance for a non-cyclical industry, the production control system to handle small-lot sizes, the wage system to minimize turnover each and every fundamental manufacturing policy designed independently by industrial professionals to maximize or minimize according to their professional training and the industrial management conventions developed over 75 years. Every system pulled its own way and the plants, run by conventional industrial management concepts, were not very good at anything and were unable to compete with foreign imports.

The class saw that the wisdom of industrial engineering, of control and scheduling experts, and of labor economists did not always work. And they saw that economists and accountants and financial experts pushed production managers toward decisions that all looked like good business, but often simply did not meet a company's strategic realities.

To illustrate, in one case, the company, facing exploding demand for its product—a massive new-high-tech element of electric power production—decided to build a new plant in a greenfield location to maximize profits with low costs and high productivity. All decisions were based on this conventional premise: just enough capacity, computer controlled NC machinery, a low cost minimum labor force, transportation of a big product on river barges, new equipment with minimal production and maintenance costs. The trouble with all this was that it would probably have minimized costs if it had all worked properly, but it maximized the chances that delivery promises to customers might be missed.

And miss them they did because of learning problems and technological failures on the new equipment and a new, low-cost work force. In the power plant business nothing is worse than missing deliveries. Orders were canceled, the company's reputation was damaged for many years and the financial consequences were disastrous to earnings and shareholder values.

The bad decisions were manufacturing policy decisions, that is, the big, long-range, expensive, fundamental decisions affecting the structure of manufacturing: number and location of facilities, make versus buy, capacity, choices of equipment and process technology, and basic systems for production planning and control, human resources policies, organization, and financial controls. This company had made its decisions trying to maximize the wrong objective (i.e., profits) instead of the critical strategic objective of minimizing any risk of missing deliveries.

So with one class to go we were all on new high ground: smart production people make dumb decisions if those decisions are premised on maximizing (or minimizing) outcomes that are dysfunctional to the firm's competitive success. We were onto the "why" of the cases; left to work out was "So how should we manage manufacturing so this does not happen?"

It was not all so clear. I knew that some in the class were wondering and would raise up the conundrum: "How can any good production manager fail to maximize productivity?"

Day 8 dawned. Early, in my office alone, I experienced the usual pre-class pressure for "really understanding all this myself." Business as usual. I asked myself what I would answer as a student if I were asked what I was about to ask the class: So how can top management manage manufacturing so as to prevent these fiascoes we've been studying?

How was top management doing it now? They weren't. They concentrated on the big, strategic problems of finance and products and markets and marketing. Production was technical, engineering, routine, standardized, repetitive, lots of people, training, discipline, grievances, inspection, inventories....none of this was top-management stuff. Delegate, son, delegate.

But the bad results in these cases were so bad they became strategic, setting the company back competitively, in markets, in financial results, and in the stock market. And the causes were poor manufacturing policies, those expensive, long-range structural decisions with massive, pervasive on-going consequences.

Pow! Wow! That was it. Top management should manage manufacturing by making sure those manufacturing policy decisions were right. "Right" would be when the manufacturing function worked. And what made it "work"? It worked when it fitted and supported or created corporate strategy.

But why could not the conventional premises and practices of production management be depended upon to make manufacturing "work"? This question was also hanging out there from the first seven classes. What was their central premise? It was that low cost and high productivity are always key success criteria. But what about delivery reliability, or quality, or minimizing investment, or short lead times for new product introduction, all criteria that had emerged in one or more of the cases? It was suddenly clear. There were tradeoffs!

A given manufacturing system could not perform equally on all success criteria. Someone had to decide. All-purpose plants couldn't succeed anymore. They had to be designed for a purpose. And what purpose? The company's competitive strategy.

And that defined a manufacturing task...what it was that manufacturing had to be especially good at to make manufacturing a competitive weapon.

There it was. I had it now: A manufacturing strategy is a set of manufacturing policies designed to maximize performance among tradeoffs among success criteria to meet the manufacturing task determined by a corporate strategy. Top management's job is to ensure that there is a coherent manufacturing strategy in which all manufacturing policies are designed as a unit to support or lead the corporate strategy.

I was now ready for the eighth class. It was a great class for the instructor, and for the students, too. They seemed almost as excited as I was. Almost.

I now had a product, a set of ideas that fit with the facts of current industrial results, and seemed to provide answers to "why" we were slipping: old industrial engineering concepts were no longer adequate for competing against the new generation of capable, low-cost and fast, flexible, high quality foreign producers. And I could now answer "what should be done:" (focus all manufacturing policies toward a strategic company objective because a factory cannot excel on every success criterion).

GETTING THE IDEAS INTO PRACTICE

The year was 1968. I had been in academia eight years. But I finally had something exciting, and, it seemed to me, important to say. Why had it taken so long? More on that later, After the AMP class, in late spring, I could hardly wait to write up my new theory of manufacturing management. I had so much to say, though, that I spent much of the summer writing, but at the end of August I had over one hundred pages but no article. It simply would not come together. It was a heap of ideas and examples, but disorganized. I was as excited as ever but could not seem to get it together into a straightforward manuscript.

Disappointed—it seemed to have been a summer wasted. But when my wife had to leave to get the children back into school and I could stay in Maine one more day, I decided to try one more time. The next morning I sat down at the kitchen table in the bright sunlight and in five hours never put the pen down. In that time I wrote the "Missing Link" article, the article that put all this, or most of it, together. Grinning, I recall, a most self-satisfied grin, with article in hand I jumped in the car and happily headed for another year at the HBS.

When the article was published the next spring (1969) in HBR one colleague told me that he liked it, saying "you are really on to something there, Wick." I report this not to be sour or disappointed for, believe me, most of us in the Area were close, collegial and genuinely friendly. I felt respected and appreciated. But, in retrospect, the fact of their silence simply reflected that they, like most operations professors were perfectly happy with the old theory of manufacturing in which the mantra was "productivity, efficiency, mass production, volume, long runs, time study, standards, continuous improvement, buffer inventories to smooth production, assembly lines, straight lines, and supervision. Do it all. Hire professional specialists for each factory function and let them maximize away. Squeeze out every drop of waste. Sales and Marketing are the traditional enemies of productivity and efficiency. Keep the customer away and we'll run in the black."

This is what they believed and that is what they taught. My ideas were just not significant to them. My concepts attracted no immediate interest in academia, not even in management-centered HBS. My colleagues had had their doctoral training in these mantras and once some academics have had doctoral training in XYZ, it is my observation that it is very difficult throughout their subsequent careers for them to get away from XYZ. XYZ is what is believable, that's what is interesting, and that's what they wish to study.

The doctoral years in a good doctoral program are intensive and very formative. The program and the process require such an intensive investment, generally with influential teachers who are demanding, and the result is the formation of a good deal of solid expertise. It may be narrow and deep, but in a good program it is exciting and extremely satisfying to become very good at something. And that something is with many Ph.D.'s forever. So when you try to get them to invest deeply in some other approach to their field or a different theory of how it all works, it can either be uninteresting or threatening or defy their premises and assumptions about their chosen work.

I think I escaped such an indelible imprint from my doctoral program because I was always skeptical and even humorously caustic about academics. Although I enormously admired many of my HBS faculty, I admired most the ones who related best to and focused most on real-life managers, and least, those faculty who were narrowly expert in techniques of management or analysis.

Probably my imprint came earlier from Eliott Dunlap Smith, my MBA professors, and the Honeywell experience. All that taught me the difficulty of being a great executive, the moral responsibility of a manager, and the tremendous impact of managers on a company, an industry and the economy. With that kind of imprint before I came to a doctoral program, it is possible to conclude that, at least in some respects, my doctoral program was a failure in that it did not change my pragmatic point of view.

I respected the tools and techniques of industrial management that I was taught, but they never seemed as exciting as top management problems. They seemed like implements of housekeeping. My interest was "architecture" and I came to see that all the "housekeeping" in the world could not make a plant competitive if the architectural design was wrong. Like a house or a bridge or an airplane, plants had to be designed for a particular use. The worst ones were those that tried to do everything and did nothing well.

In industry the "Missing Link" article caught on like wildfire and, to my great surprise, the phone began to ring and I was soon caught up in the center of fad life. There was a flood of speech, seminar and consulting invitations and lectures at other campuses. The ideas struck some kind of a chord because American industry was in trouble and managers were ready to try most anything. Getting them to really understand that they were the problem was more difficult.

In fact, the "manufacturing in the corporate strategy" (MCS) approach relentlessly demands whole new premises, insights,, and skills of industrial managers, and these behaviors run counter to nearly a century of contrary, well-reinforced habits and beliefs. As a result the consulting experiences proved the most demanding and therefore the best laboratories for further developing my ideas.

One consulting assignment was particularly formative. Manufacturing was a consistent problem in all five divisions of a high-tech company. Their approach to manufacturing was to centralize and consolidate all production in one plant. Their purpose was to minimize capital investment, share facilities, keep indirect labor and overheads low, and shift workers around between the five divisions to offset shifting workloads. The scheme was an accountant's and finance VP's dream, the epitome of the industrial engineer's philosophy, but the plant's performance for any division was abysmal. Division A complained about long lead times, Division B about missed delivery promises, Division C about bad quality, Division D about slow and uncooperative new product development, and Division E, perhaps surprisingly, about high production costs.

Every division manager told me and the president that manufacturing was a competitive millstone. The president said "Professor Skinner, we don't have a philosophy of manufacturing." When I asked him what he meant by a philosophy of manufacturing, he said, "Professor, I don't know what I mean but I know we don't have one."

Actually they did have one, as described above, and it was the product of financial rules of thumb. What they needed were five strategies of manufacturing. Each had to be designed to fit and support a unique divisional situation comprised of specific competitive, economic and technological realities. They seized upon my advice with astonishing alacrity, led of course by freed up division managers, and all ended well. The improvements in performance of the five, organizationally separated operations was just as expected by the MCS theory, though nearly incredible to the overjoyed but surprised president and his financial experts.

Thus was born the notion of the "focused factory" and when this concept was written up and published (HBR, 1974) it was even more circulated and celebrated than the "Missing Link." The ideas in each article are really one and the same, but "The Focused Factory" deals more with the "what to do." A catchy phrase (my worst critics admit that at least my titles are great), it caught the attention of not only production people but top management and this led to more challenges of implementation.

One such challenge was at the Copeland Corporation, a leading manufacturer of large refrigeration and air conditioning compressors located in Ohio. There they had, would you believe it, one humungous large and, of course, unfocused factory. So the CEO built a new, focused factory for their major product line in Alabama. This investment, which used every dollar of raisable capital and truly bet the company, fortunately proved to be an enormous success. Its particularly important achievement was that it produced unexpectedly high levels of reliable product, a performance feature of strategic importance for refrigeration compressors, where field failures are costly. Two more focused plants were built and five years later, after two big competitors dropped out of the business rather than trying to compete, Copeland's market share, worldwide, had risen from 15% to 60%.

So, just like Copeland, MCS and "the focused factory" took off and as they did, I added to the concepts and fleshed them out with many more articles and two books. In both books I offered several chapters aimed toward helping managers in the actual process of developing a manufacturing strategic, starting with a manufacturing "audit" and leading to a menu-choosing of manufacturing policies.

The notion is that there are usually four or five alternatives to choose among for every manufacturing policy decision. When the policy designer defines the strategic objectives and economic and technological constraints the best menu choice typically follows. More on this later because history indicates that many managers have big problems in bridging from "the manufacturing task" to designing appropriate manufacturing policies.

A CIVIL WAR IN ACADEMIA

Now, back in academia, it was another story. The Manufacturing Policy course was as or more successful than ever and the first year course began to use the "Missing Link" as a course-ending reading. (Students complained, "why didn't you give us this to read at the beginning of the course?" They liked it great deal, but, of course, at the beginning rather than at the end it would not have meant anything to them). But within the Area things were not very good. A big, ideological, bitter fight was looming up.

With the success of the MCS concepts in industry, in the classroom and in the business press, it might have been expected that there would be changes in how we in the Production Area went about our work. The new ideas were accepted, no one argued with the concepts or said they were wrong or unimportant, I was congratulated by many colleagues, and, as noted, some used my articles in their courses. But the bulk of our members kept right on doing what they had been doing right along with no change whatsoever.

They were studying and teaching simulation, job-shop scheduling, work sampling, queuing theory, operations management in services, government, hospitals, and international settings. This variety of settings was good and proper but what is interesting now is that they were still using the old industrial engineering paradigm of breaking the job down into small parts and improving the efficiency of each part. But what about the whole? What about the key, strategic "task" of the unit? What about tradeoffs? What about "focus?" These fundamental ideas of MCS were totally unrealized in the work of most of the area, who plugged away unthinkingly glued to the traditional industrial engineering conceptual model. Curriculums and thinking patterns were as stuck as ever.

Here is the traditional academic tradition at work. Professors each do their own thing, even in continuing premises and ideas and conclusions that are wrong or out of date. We do research to add new knowledge and insights to our profession, but it is usually so narrow and deep that it misses what goes on peripherally to our own cozy tunnels.

I was an accomplice to this stuck-in-the-mud process in that I obeyed another academic tradition, that of not harassing one's colleagues to follow one's "great new ideas." The assumption, not a bad one, is that if the idea is really that good, others will pick it up. It is not good form to get on a soapbox and try to sell your ideas to uninterested colleagues. If they ask, O.K. And, anyway, I was too busy in my new popularity outside the School to seek new converts right in my own back yard. A few came and asked and, pleased, I tried to be helpful and convincing.

Now another set of academic traditions came into play: how do new faculty get selected and hired, and, second, how do senior faculty decide who gets promoted? The tradition, of course, is total democracy at work. Everyone gets involved. Lone wolves are forced into the pack. Snarling and circling, their instincts are clear: select young faculty who share your own interests and beliefs, and promote those who have proven themselves to support your views of the field. A lot of diversity is bad.

So when we full professors came to the appointments process in 1972, the rubber hit the road. I had a few converts to my ideas, more than I realized, but the ideological issues did not center on those. They focused clearly and simply on whether the future of the Area lay best in "quantitative" or "management" territory.

Each candidate was categorized beyond a doubt and we lined up predictably. When the "quantitatives" in full view shot down a "management" as he came up for a full professorship after nine years in the process, the Area exploded into an open, shooting war. There were quarrels over curriculum and new courses and course names and new hires. The "quantitatives" had a serious problem because the few "management" courses, particularly Manufacturing Policy, were going well with good student reviews and high enrollments whereas the "quant" courses did poorly. And the required first-year course, which was dominated by the "Quants" ranked number thirteen of the thirteen first-year courses.

There was also a total split over changing the name of the area, dropping the name "production." We made such a fuss that the younger faculty dared not to vote against us and the name remained unchanged.

It turned out that the younger faculty were the keys to resolving the split. We elders had them in a no-win position. Who could get promoted in such a situation? They appointed several delegates and went to the Dean, Lawrence Fouraker. Now it was his problem.

His solution, after interviewing quite a few of us, was to ask me to take over as Area Chairman. For once in academic politics I had been bold and had said to the Dean when interviewed, "What does it take to be appointed Area Chairman?" pointing out as modestly as I could my successes with MCS ideas and related courses and the reaction to my ideas outside the School. Though correctly polite, I'm afraid that I was quite brazen as I assured the Dean that I could restore order and civility. The next day I was made Area Chairman.

ONWARD AND UPWARD

The process of renewal was quite easy. With the gracious support and total cooperation of a leader from the other side, Dick Rosenbloom, we just decided as an Area that we should enrich ourselves and our work by learning from each other and make this possible by employing and promoting competent and well-qualified people of every stripe. We quickly agreed that about 20% of our people would have a primary focus in each of the following sectors: production management, service operations, international operations, quantitative analysis, and because of particular present interests, in operations scheduling and inventory control.

We further agreed that the percentages were never to be specific, that any Area member should feel free to move about, that the first-year course needed to be retooled, and that each member of our group, having been carefully selected and coached, deserved full respect and all possible support for his or her teaching and research. We agreed that we would all support success. Whatever worked well would benefit us all. Let the market prevail. The civil war ended within days.

Of course what had caused the civil war was the realization for all of us that we had set up a zero sum game. The quants felt that the Area had to change wholly and completely. We management types were made to feel old-fashioned, for the quantitative people were genuinely sure that we were just hanging on to old, outdated concepts and techniques and we had to go.

Their total lack of awareness of the breakthroughs and the success and vitality of the new ideas creating the whole concept and techniques of manufacturing strategy is now astonishing. I must blame myself for not getting across to others the power and excitement of the new theory of how to manage manufacturing. It got across to other campuses, to big consulting firms, and to managers all across the country, but not to colleagues who had other interests and training. My excuse is that the academic culture as I read it and felt it called for leaving colleagues free. The civil war came, though, when they wouldn't leave us free to promote a deserving candidate and he was turned down.

I served as Area Chairman for about three years and can say that after my regime was over the Area went on to do even better. We were in gear. Once we had agreed on the advantages of diversity and openness we did let market forces prevail and such an evolutionary process led to new courses, new people, and the survival of individuals with skills and ideas that worked.

Under subsequent leaders and, particularly Bob Hayes, Earl Sasser, and Kim Clark (all of whom I claim with immodest pride as my progeny) year by year we got stronger and stronger. The most able people attracted younger ones with relevant interests, new hires found excitement in management issues. Extraordinary attention was placed continually on the development needs of nontenured faculty.

In ten years we had the most productive and effective group of faculty at HBS as judged by course ratings, research impacts, and the number of students in elective courses. We were aided, of course, by the new attention top management placed on operations management when the requirement for excellence in manufacturing became a clear necessity for survival in the global economy.

My proud legacy is a group of younger colleagues who grabbed the baton and took it much faster and further than I had been able to do. They expanded the ideas, added new ones, made the implementation more explicit, wrote articles and textbooks that made much more useful and precise my struggling attempts to understand and teach about the management of technology, and, unlike so many in operations management, resisted the temptations to make fads out of Japanese management techniques.

One of these younger colleagues, Kim Clark, went on to become Dean and four others were appointed Senior Associate Deans. We were loaded with talent in the Area and marvelous talent developed elsewhere all over the world. These colleagues took up and advanced the manufacturing strategy concept in their courses and consulting and created a massive literature. The talent list is long because the field and its practitioners have grown over the years. These are the people who have led it. And along the way they have been politely, but firmly helping me to learn more and express it better.

CONCLUSIONS

What Happened?

I offer three sets of conclusions, one for each of the three areas in which this story has taken place: personal, the field of industrial management, and academia.

Appraising each in turn, what happened was very good in personal measures, quite good but certainly not an overwhelming victory in the operations field, and surprise, surprise, left no mark whatsoever in how academia is managed.

1. Personally, of course it's been a great trip. The ideas were worked out, slowly to be sure, but they got written up and disseminated, attracted thoughtful interest and clearly have influenced practitioners and scholars. Companies got changed, courses got retooled, hundreds of articles and more than a dozen books have been written by colleagues who took up and advanced these concepts.

I do regret showing pride but I am pleased that as of this writing 509,884 reprints of my *HBR* articles have been purchased, including 158,692 "Missing Links" and 121,402 "Focused Factories." About 25 colleagues all over the world have been active teachers, consultants and writers concerning manufacturing strategy.

The original work was accomplished with no backing, involvement, or interest on the part of anyone in my Area at the School or indeed at any school of management. The thinking process, however, was stimulated and made to work by the teaching process and great students. Whereas my particular ideas and their slow development were not supported by Area colleagues until they caught on elsewhere (1970), however, after that my younger colleagues were enthusiasts and I also received total support from the School and Area colleagues in other ways.

I was given ample research and case/course development time, I was warmly praised and encouraged for my results in the classroom and, somehow, I got promoted to full professor (1968) based on teaching and "promise." I suppose now that it was the hope that maybe I'd do at least something with my ideas which seemed to work so well in the classroom. (The reader should understand that 95% of my published articles and books came after, repeat after, I became a full professor. Who could ask for more support from an academic institution?) I believe that some full professors from outside the area plus two in the area bet on me because I was on the right side as they saw it in the forthcoming civil war.

Anyway, finally, once I published the "Missing Link" and we won the civil war, all else followed. We hired and promoted faculty who were management, teaching, and broad rather than narrow in their interests. They prospered and produced, the courses went better and better, they took my original work and greatly expanded and improved it, and the rest is all good history. We were rich and got richer. Bob Hayes should be given especially great praise for all that happened because of his intellectual leadership and tireless devotion to the development of younger faculty.

2. That was the "very good," the personal side of the story. The industrial management side I classified as "good but not an overwhelming victory." As stated above, the impact and penetration of the MCS concepts and techniques have been quite significant in industry, the literature of industrial management, and academia. Nevertheless the practice of operations management is by no means dominated by MCS. In fact, although it is clearly well recognized and respected, and the theory is of long standing duration, it has not replaced "productivity" as the practi-

tioners' dominant philosophy and methodology of the field. The McKinsey Prize judges who awarded me that prize in 1986 (for the first and only time) for "The Productivity Paradox" were in the minority!

What dominates, regrettably, is essentially what dominated me at that seminar in 1960: advanced manufacturing techniques (AMT's)! This is the heritage of industrial engineering thinking, starting with Frederick Taylor and followed by the Gilbreths and dozens of other efficiency engineers with an enduring emphasis on "continuous improvement" of every nook and cranny of a factory.

Each decade brings new AMT's and over and over, if they are any good, and most of them are, they become fads and installed willy-nilly everywhere by eager consultants and bright young engineers. We have had, over 100 years: scientific manufacturing, time study, motion study, pre-determined standards, value analysis, quality control, PERT, work sampling, economic order quantity, inventory management, MRP, quality circles, and etc., etc. each an AMT in its time. It goes on today, perhaps with more market-driven fervor.

As each AMT becomes popular they cease to create competitive advantage. Worse, employed superficially and without explicit design of a set of appropriate manufacturing policies, they are dysfunctional and damage strategic performance.

The Japanese AMT's, good as they are, could not have come at a worse time for us MCS proponents. For when we were arguing that the way out of industrial decline was to design a coherent set of manufacturing policies to regain a competitive edge, along came the Japanese AMT's and managers grabbed at them because they thought that if we could copy them and employ best practices we would be O.K. again. So the consultants, led by the big accounting companies advertising "benchmarking," "world class," and "best practices" have full blast sold J.I.T. (Just-In-Time) and TQM (Total Quality Management)and "Lean" and "flexible," all the other thirty AMT's since MRP2 with great success.

Everybody copies everyone else and, chasing with a late start, no competitive advantage is gained. Our factories are uniformly unfocused, and, filled with conflicting AMT's, are chock-a-block with inconsistent, non-coherent manufacturing policies. Meanwhile the Japanese have kept improving faster than western manufacturers and only a favorable exchange rate and a strong domestic economy have made American firms competitive in many industries. The U.S. manufacturing trade balance is worse than ever.

In fact, the rush to AMT's has been an unbroken industrial management tendency for a century, since the beginnings of "Scientific Management." Reaching out for a new management technique has always been an irresistible, seductive temptation, an habitual tendency of operations people. And the presumption that techniques create competitive advantage has kept on overpowering the contrary concepts of manufacturing strategy. We have made good progress in changing the thinking of many industrial managers and professors, but in the practices of industrial managers our approaches, while growing, but are yet in the minority.

3. While MCS has had clear success in the literature and in the work of about twenty-five leading professors and their courses, most operations management courses go on emphasizing the latest AMT as if these techniques create competitive success. Academics in the POM field are interested but seem largely unscathed.

One would think that research and teaching in professional schools of management would be "scathed" by the successes of certain schools that have had significant influence on the thinking and practices of the profession. But what prevents more individuals and more schools from exerting actual influence on the practice of management is, of course, the traditional academic promotion process.

To get promoted one has to do "research" and "get published" and "good research adds to knowledge" and is "true," that is, provable. Naturally, then, the research gets more and more into minutiae, constraints are set up to allow it to be provable and the libraries and journals of the world fill up with trivia. Worse, young scholars are trained and, as we said earlier, with premises and practices and skills that limit them for life. And they go on to clone the next generation.

The incentive system generally drives performance. We academics, or, I will now say, you academics, have trapped yourselves with your own, chosen, tradition hardened promotion standards. Only you can change them.

I am shamelessly chauvinistic, I know it full well. But I must state that the Harvard Business School is different and better because we have no departments, we try to avoid minutiae, we get out in the field for data, we write hundreds of cases every year, we try to listen to and help managers, we promote based on effective impact on students and managers, and we turn down candidates for promotion if the candidate publishes trivia.

It is clear to me that my work, with whatever its balances of success and failures, was only made possible by being on the faculty at the Harvard Business School. And my colleagues at that first, disastrous seminar, one dark evening in December, 1960, did a job on me that saved me from more fiascoes. They taught me that night that changing old ideas is enormously hard and that half-baked or incomplete research findings wouldn't get very far. Their harsh criticisms woke me up and but they spurred me on.

Somehow they told me to keep working until I got it right. They did not know it would take eight years.

Q. Well, professor, your bottom line?
A. Those academic traditions were not so bad after all.

Thanks, everybody.

Wickham Skinner
Harvard Business School
November 30, 1997

PUBLICATIONS

1959

Honeywell chooses plant site. *Industrial Development* (February).

1960

Wanted—frontier managers. *Virginia Law*, DICTA, April.
Critique: Management in the industrial world. *The International Executive* (February).

1964

A test case in Turkey. *California Management Review* (Spring).
With A.R. Dooley, J.H. McGarrah, J.L. McKenney, R. Rosenbloom, & P.H. Thurston. *Basic problems, concepts, and techniques.* New York: Wiley.

With A.R. Dooley, J.H. McGarrah, J.L. McKenney, R. Rosenbloom, & P.H. Thurston. *Wage administration and worker productivity.* New York: Wiley.

With A.R. Dooley, J.H. McGarrah, J.L. McKenney, R. Rosenbloom, & P.H. Thurston. *Operations planning and control.* New York: Wiley.

With A.R. Dooley, J.H. McGarrah, J.L. McKenney, R. Rosenbloom, & P.H. Thurston. *Production operating decisions in the total business strategy.* New York: Wiley.

Managing international production. *Harvard Business Review* (September/October).

1966

Production under pressure. *Harvard Business Review* (November/December).

1967

With A.R. Dooley, J.H. McGarrah, J.L. McKenney, R. Rosenbloom, & P.H. Thurston. *Basic problems, concepts, and techniques.* New York: Wiley.

With A.R. Dooley, J.H. McGarrah, J.L. McKenney, R. Rosenbloom, & P.H. Thurston. *Wage administration and worker productivity.* New York: Wiley.

With A.R. Dooley, J.H. McGarrah, J.L. McKenney, R. Rosenbloom, & P.H. Thurston. *Operations planning and control.* New York: Wiley.

With A.R. Dooley, J.H. McGarrah, J.L. McKenney, R. Rosenbloom, & P.H. Thurston. *Production operating decisions in the total business strategy.* New York: Wiley.

Procurement for international manufacturing plants in developing economies. *Journal of Purchasing* (February).

Contribution of the college business manager. *Council for the Advancement of Small-Colleges Newsletter* (July).

Control in a multinational corporation. *Worldwide P&I Planning* (May/June).

1968

American industry in developing economies. New York: Wiley.

With D.C.D. Rogers. *Manufacturing policy in the plastics industry.* Homewood, IL: Irwin.

With D.V. Rosato. *The plastics industry.* In J. Goldhar (Ed.), *Environmental effects on polymeric materials.* New York: Wiley.

1969

Manufacturing—missing link in corporate strategy. *Harvard Business Review* (May/June).

1970

With D.C.D. Rogers. *Manufacturing policy in the oil industry.* Homewood, IL: Irwin.

With D.C.D. Rogers. *Manufacturing policy in the steel industry.* Homewood, IL: Irwin.

The stubborn infrastructure of the factory. Numerical Control Society.

1971

The anachronistic factory. *Harvard Business Review* (January/February).

1972

Production and operations management at the Harvard Business School. *HBS Alumni Magazine* (August).

How most companies mismanage their factories. *Executive Voice, Fortune* (May).

1973

After seven lean years. Academy of Management *Proceedings* (August).

Perspectives on operations management for the 1970's. American Institute for Decision Science *Proceedings* (November).

1974

The focused factory. *Harvard Business Review* (May/June).
The decline, fall, and renewal of manufacturing plants. *Journal of Industrial Engineering.*
Closing the gap between corporate strategy and manufacturing performance. AIEE Convention *Proceedings* (November).

1977

With A. Dooley. Casing casemethod methods. *Academy of Management Review* (April).
Preface to the production management series. *Harvard Business Review, 3*(May).
With E. Sasser. Managers with impact: Versatile and inconsistent. *Harvard Business Review* (November/December).
Why our factories have been failing us. American Institute for Decision Science, *Decision Line* (November).

1978

Manufacturing in the corporate strategy. New York: Wiley.

1979

The impact of changing technology on the working environment. In J. Rostow & C. Kerr (Eds.), *Work in America: The decade ahead.* New York: Van Nostrand Reinhold.

1980

With M. C. Lauenstein. The strategy of superior resources: An elusive objective. *Journal of Business Strategy* (February).
Manufacturing in mature industries. *Journal of Business Strategy* (February).
Factory of the future: Always in the future? In L. Kops (Ed.), *Towards the factory of the future emergence of the computerized factory*

and its impact on society. American Society of Mechanical Engineers.

1981

Big hat, no cattle: Managing human resources. *Harvard Business Review* (November/December).

1982

The impact of new technology: People and organizations in the service industries. Elmsford, NY: Pergamon Press.
Productivity is the wrong objective. *Wall Street Journal* (March 16).

1983

Technology and the work environment. In T.R. Martin (Ed.), *Stewardship: The corporation and the individual.* New York: ICCG Productions.
Getting physical: The strategic leverage of the operations function. *Journal of Business Strategy,* 3(4), 74-79.
Strategies for excellence in old-line companies. *Proceedings of the Innovations Management Conference.* OH: Case Western Reserve University.
Wanted: Managers for the factory of the future. *Annals of the American Academy Political and Social Sciences* (November).
The productivity disease. *The Princeton Papers.* Mississagua, Ontario: Northern Telecom, Ltd., September.
Seven initiatives from the operations function. *Operations Management Review,* 1(4), 4-11.
Comments and suggestions concerning a conceptual framework for the factory of the future. *Conceptual Design for Computer Integrated Manufacturing,* pp. A 2634, materials laboratory, Wright Aeronautical Laboratories, Air Force Systems Command, Wright Patterson Air Force Base, Ohio. Document ITR 110510007U, July.
Management of international production. In D.N. Dickson (Ed.), *Managing, effectively in the world marketplace.* New York: Wiley.

1984

Reinventing the factory: A manufacturing strategy response to industrial malaise. In R. Lamb (Ed.), *Competitive strategic management* (pp. 520-529). Engelwood Cliffs, NJ: Prentice-Hall.

Operations technology: Blind spot in strategic management. *INTERFACES, 14*(1), 116-125.

Reinventing the factory. *ISSUES Journal for Management, 2*, London.

How America had it made. *The New York Times*, Sunday Book Review (September 2, pp. 10-11).

Operations technology—blind spot in strategic management. In A. Hax (Ed.), *Readings on strategic management* (pp. 167-176). MA: Ballinger.

[Foreword] *Understanding the manufacturing process* (by J. Harrington, Jr.). New York: Marcel Dekker.

1985

The taming of lions: How manufacturing leadership evolved, 1780-1984. In K. Clark, R. Hayes, & C. Lorenz (Eds.), *The uneasy alliance: Managing the productivity—technology dilemma* (pp. 63-110). Boston: Harvard Business School Press.

Manufacturing—The formidable competitive weapon. NY: Wiley

Break the habits of mass production. *The New York Times* (Sunday, August 25).

Corporate attitudes toward introducing new manufacturing technology. In *Education for the manufacturing world of the future.* National Academy of Engineering. Washington, DC: National Academy Press.

Make it or sell it—don't keep track of it. *Harvard Business Review* (September/October).

1986

Implementation of operations strategy. *OMA Review, 4*(2).

The role of the Department of Defense in supporting manufacturing technology development. Report of Committee on the Role of the Manufacturing Technology Program in the Defense Industrial Base. W. Skinner, Chairman. Manufacturing Studies Board. Commission on Engineering and Technical Systems, National Research Council, Washington, DC.

The productivity paradox. *Harvard Business Review* (July-August).

Boosting productivity. *Boardroom Reports* interview (November 15).

1987

Manufacturing is U.S.'s formidable competitive weapon. *Appliance Manufacturer* (March).

With D.M. Ruwe. Reviving a rust-belt factory. *Harvard Business Review* (May-June).

A strategy for competitive manufacturing. *Management Review* (August).

Wanted: A new breed of manufacturing manager. *Manufacturing issues.* Cleveland, OH: Booz, Allen & Hamilton, Inc.

Manufacturing: Corporate millstone or competitive weapon. *Journal of Melbourne University Business School, 10*(2).

With K. Ferdows. The sweeping revolution in manufacturing. *Journal of Business Strategy, 8*(2).

1988

What matters to manufacturing. *Harvard Business Review* (January-February).

The competitive problems of US industry. *Valve Magazine* (April). Valve Manufacturers Association of America.

[Abstract]. With G.R. Bitran. Operations research in manufacturing. *OR/MS Today* (April), 40.

A recipe for manufacturing excellence. *Technology Strategies*. No. 31, May, 1. Strategic Direction Publishers, Zurich.

Is an industrial renaissance underway? *Production Engineering* (July).

1989

Manufacturing management for the 90's: A strategic perspective. *Proceeding* of the *Conference on Manufacturing Management in the Nineties.* University of Toledo.

Forty eight words. *Academy of Management Review, 14*, 292-294.

1990

Production and operations research needs. *Operations Management Review,* 7(1 & 2).

The productivity paradox explained. In *The quality and productivity equation* (pp. 147-157). Cambridge, MA: Productivity Press.

1991

Loose cannons or popguns: Directors & the R&D program. *International Journal of Technology Management.*

Precious jewels: Companies which achieve competitive advantage from process innovation. *International Journal of Technology Management.*

Missing the links in manufacturing strategy. In C.A. Voss (Ed.), *Manufacturing strategy: Process and content.* London: Chapman & Hall.

1994

American industry's comeback—How to get back in the race but not win. *Strategy: Quarterly International Network Review (*Summer).

Re-engineering in the operations management profession. *Operations Management Association Forum.*

1995

American industry 1995. In **Fifty years out—1945** (pp. 35-38). New Haven, CT: Yale University Press.

The high cost of order. In C.S. Lawson (Ed.), *Gold from aspirin: Spiritual views on chaos and order from thirty authors.* West Chester, PA: Chrysalis Books.

1996

Introduction to the production and operations management society journal special issue on manufacturing strategy. *Production and Operations Management Society Journal* (Winter).

Three yards and a cloud of dust: Industrial management at century end. *Production and Operations Management Journal* (Winter).

Manufacturing strategy on the "S" curve. *Production and Operations Management Society Journal* (Winter).

Appendix

Contributors to Volumes 1-5

VOLUME 1, 1992

H. Igor Ansoff
Chris Argyris
Bernard M. Bass
Robert R. Blake

Elwood S. Buffa
Alfred D. Chandler, Jr.
Larry L. Cummings

Keith Davis
Fred E. Fiedler
Jay W. Forrester
Robert T. Golembiewski

VOLUME 2, 1993

Frederick I. Herzberg
Robert J. House
Edward E. Lawler, III
Paul R. Lawrence

Edmund Philip Learned
Harry Levinson
Edwin A. Locke
Dalton E. McFarland

John B. Miner
Henry Mintzberg
William H. Newman
Charles Perrow

VOLUME 3, 1993

Lyman W. Porter
Edward H. Schein
William H. Starbuck
George A. Steiner

George Strauss
Eric L. Trist
Stanley C. Vance

Victor H. Vroom
Karl E. Weick
William Foote Whyte
James C. Worthy

VOLUME 4, 1996

Kathryn M. Bartol
Janice M. Beyer
Geert Hofstede

John M. Ivancevich
Fred Luthans

Jeffrey Pfeffer
Derek S. Pugh
John W. Slocum, Jr.

VOLUME 5, 1998

Arthur G. Bedeian
C. West Churchman

David J. Hickson
Thomas A. Mahoney
Andrew M. Pettigrew

Karlene A. Roberts
Wickham Skinner

NAME INDEX

Management Laureates
A Collection of
Autobiographical Essays

J

A

I

Edited by **Arthur G. Bedeian**, *Department of Management, Louisiana State University*

REVIEW: "The collection of autobiographical essays is a creative project. No other publication in management has asked leading contributors to reflect on their experiences and the factors and forces that influenced their professional and personal development. Each essay is accompanied by a photograph and complete bibliography of each individual's work. The 42 autobiographies represent the editors selection of management laureates, those who have achieved distinction in research and publication, teaching, and consulting. These laureates are holders of distinguished professorships--almost all are Fellows of the Academy of Management, some have been presidents of the Academy of Management, and others have distinguished themselves professionally. It would be difficult, if not impossible, to read one of our scholarly journals without finding at least one of these individuals cited. . . ."

—*The Executive, Daniel A. Wren*
University of Oklahoma

P

Volume 4, 1996, 313 pp. $86.25/£55.50
ISBN 1-55938-730-0

R

CONTENTS: Preface, *Arthur G. Bedeian.* Challenged on the Cutting Edge, *Kathryn M. Bartol.* Performing, Achieving, and Belonging, *Janice M. Beyer.* A Hopscotch Hike, *Geert Hofstede.* Roots, Wing, and Applying Management and Leadership Principles: A Personal Odyssey, *John M. Ivancevich.* A Common Man Travels "Back to the Future", *Fred Luthans.* Taking the Road Less Traveled: Serendipity and the Influence of Others in a Career, *Jeffrey Pfeffer.* A Taste for Innovation, *Derek S. Pugh.* Never Say Never!, *John W. Slocum, Jr.* Index.

E

Also Available:
Volumes 1-3 (1992-1993) $86.25/£55.50 each

S

S

JAI PRESS INC.
100 Prospect Street, P. O. Box 811
Stamford, Connecticut 06904-0811
Tel: (203) 323-9606 Fax: (203) 357-8446

J A I   P R E S S

New Approaches to Employee Management

Edited by **David M. Saunders**,
Faculty of Management, McGill University

Volume 4, Expatriate Management:
Theory and Research
1997, 270 pp. $78.50/£49.95
ISBN 0-7623-0014-0

Edited by **Zeynep Aycan,** *Faculty of*
Management, McGill University

CONTENTS: Preface, *Zeynep Aycan and David M. Saunders.* Predicting Expatriate Adjustment: A Critical Review of Literature and A Conceptual Framework., *Zeynep Aycan.* Rethinking the Strategic Management of Expatriates from a Nonlinear Dynamics Perspective, *Mark E. Mendenhall and James H. Macomber.* Personality Determinants in the Prediction of Aspects of Expatriate Job Success, *Deniz S. Ones and Chockalingam Viswesvaran.* Expatriate Selection in Multinational Companies: Possibilities and Limitations of Using Personality Scales, *Juergen Deller.* Assessing Expatriate Success: Beyond Just "Being There," *Paula M. Caligiuri.* A Comparative Test of Alternative Models of International Assignee Job Performance, *Winfred Arthur, Jr. and Winston Bennett, Jr.* Empirical Investifgation of the Host Country Perspective in Expatriate Management, *Handan Kepir Sinangil and Deniz S. Ones.* Training Needs for Expatriate Adjustment in the People's Republic of China, *Georgia T. Chao and Yen Jun Sun.* Spousal Assistance Programs: An Integral Component of the International Assignment, *Mary T. Pellico and Linda K. Stroh.* Current Issues and Future Directions in Expatriation Research, *Zeynep Aycan and Rabindra N. Kanungo.*

Also Available:
Volumes 1-3 (1992-1995) $78.50/£49.95 each

JAI PRESS INC.
100 Prospect Street, P. O. Box 811
Stamford, Connecticut 06904-0811
Tel: (203) 323-9606 Fax: (203) 357-8446